PRECIOUS BOOKS

PRECIOUS BOOKS

Name: In Search of A Holy Land
Author: Lauren Booth
İnside & Cover: Mevlüt Sami Ertem
ISBN: 978-1-7393841-1-1
Print: June 2023, London.
Print: Office Print House
Publisher: Precious Books
          64 Holly Park Road N11 3EY London - UK
Web: www.preciousbooks.co.uk

In Search of A Holy Land

An adventure story to faith

Lauren Booth

PB
PRECIOUS BOOKS

Lauren Booth

Lauren Booth is a highly sought after writer, presenter and public speaker. The fifth daughter of socialist actor Anthony Booth, she grew up in Hampstead, London. Initially focusing on performing arts, Lauren went to a UK drama school and toured plays in France and Austria before turning her attention to writing.

After a successful career as a columnist, TV and Radio presenter for, amongst others, BBC Radio London, Mail on Sunday and political magazine the New Statesman, Lauren was commissioned to report from Occupied Palestine. That experience impacted her beliefs and the direction of her work.

In 2010, she accepted Islam, subsequently spending time in both Qatar and Palestine.

Lauren wrote and toured her first stage play in 2019. 'Accidentally Muslim' is a one woman show which received critical acclaim at the Edinburgh Festival Fringe.

She has two children and now lives with her husband in Istanbul, Turkiye, where she produces articles and short films on modernity, faith and Islamic world history.

"Booth is a gifted storyteller, whose honesty of testimony and ability to recreate moments from her life draw you in." (The Scotsman)

CONTENTS

FOREWORD

In the nineties, I was asked to write a diary about my accidental (unauthorised) public role as 'Blair's sister-in-law'. Back then, publishers wanted tittle-tattle, a cartoon version of the celebrity culture in the shallows of which, I gaily paddled.

'No thanks,' I said. The last thing the world needs is another gossipy, name-dropping, tell-all.

The idea of writing a memoir though, was resurrected for me later, during a speaking tour of the United States. In a gym attached to a mosque, I presented some of the weird and wonderful events I'd lived through, from the rainforests of Australia to the deserts of Egypt. During the Q and A session, a boy of eight jumped up and down until the screeching microphone was handed to him.

'Excuse me,' he said. 'Did any of that really happen?' The consensus from the floor was that if I had lived those experiences, a memoir would be a duty.

Back home, I decided to check my memory wasn't completely skewed by years of alcoholic nights out. Sat on the floor with my daughters, I rifled through decades of scrawled upon scraps of paper bound into broken, sand-dusted and water-damaged, notebooks. After an hour of laughter (theirs) and some nostalgic tears (mine), we had to admit - as unlikely as it seemed the stuff I'd said, and much more, really happened.

'Dibs - I get the diaries when you die, Mum' my eldest, said. Charming.

As for Islam, if you'd asked me about the worlds fastest growing faith when I was 15, I would have said it was 'foreign' and mostly meant girls had to become doctors, dentists or subservient, docile, house slaves.

Islam, as a practical way of life, reflecting an ancient ethical example, was completely unknown to me until I was 38 and travelling across the the Occupied Palestinian Territories. There, my lack of knowledge of the journalistic etiquette of penning a story from the West Bank, put me in what would be considered risky, but were ultimately, enlightening, situations. My lack of training, allowed me to listen to the indigenous people of the region, whose stories were noticeably at odds with the political rhetoric and my own preconceptions.

That experience awoke in me an empathy for others, which my life as a 'celebrity' columnist had, long since, dulled.

The Muslims I met, living under Occupation, failed to live up to their terrifying status. They tried to guide me away from my own building anger at their reality, towards the calm reflections and hope that sustains them. My travels to other lands and into the homes of Muslims based in the UK, confirmed a different way of thinking and behaving could be possible - even preferable.

Inevitably, I picked up the book of guidance: The Holy Qur'an.

In western terms, the life described here began as a gritty soap opera. It proceeded (for a bit) as a glossy rom-com, then revealed itself to be exactly the same as your own. This is a short trip from womb to tomb, encompassing a quest for purpose and meaning.

Anything good or beautiful within these pages is a blessing from Allah. He alone do I thank and He alone do I praise for all things. I seek forgiveness for any errors. Any good found in this work is entirely due to the Almighty who is self sufficient with no partners.

I want to recognise special people who have supported me before and during the writing journey.

I dedicate this to my grandparents Frances and Spike, who taught me special stuff like manners, duty and how to enjoy a long walk (even beside a motorway).

To Mum, who forgave me – and boy did I need her forgiveness!

To Dad, who taught me epic storytelling and empathy for the poor.

To my daughters, who I love without limitation.

A special thank you to sister Anisa, who teaches me that ethics are in the doing, not in the saying.

To all my sisters - deep love and respect for the roots that bind us.

To Birdy, for her brilliant observations.

To KAJ for being the man who takes care for me. His guidance and wisdom give my dreams a chance.

I dedicate this book to the people of Bilad al-Sham who await and will most certainly receive justice.

There's a lot of mentions of God on the way, so buckle up. Let's travel together a while.

In peace and solidarity.
Lauren Booth
This is your invitation

PROLOGUE

> But they planned, and Allah planned.
> And Allah is the best of planners.
>
> **Qur'an 8: 30**

Getting out of the car, I almost stepped on a mother feeding her children flat bread and meat on the warm tarmac. Tents cluttered around the base of the concrete stairs leading to the site my hosts and I were rushing towards: the biggest domed building I had ever seen without Princess Diana sitting in front of it. I had forced myself into a volume of black material, in order to blend in with the crowd. It tangled my legs, so I almost fell backwards into the sea of women climbing the stairs behind me.

I had been coerced into becoming a floating shape by Nargess, my 22-year-old colleague at the Iranian news channel, Press TV. She'd invited me to take a mini break with her and 'Mamma' after we'd finished reporting on pro-Palestine marches for the news the day before. Nargess was a great laugh. Full of cheek, with a unique accent that was part north London, part urban Tehran. She could hardly contain her delight at how weird I looked elbowing the black sheet, a *chador,* over my head on the back seat of our taxi. I had half strangled myself in the process.

We had been driving for four hours from the Iranian capital when our driver thankfully pulled up alongside this monochrome mass of humanity we were now a part of. I took in the scene. thousands of women in head-to-toe burkas, dragging children through a heat that didn't seem to accept it was now evening.

It was an *iftar* in Ramadan, the moment when Muslims break their day-long fast and eat together. The month of fasting was not a welcome element to my visit. There hadn't been a lot of food on offer at the news centre when I was filing my reports, which I respected, but it wasn't the first Muslim country I had been to, either. As always, my attempts to fast 'in sympathy' had been met with secret cups of tea to 'save me any trouble'. However, when the time for breaking the fast had arrived I had been looking forward to a shared spread of Persian delights. Instead, on a conference table in a back office, everyone on shift had gathered around for a bowl of meat- filled porridge. The news team consumed plate after plate of the grey gloop as I listlessly stirred mine around, hoping it would vanish all by itself.

'Do you like the special Ramadan food?' asked the executive producer, Hamid.

'Never had anything like it,' I replied truthfully.

'This is a delicacy we save for Ramadan!' He told me. I wasn't surprised.

We arrived at the city of Qom just as the call to prayer began. The gigantic mosque we were climbing solid stone steps to reach was a shrine. The learned daughter of a famous scholar was buried here and it was tradition to ask her for favours, which she would then ask God to grant.

The sound of the call to prayer echoed overhead: *'Allahu Akbar Allahu Akbar, la ilaha illa Allah.'*

The strange key changes floated on the warm evening air, carrying its usual enchantment. However, there was no time to pause to admire it. Arriving at the top of the steps, sweating and out of breath – me not her – Nargess reminded me of the plan: 'We'll pray, you look around, then a quick bite to eat in the city centre and we can sleep the rest of the way to our five-star hotel in Esfahan'.

What could possibly go wrong?

All I to do was to pass myself off as a Muslim for an hour. If my disguise failed, I could be accused of spying for foreign interests and arrested. My transformation from western city journalist to giant penguin convinced me the modest look did *not* suit me. The chador had been (predictably) too short for my height, leaving a good three inches of awful, pasty white shin on display. Tugging the material down to my ankles my blonde fringe slipped out from beneath the hood, instantly giving me away as an intruder. Was it possible to suffer an epic fashion fail in a sea of women dressed identically? Apparently so.

I had to wear the chador to cover my 'other-ness'. I was not permitted to be at the shrine, where this serious religious gathering of Shia pilgrims was taking place in the most holy month of the Islamic calendar. Not that I was interested in the religious side of things, this strange pilgrimage was only a touristy day off while I was abroad. And possibly a great colour feature for a newspaper back home.

As the crowd jostled to enter, I wondered what I was about to witness. I had no idea what sort of things went on inside a mosque in the Holy month. Did Muslims kill goats in the mosque or was the whole 'streets-of-blood' thing done elsewhere? I had no idea.

Of course it would have been simple to have asked Nargess. I didn't because I get sick at the sight of blood and if she had said yes to the lamb slaughtering stuff I would have lost my nerve straight away. I shuddered, despite the heat of the bodies pressed all around me at the final archway. I felt like the Jodie Foster character in *Silence of the Lambs*. My inner journalist whispered: this could be great story! I took a deep breath and patted the iPhone in my handbag, intent on recording secret footage.

Doves circled overhead and watched our progress as step by step we shuffled towards the vast green dome. From time to time, local eyes peeping from between black scarves looked me up and down. The eyes were a mixture of confusion and amusement. At any moment I could be found out. At last we reached the 20-foot high white entrance. An armed guard, a Tom Selleck lookalike (with a mono-brow), looked disturbed by the sight of me. I couldn't blame him, I was a giant flightless bird belonging closer to the North Pole than this steamy place. He played with one side of his moustache, considering what to make of me. Clearly, he was running through the option of pulling me aside against the delay that would cause to the thousands of tetchy, hungry pilgrims. Women were pressing forward from all sides, so perhaps I'd be crushed to death before the guard even had time to drag me away, never to be seen again.

'Tom Selleck' grunted permission for me to cross the threshold of the shrine-come- mosque. The human wave lifted my feet off the ground for a moment beneath a dazzling sky of endless mirrors. I was instantly hit by the heavy aroma of Myrrh and drifted off. In ten hours I would awaken from a deep sleep, not in the five-star comfort of the Hilton Hotel in Esfahan, but under these same mirrors. I would put freezing water from a cracked basin on my hands, my face, my forearms, head and feet. I would wake up to a new mind-set, my heart certain of the pillars of faith from a book which, till then, had terrified me.

CHAPTER 1
PAPER ASPIRATIONS

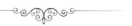

'Then he gave me his autographed
picture. And these three rusty nails.'

Roger McGough

In 1967, Highgate was a pretty cobbled village on the edge of a heath where my father, actor Anthony Booth – at the pinnacle of his fame (yet financially broke) – missed my own premiere in the maternity department of Whittington hospital. My mother, Pamela Riley (born Cohen), gave birth to her first daughter, Sarah Jane, with only my grandfather at the hospital to congratulate her. She was immediately anxious about the absence of the handsome, flighty father-to-be, and hours after my birth and freshly stitched, she fled the hospital in search of him. She suspected he had sneaked out to some party or premier, leaving my new-born self to spend that first night in a hospital cot to 'cry it out', which was the neo-natal fashion at the time. Years later my mother would show me the note she had found taped to the end of her hospital bed on her return the next morning: 'Enjoy the party! Hope you have a haemorrhage, love Nursey.'

My father was enjoying success in a TV show called *Till Death us Do Part* when I entered 'stage right' in my pushchair and intervened temporarily in his life. The part of the 'Randy Scouse Git' (translation: Lecherous, Liverpudlian Lout) was specially written for him by the screenwriter Johnny Speight as a foil to the main role of the racist, right-wing bigot, Alf Garnett. My father would admit, with his charming smile, the 'Scouse git' role suited him to a tee.

We moved several times in my early years, from pleasant Victorian house to rented apartment, each move dependent on my father's wavering popularity and his determined inability to put aside some of the money from this brief fame for the (as it turned out) many and torrential 'rainy days' to come. By the time my baby sister arrived in 1970, our parents were miserably resident in the bedsit upstairs in my maternal grandparents' semi-suburban home. It was not an especially happy time for the young family.

The traditional values of Sid and Frances Riley were at odds with the 'Come the Revolution' rhetoric and political activities of their 'son in law'. Even that misnomer was a cause of bitterness, for my parents never actually married. The British way of life of was changing; in the 1950s, society dictated your social status and one's expected code of conduct in personal affairs was still broadly attached to Christian values. One man for one women, for life, in marriage. The 60s would usher in a 'who cares' rejection of forever-ness in relationships. It was 'you only live once': YOLO 1.0.

My father, true to his 'Scouse git' title, couldn't have married anyway as he was not yet divorced from his American wife and mother of their two daughters, who had returned to America after they split. A pattern was already forming. We were not his first, nor his last, attempt at family life. In the early 50s my father met a pretty Northern girl who was also an aspiring actress. They married young and had two daughters. As his career in film and on stage began to take off he would tour and then work in London, leaving his lonely wife at the home where he had been born, overseen by his Liverpool-Irish mother, Vera. The intervals between my father's visits back to Liverpool became longer and longer. After two or three years they more or less ground to a halt, he was too 'busy'. Mother and daughters were left to survive as best they could in Waterloo, a less than salubrious area. The cramped home, a traditional two-up two-down mid-terraced house, was also shared by his younger brother, Robert, another aspiring actor.

Back in North London, the 70s rolled on. It was an era of which my grandmother, hunched over endless cups of tea, high-tar cigarettes and her personal Ouija board, called: 'Godless times.' I was by all accounts a 'bonny' baby who rarely, if ever, cried. I had a mop of dark brown hair, beneath which my mother said 'determined' brown eyes looked straight into a person's heart. The single close up photo that existed of me, long since lost, showed a boyish 1-year-old, sitting straight backed in a white lace dress staring directly at the person taking the photograph, her lips pulled thin into an exact replica of my father's. This kid is 'going places', my parent's groovy friends would say whenever it was, very occasionally, shown.

In 1970, Sid and Frances wanted no part in any revolution, 'sexual' or otherwise.

It was kept a secret from my sister and me that our 'real' grandfather had been a smart young man from the only Jewish family in Rhyl. The marriage had ended in divorce and a bitter custody battle over my mother, which caused an unforgiving suspicion of men and 'foreigners' to take root in my grandmother's character forever after.

When I was four years old, my parents had a momentary flurry of cash after my father signed a deal to appear in a series of movies known as the *'Confessions'* films, four cheaply- made, poorly-scripted 'comedies'

My father was embarrassed to have to make the trite, things, but we were so broke he had no choice. He was paid the princely sum of £5,000. Early in 1971, my mother and grandfather went hunting for a beautiful place where she could (perhaps) finally persuade her unreliable boyfriend to settle down.

Built in the early 1900s, Heathcroft was an elegant block of red-brick apartments with high ceilings. There were three open lawns, rose gardens and a posh-sounding 'Porters Lodge', where mail and cleaned linen were delivered and collected. A van came twice a week, bringing basics door to door including milk and eggs. A real step up in the world after my grandparents' bedsit.

Number 79 was on the top floor of one of the imposing, elegant buildings. It had a dark wood front door, an external lock-up, where paraffin for the heaters could be stored, and a brass letter box. This series of comedy films that were popular in the UK from the 1950s to the 1970s.

After we moved in, Dad bought a second-hand Jaguar. Life looked grand.

New End Primary school, Hampstead. It was the school of choice for a number of actors' kids, For a while, even the legendary Hollywood star Lee Remick was a fawned over playground mum.

Marching up the flowering high street with my Dad's hand in mine, I had the world at my feet. I felt gloriously fashionable in my red corduroy dungarees and matching Kickers, strolling amongst the actors and poets of the fashionable suburb. My hair was red- brown, shoulder length and pulled into bunches. With dad on my arm I felt great. Who cared if we took the bus because we had no cash for petrol for the gas-guzzling Jag? We would hop aboard the single decker 268 bus, because we wanted our 'special driver'. At 8:22 in the morning, the 268 would rip up the hill like a sports car at Brands Hatch.

'Bloody hell kid, he's going for it today!' Dad would grin, lighting a roll-up.

The driver would open the doors and turn his handsome smile our way, I loved his thick

'How ya doing, Evel Knievel, don't drive too crazy today all right, I've got a smashing hangover,' Dad would wink. 'Evel Knievel' would take his cue and before we could take our seats the bus lurched forward, propelling us down the aisle, laughing, into the seats. Everyone on bus (including the dangerous driver) loved my father. 'What a character,' the other passengers on the 268 would say in earshot, as we sat down.

The epitome of 70s panache, he'd swing down the road, my little hand adoringly clutching his, his shoulder length blonde hair bouncing off the neck of a beige roll-neck sweater. I would hear women audibly gasp as we went by. At other times, walking through Golders Green to shop at Mac Fisheries or browsing the high street for the Jewish food he loved, passers-by in plaid coats or working men's boots would wave and shout: 'All right Tony, stay away from the women now mate!' The teachers in the staff room, the geezers outside pubs, the man in the butcher's shop where we got sausages, and every newspaper seller who had a kiosk in North London – loved him to bits. At a time when film stars were becoming distant hyped-up figures, with, Tony Booth was a down to earth, man-of-the people, TV star. The general public never suspected that under Dad's flared jeans, my father routinely wore less than fashionable, yellow striped pyjamas. Nor did they seem able to tell, as I could, that beneath the cheap cologne there was an alcohol-based tang from the increasing amount of alcohol he relied upon to cope with the fact his once promising career was derailing. By the mid-70s, my father was an out of control 'social' drinker. His refusal to toe the establishment line by agreeing to such things as standing up for the national anthem at film premiers earned him almost as bad a reputation as that of an abusive drunk. When *Till Death* ended after seven smash hit series spanning a decade, he was forced to 'sign on' at the Labour Exchange, receiving money from the government. *Confessions* films aside, we relied on these payouts for the next eight years.

One day, when I was around nine years old, my father was rooting through a hall cupboard looking for the missing pages of a script he'd been sent to look at by his agent, Lee. He was desperate for work and the kitchen fridge boasted one egg, two beers and half a tomato from a bygone era.

Each day, letters came that the adults couldn't face. These were shoved into a bulging drawer in the hallway. My father swore under his breath as pages were scattered on the floor, counting. '16...17... 47... 81 ... did they let some idiot child of the landed gentry send this out?'

I stood behind him, a sickly feeling climbing in my throat. Quietly, I tiptoed away to my room. On my bed was the dolly paper chain I had made earlier that morning. On one side they had pencil clothes drawn on, which I liked. There was a pair of dungarees for the girl one, plaid trousers on two, three had a swimsuit in stripes. I turned my artwork gently over. The other side had typing on it. I read some of the words out loud.

'Sarah! Come here love, tell me if I've counted this right will ya?' I shoved the dolly chain under the bed covers, Dad would understand wouldn't he? The paper had been a treat, we never had anything to draw on or My Tiny Tears doll had limbs with tattoos on as my baby sister used her as a jotting pad. I hadn't known the stack of pristine pages in the hall cupboard had been a new script. Besides, Mum always gave us the old ones to use as drawing paper. I walked round the corner of my room and peeped back into the hall, where Dad was muttering options. How to turn up to an audition with half a script and lines unlearnt? I stood behind him and stroked his shaggy, bleached blonde hair.

A tiny black and white photo resting on his lap caught my eye. I reached round his waist and examined it, as if it were a rare fossil. Two little girls in quaint dresses, matching straight fringes and floppy bows in their hair smiled back at me. 'Who are these funny little girls Dad?' The dresses were dated compared to the colourful seventies clothes I was used to seeing. The girls were probably ancient aunts or something.

He pulled me onto his lap. 'These ...' He paused. 'These ... are your older sisters, Sarah. That ... that is Cherie and the smaller one is Lyndsey. You know Cherie, she comes to babysit sometimes. Well, she is your sister. Isn't that great? And one day you'll meet the others and you'll get to know them too. And they'll look after you and you'll all look out for each other. Isn't that great?'

I held my breath, I was waiting for the punchline to the teasing. He liked to tease me, I'd been called 'Jimmy' for as long as I could remember. 'Come 'ere Jimmy,' he'd say in a Scottish accent whenever we watched football together alone at night. Neither of us knew where the nickname had come from but he'd teased me with it and it had just become our joke. Now he was joking that my occasional babysitter, Cherie, was my sister? She was a just a family friend. I liked her. She had come over and been nice. She wore bells for jewellery. I remembered her smile, her straight jet black hair. We didn't look alike. More importantly, I was the eldest! How could a university student be the child in that photo from the olden times?

I went to my room and reached under my covers for the dollies made of script paper. I threw them into his lap. He held them up, pretending to admire them. The sunlight made the shapes opaque, catching the typing on the other side. He slowly turned it over. He read some of the words. Then he leapt to his feet and lunged for me. I was already sprinting to the other side of the table. He chased me round and round, fast in his fury. 'Mum, Mum!' I shouted, 'Dad's going to hit me!' He never had in the past, though this time looked likely to be the first. Mum entered to a scene of squealing chairs and Scouse cussing. He lapped the oak dining table again, she stood in front as he tried to grab the straps of my dungarees.

'Tony stop! Stop! You will never hit these girls do you hear me? You'll have to get through me first.' I hid under the table, panting. Mum led Dad, head bowed (about the script not about wanting to clout me) to the living room phone, where he could call his agent, Mary Lee, and face the embarrassment of asking for a duplicate script to be printed and posted.

I crawled from under the table and went to lay on my bed. I stared at the chipped, crumbling ceiling, two faces seared into my mind's eye. How much I hated those knobbly-kneed strangers with their stupid bow-heads. How they must have felt hearing about more children, younger than they were, actually living with the father who had left them, did not cross my mind. I learnt to live with the fact by leaving the room every time the other girls' names came up and pretending it wasn't real.

Until the accident.

***

My days at primary school were a free-for-all amongst the trendy-kid set. I learnt to write essays and explore thought, I loved education and my father was the most inspiring teacher of all. His opinions, his historical knowledge and his care for the 'working class' and anyone under oppression were to have a lifelong effect on my outlook. Outside school hours, things were less rosy. Our once bright and beautiful flat had become a run-down mirror of my parents' relationship. The walls went from cheery yellow to a glum and depressing dark brown.

'Can't see the smoke stains,' my mum would say, painting the walls herself. Sainsbury's shampoo became Fairy Liquid from the kitchen, stripping our hair of shine.

The revelation that our family's life was blighted by poor finances came one afternoon while I was sitting on the toilet. I had put my hand down the side of the yellow enamel, feeling around for toilet paper, and found newspaper instead.

Anyone who has had to use newspaper for this purpose knows it doesn't work. Grimly I washed my hands, stopping at the tarnished bathroom mirror for a little am-dram chat with myself.

I was every inch an actor's daughter. 'This is *not* fair.' I whispered at the brown eyes staring back at me.

'It's inhumane to live like this. I wish, I wish I had normal parents, who went to work, came home, cooked dinner, watched TV and went to bed at a normal time and ... and ... could afford loo roll!' I closed my eyes tight, forcing a tingle to climb behind them. Tears were forming.

In a rage which was only part pretend, I grabbed the remaining newspaper and marched to the living room where Dad was in his 2–4 pm phase of the day: Chain smoking and watching the horse racing. I deliberately stood in front of him, blocking his view of the screen, and crossed my arms.

'Dad,' I said.

He leaned to one side so he could see around me to the horses parading ahead of the 2:45 at Newbury, glancing edgily at the betting odds in the newspaper and opening another can of the yellow, bile-smelling poison known as 'beer'. 'Dad!' I said louder.

'Out the way, kid.' This was a warning.

'No!' I stood my ground.

'You what?' I had his attention now, at least until the next race was called. There was no time to waste:

'Dad – I hate being poor!' I wailed, putting dramatic expression into the words and leaning my body towards him in what I hoped was an approximation of a desperate match-girl from the Victorian era.

'How do you mean, you're poor?' He sat forward from his slump, a curious half smile on his lips.

'Look at this!' I dramatically pulled the bundled newspaper from behind my back. 'We are poor because we use Fairy Liquid as soap and newspaper as toilet paper and ...'. Words failed me. Didn't he see the cigarette holes in the filthy living room carpet? Was he oblivious to the beetles which had swarmed over Lucy's cat bowl? Did he really not notice the stinking, unwashed dishes piled high in the sink, or the empty, vomit-smelling fridge?

'I see.' He crossed his long legs and leant back into the sofa. There was a long pause. I didn't have much idea about my father's childhood in wartime Liverpool. His father, had been injured at work after leaving the Merchant Navy. His mother had taken in washing and done part-time work. No one had moaned about being poor. Others were homeless after the German bombing. Dad had been pulled out from a promising school career to work for the family. He knew what I didn't. That his first wife, Gale, and his daughters, Cherie and Lyndsey, had less than I had. The house in Ferndale Road was overcrowded, with an outdoor lavvy. The women-led family were busy doing the Northern thing of 'getting on with it.'

'You think that because we use newspaper when we go to the toilet instead of fancy, pink stuff, that somehow that makes you poor – is that it?'

When he said it like that, it sounded stupid. I gulped. 'Ye-es.'

He strode over and snatched the paper holding. 'And what newspaper is it that you dislike using as loo roll, Little Miss Fauntleroy. Is it the *Sun*, or the *Mirror*?'

He knew it was the *Guardian*, it was the only paper allowed in the house now the hated Margaret Thatcher was in power.

'It's *The Guardian* Dad, but that's the not the point ...'

Bending down, he put his hands on my shoulders. 'Look around you kid. Look at where you live, look at the nicey, nicey school you go to, look at the types of friends you have like what's 'er name ... Olivia? Christ sake! This ...' he shook the *Guardian* pages in front of my nose, 'This is a broadsheet you're using to wipe your dainty southern derriere. This, my girl, is the toilet paper of aspiration! If we ever have to use the *Sun*, then you should be worried!'

He finally spotted my tears (becoming more real by the moment).

'Do you understand, kid? It's all about education and prospects. And you ...' He gave me an appraising look, 'you have white skin, you live in England, you're pretty and clever enough. Guess what – you've won the lottery of life. There's millions and millions of kids worse off than you. It's not where you start, it's where you end up. And you. You are gonna change the world.'

He grinned lovingly at me for a moment.

'Now out the way, we're broke not poor. There's a world of difference and I've got a bob each way on the next race ...'

My father was right. Not having the finer things in life was no handicap so long as I had a smart mind and big dreams. I needed to be more grateful instead of wasting precious moments moaning about things not being 'perfect'. That day I decided that having belief, confidence and ethics was the way to navigate the world.

CHAPTER 2
KEEPING THE FAITH

'Then fancies flee away! I'll fear not what men
say, I'll labour night and day to be a pilgrim.'

John Bunyan

When I was a kid, worrying about things at bedtime was only for adults or while cramming for the few hours before a test. Otherwise my mind was free to roam, bored at first, then towards interesting topics which adults forgot to explore as they worried about money or the likelihood of nuclear war with the Soviets. Children are being starved of imagination because of screens in their bedrooms, screens everywhere. When I was eight years old, having been sent to bed with 'no messing around' after the *Nine O'clock News* there was never anything to do but lie there and think.

Thinking is a big deal. It's a bit like boredom, only better, though both have the same starting point: having absolutely nothing to do. My bedroom was a perfect starting point for boredom. There was a single bed, a second-hand wardrobe, a cracked sink. Finding nothing to occupy it, my mind turned to the big questions that demanded universal answers. These began and usually ended with: What is really out 'there'? I would lay in my bed trying to grapple with how the universe never, ever came to an end. Never. Ever. Admittedly, I didn't have much distance to measure this 'forever' against. During the summer, Nan and

Granddad would take my sister and me to Bournemouth on the south coast, which was considered 'not too far'. However, the 11-hour slog up the A1 to Rhyl, a journey of some 230 miles, was known to be 'a long way'. 'Forever' would be double that and then some.

This thought, far more than death (which is easy to ignore at eight), tormented me. I would try hard to make my soul, my consciousness, leave my body so I could look down on myself and then float away. I thought it would work if I closed my eyes and lay really still, but it was never enough, of course, because the soul is stubborn. So I tried to visualize my essence leaving my sleepy body behind to fly out of the broken window-pane of my room. The crumbling panes in my room caused the glass to rattle and fall out on windy nights and Mum boarded up the holes with flaps of cardboard which let in the wind and the cold. Never mind that, I knew such distractions stopped the process. I lay on my back, urging my soul to leave my body. Up through the night sky I would suddenly burst, soaring past eons and eons of stars. Silent, cold air would brush my cheeks as I sought and sought for an answer which my child's brain could manage.

There *had to* be an end … to … being. Everything, even anything, could not just continue forever, it didn't make sense. Every time I threw my 'self' forward in space I ended up at a brick wall. A literal, visualized brick wall, with a sign on it that said: 'End of the Universe Here. Stop.' This was most probably a result of my watching the famous sci-fi comedy *The Hitchhiker's Guide to the Galaxy* on BBC2. It was a frustrating taunt that wouldn't go away. Unable to come to the end of the universe in my imagination, I would lie there and then, stone-still, try to go backwards, to the beginning, to the heart of everything; to the moment of creation.

Dad had gone through a messy spiritual divorce from the Catholic Church long before I was born. Now he talked endlessly about the untapped power of the mind. Presciently, he would say: 'Mankind's on the wrong track kid. They're all obsessed by machines and electronics. What we should be doing is finding out why we are here in the first place. What's our true purpose? We need to look at the untapped power of the brain.'

On the evenings when there wasn't enough loose change for the pub, we would sometimes do experiments in mind reading using a pack of cards. We'd sit cross-legged together on the musty living room rug. Holding up a card to his chest, he would look at me intently.

'Now Sarah, use your mind's eye. Really concentrate on what I am sending over to you. It's a picture, try and see it and then say the FIRST card that comes into your mind.'

This was the age of transcendental meditation, gurus, chanting and ganja-induced highs.

God may have been out of the picture for the adults around me, but the material world was shown to be just a façade, to be transcended – if you had the tools. Or the narcotics.

'Five of diamonds!' I said.

'No. Let's try again.' He picked a card, stared at it, put it against his chest and turned his green eyes on me. I didn't care about the card game, but I relished our time together.

'Diamonds?' I tried, slowly.

'Yes! Come on ...'

'Seven?'

Sometimes I'd get none and just occasionally, when the room was still and the large girls who lived downstairs weren't 'clumping up and down' as Mum put it, we'd get a run of six, seven, eight cards correct. Then my dad would hug me tight. 'You and me kid,' he'd say, 'we're gonna change the world.' With no acting work on the horizon he had turned his hand to writing and we spent a good deal of time at the Colindale Newspaper Library. He was researching arms links between Libya and Northern Ireland for a book he'd almost finished.

In the spring of 1979, my career in the Golders Green Brownie troop scaled new heights. Our leader, Brown Owl, a modest and kind-eyed lady with fashionably short hair, elected me for the honour of presenting the Brownies flag to the church altar. I nervously asked my parents to attend, fully expecting them to say no, as this followed on the heels of a huge row between my parents and my grandmother. Frances, fearful of the Godless environment my sister and I were being brought up in, kept pushing us to be baptised in a church. My parents utterly refused. This led to the infamous incident where my father, not totally sober, held one of our heads under the tap in the kitchen. With my grandmother watching in apoplectic fury, he splashed water over our hair and yelled: 'The father, the son and the holy spook. There, baptised! Happy now?'

Nan would later tell this tale to me in the safety of her own home and my neck would prickle with terror. Had all of our eternal souls been compromised? Was Daddy going to Hell? Was I? This memory would send me rushing to the bedroom to pray fervently in private, so I was shocked when Dad said yes to a family outing to church.

The ceremony was a classic C of E standard of the time and the Brownies and Girl Guides were drilled relentlessly during the Wednesday evening meetings about what would take place. It was known that all the parents, plus well-to-do local dignitaries, would be present. In home- made Easter Bonnets, young children carrying posies of spring flowers would make a procession down the aisle, bobbing (curtseying) as they reached the altar, then skipping to the second row of proud bankers and owners of rose gardens. The cute smaller girls in their yellow bonnets, decked with homemade eggs and bunnies tied up with yards of ribbon, would make their way back to their parents to coos of, 'ah, bless them.' This was a quarter of a century or so before the smartphone, so no videos were ever taken. Besides, no one would have dreamt of desecrating the ceremony by taking a camera to church on such a holy day.

The big day came and everything was going well. The event had a traditional, English stiff upper lip-ness to it and Easter in the Church of England always had a part reverent, part jubilant atmosphere. A man had died on the cross for our sins. That made him God, although he had already been a part of God all the time. This concept was beyond my 10-year-old brain, so I would file it with the 'end of the universe' mystery – but with one vital difference. There definitely, certainly, had to be a beginning of time and space, I just couldn't grasp it, but the Trinity made the Lord's Prayer (which I loved) a bit goofy. Jesus was a man, a servant of God. He had kneeled before a crowd to teach them how to pray to God, which is why it made sense for the Lord's Prayer to begin 'Our Father, who art in Heaven'. He was teaching his followers that God was the benevolent ruler of every single person on earth and that He was, crucially, both in an unseen realm and in a different dimension to human beings. If Jesus were God *himself*, then he would have told his followers to kneel before him and say: 'I am the Father, who art right now here on earth, hallowed be *My* name, My Kingdom Come, My will be done.' I ignored the Trinity and prayed to God alone.

At the back of the church, my knees trembled and my right hand quivered on the flag staff. A powerful sense of awe and fear came over me. I was before a symbolic representation of The Creator: The Power and The Glory, He was before me (unseen), watching as Sarah Jane Booth presented our Brownie squadron in service to Him. I thought I was going to faint with the weight of the duty. He was the Mighty, the Judge, the Great; God was One and He was watching me plunge the flag into its holster.

I was so deep in reverence, I only just about noticed the other girls peel away as we stood in front of the altar. I stood there, terrified. Behind me, my father's acting sensibility noticed the minuscule hesitation, and in his legendary (very loud) stage whisper he urged: 'Don't dry up now, kid, embrace the nerves, you can do it!' After a small pause, and to the congregation's relief, I heaved up the flag and brought it down again into its new rightful place to the right of the altar. All I had to do then was turn around and walk to the rear of the church.

Around this time, there were a spate of films that effected a generation. These were the Hollywood and British-made blockbusters about Biblical characters and the Tudor royal family. Famously, Charlton Heston played Moses, with his long locks flowing in the breeze and God above him in the storm clouds issuing edicts and warnings for the Children of Israel. Meanwhile, British studios made movies about long dead rulers such as Queen Elizabeth I and Henry VIII – to the English they ruled as God's chosen appointees.

Standing before the altar, I felt this was all wrong. There had not been the reverence to the ceremony I had expected. I was disgusted at the girls who had simply turned their backs on the Lord, then skipped away. Hand quivering on the staff, about to let go of the flag, my mind fixed on the way Elizabethan courtiers in the films bowed and grovelled backwards from the Queen. I instantly knew that this was the level of respect that was called for. I wanted to show God I was a girl who really respected Him more than some King or Queen of England. I made a waist deep bow. The congregation behind inhaled. Then, tiny step, by tiny step I inched my way back up the red carpet of the aisle almost bent double. Right foot back, left foot together, right foot back … after a metre or so of my reverse parade, titters, muffled by polite coughs, were heard from the congregation. I continued, backward I shuffled 'right, together, left, together.' I remember a feeling of heaviness, a fuzzy distance from the world of coats and handbags. 'Right, together, left, together.' God was worth every mocking giggle.

Suddenly, the jewelled hand of a Brownie mum grabbed my right arm and heaved me onto a pew with an accompanying tut, loud enough to cause an echo. I looked at my hands, a flush heating the back of my neck. The vicar keen to pick up the pace, the jolly atmosphere of his Easter Sunday service suddenly flattened by unexpected seriousness. We rose to our feet for the Brownie troop's favourite hymn, 'Lord of the Dance', it was a rare treat which allowed smiling and even a bit of swaying from side to side ('but not too giddy,' Brown Owl had reminded us). Afterwards, parishioners milled around in front of the stone grey church, on a small verge directly opposite the famous Hippodrome concert hall. The sun was shining as toddlers, finally hat-free, tumbled and played on the newly-mown grass.

My father, predictably, was mobbed by star struck mums and dads. He saw me and gifted me a smile, which showed his dimples. I ran over and he ruffled my beret until it fell off.

'Yeah kid, yeah! I get it, totally, you were right! If Kings and Queens get treated like that, He, up there (he nodded at the sky) deserves way more! You were great kid – right on, right on!' He was punching the air, to the bemused suspicion of the more conservative parents. I knew Dad would understand what I'd been trying to do. If you were going to do anything – even religion – do it in a big way, don't patsy around.

CHAPTER 3
HOT AS HELL

'If we don't know many things about Mister
God, how do we know he loves us?'

Sydney Hopkins

Later that year, in November 1979, tragedy struck. My father had collected the bi-monthly money he received for food and bills that morning, but he hadn't come home to share it. Instead, he was missing again. At nine o'clock my mother, jittery and depressed, called me into the hall. The heavy wooden front door had two locks and she turned the iron key in the top one, an ominous sign; Mum was the only one with the knack of unlocking it. She looked down at me and sternly warned: 'Don't let your father in when he gets back. Whatever he says. Do you understand?'

'Okay Mum,' I replied.

'I mean it. Do NOT let him in. I've had enough!'

We both knew that if I could manage to open the lock, I'd let my father in, half-pushing, half-carrying him to the living room sofa. I'd done it so many times before. When I opened the door on those occasions, he'd be so grateful he'd burst into tears at not having to spend a humiliating night on the cold, green linoleum of the public hallway.

'Don't let the Bastards grind you down, kid,' he'd slur, as I stroked his hair.

'And this above all things – to thine own self be true!' Advice from Polonius, the faintly ridiculous, pompous courtier in Shakespeare's *Hamlet*. Before his red eyes closed, he'd hug me until I thought my ribs would break and whisper: 'You and me, kid – we're gonna change the world!'

That night my mother went to her room to take the sleeping tablets prescribed by a doctor (eventually) and lay, fully dressed, on her bed in a semi- comatose state.

Around midnight, a commotion at our front door woke me up. I ran to the front door to try and let my father in. Fiddling with the lock, I was shocked when a stranger spoke directly to me through the letterbox: 'Open the door, little girl, and let your daddy in or we'll have to burn it down like we do in Ireland, understand?'

I froze in terror, unsure if I was awake or having a nightmare. My Dad was speaking to another man and I couldn't make out what they were saying. I pinched myself, I was awake. There were dragging sounds, of metal on lino, then the sound of the hatch on the roof outside being opened. Did I open the door to the men or not? It was a redundant question as the lock was jammed anyway. I could smell whisky fumes coming through the letter box. My 8-year-old sister appeared next to me, crying and rubbing her eyes.

'There's a foot in my roof and stuff fell on me. I think it's Dad. Mum won't wake up.'

I ran to my sister's bedroom. There was no foot over the bed any more, just a gaping hole. Overhead, we heard heavy footsteps as our father fought, in match-lit darkness, to navigate his way through the loft towards the hatch which opened into our hall. Scared by the man at the front door, I sent my sister to our parent's bedroom. 'Ignore it,' I said, 'it's Dad'. We were used to having to ignore music or arguments late in the night. This was different, though, strangers were involved.

I went to bed, throwing the covers over my head and praying to God to make the night end. I had a sick feeling it was only the beginning and my ears were hyper-sensitive, alert to the slightest sound. A few minutes later I heard a crash. I ran back to the front door. There was a noise outside, like my father's voice but high pitched, wretched, agonised.

'Jesus, God HELP ME! HELP ME! Sarah, OPEN THE DOOR. HELP ME!'

I dragged a heavy oak dining chair to the door, but even at that height I couldn't undo the stiff top bolt. Dad's screams intensified. I was shuddering. There were men's voices outside and smoke was filling the hall from a fire in the letterbox. The men began swearing; 'F*** you idiot, what did you do?' There was running, a frantic knocking at a door, and neighbours voices. My father was still screaming and I listened transfixed in horror on the chair behind the smoking door.

Suddenly, chillingly, the screams stopped. On silent. In shock I crept back to bed and pulled the covers over my head once more. My mother woke up later, coughing from the smoke fumes. She found me hiding, grabbed me and my sister's hands and unbolted the smoking door. Before us was a scene of utter chaos. Firemen were in the hallway between our flat and that of our neighbour, Jeremy, and an ambulance siren wailed in the distance. Two huge men stood on the stairs between the landings, looking strange. From his front door a few feet away from ours, where we stood in confusion, Jeremy reached a hand towards me.

'Sarah just come this way - quick! And you, Suzie, DON'T look down!' My sister was shoved into his hands and my mother dragged me with her, but I pulled away. Terrible things happen in slow motion and I felt my neck turn, my hand leaving my mother's, as I brushed past the firemen trying to help us across, to block our view of whatever was on the landing below. I ran to the cast-iron railings searching for my father.

I looked. My father was face down directly below me, his lower legs emitting smoke, seeping a red and white fluid. He lay in a puddle of what seemed like oil and water and the air smelt of burning flesh. He was panting weakly, repeating the same words over and over and over: 'Oh God ... Oh God ... Oh God.'

A fireman grabbed me in his hands and took me into number 78, putting me on a red sofa next to my silent mother and crying sister. There was one more shock to come. Around 3 am, the three of us were huddled together in bed. My father had been taken to a 'special' hospital by ambulance. The fire at the door, which had spread via my burning father to the floor on the landing, had been extinguished. The lights were off and the burnt door was securely bolted once again. We had just fallen asleep when my mother screamed. A dark figure stood in the doorway of her room.

'How did you get in? Leave us alone!' She shouted.

'I'm not going to hurt you,' said the voice I recognised from the letter box, 'I just came to say I'm sorry. I really am.'

'Get out! Get Out!' My mother screamed.

'I'm so sorry about what we did,' repeated the retreating shadow. We heard the front door being unlocked, then slamming shut. The only sound was my mother's ragged breathing.

As my father was rushed to hospital, he needed resuscitation several times to bring him back from the brink of death. He was taken to a specialist burns unit, some thirty miles away, in the countryside. My mum went to see him, but never said much about his condition except 'still alive.' Weeks later, when he was out of danger and the sight of him was deemed not too traumatic for my sister and me, most Sundays our grandfather would drive us on the hour long journey to visit him. Doctors said 45 per cent of his body had suffered third degree burns, and my father lay, heavily bandaged from the waist down and somehow shrunken, in the burns unit of Mount Vernon rehabilitation centre.

He had suffered dozens of agonising skin grafts and had lost toes, but on my visits he would make the nurses, who all clearly adored him, giggle. His body may have been diminished by several layers, but his character still won fans. After several months, he would lean on me as he relearnt how to walk, agonisingly dragging his still-seeping legs up and down blue hospital corridors. He also needed to be weaned off the high-intensity pain relief which had helped him survive the agony of the first three months. I prayed every day for six months for him to stay alive, to return home to us.

During our walks up and down the corridor, Dad would tell me about his soul leaving his body, I believed him.

***

22nd July 1980, my thirteenth birthday, granddad Spike drove me to the rehab unit where my father proudly stood up on his own in the family visiting lounge. He handed me a white and navy embroidered cheesecloth shirt that a nurse had bought for him from a nearby market. I held my father's hand and we walked slowly up and down the corridor as usual. Each step was agony for him, but he refused to be 'a cripple' and use a wheelchair. I held back tears at the sight of his bandaged hands, his perilous weight loss, and at his normally blonde hair, now shockingly and permanently white.

A song by the band Thin Lizzy was playing on the radio at the nurses' station as we passed: 'When you begin to smile you change my style, my Sarah ...'.

'That's my song for you,' he said, pausing to look out of the window at the pleasant hospital grounds. 'I always think of you when that plays.'

After another pause, he said, 'Your mum and me, we're finished. You must have known this was coming, kid ... Look, if you want to come with me to Liverpool you can, but it won't be easy. I'm going to live with my Mum, your grandmother, Vera. You've met her, remember? It won't be easy but we'll get through. It's your choice, Sarah – me or your mum. But I'm telling you that I'm leaving London forever.'

I couldn't answer. How can you split your heart? He hobbled down the blue corridor, away from me. I chose to stay in London, with my mum, my sister, my grandparents. And Dad, true to his word, never came back.

He would phone on a Sunday every so often, when my sister and I were at our grandparents and had access to a phone. We discussed 'the night of the fire' many times. I asked him about the men with Irish voices, behind the door. About the one who had broken in later when we were in bed. Dad told me they were British soldiers from a special unit based in Ireland. That they approached him in a pub and plied him with free drink all night.

My father believed the state had tried to kill him. Either for what he had found out during his research into Irish and Libyan arms deals or for his anti-authoritarian activities. All I know for sure is that almost a decade later my father applied for and allegedly received government compensation for his injuries. On the condition that he stopped looking for answers.

CHAPTER 4
CLOWN OF RENOWN

'Life is a lot like jazz... it's best when you improvise.'

George Gershwin

The girls and staff at Copthall Girls Secondary School knew my father was on the TV. As a result my quietness was confused with snobbery. I didn't fit in at school.

It wasn't all bad. I remembered what my father had told me about making the best of things. I decided to see the fact I had zero friends, as an opportunity. I would spend break and lunch times rotating my reading between the King James Bible and the complete works of Shakespeare.

Meanwhile, I watched from a curious distance the social hierarchy of school life. Asian pupils, I noticed, fell into two categories where the majority white students were concerned. Most were given the simple title, 'Budbud Dings.'

'Budbudbudbud' was a mocking imitation of Urdu, Bangla and Hindi. The girls called this name had (it was presumed) fathers who worked on the London buses. 'Ding' being the sound of the bell that was rung when a passenger wanted the bus to stop. It was inconceivable that 'Budbud' parents had any other jobs, aspirations or talents besides running newsagents or working on public transport.

My generation in North London were on the frontline of a social Dark Age. Some of our parents waxed lyrical about Hindu gurus, or listened to Bob Marley, but to the majority of white

Britons, being Asian was a sign of social and racial inferiority. Nobody at the time cared which weird and wonderful, undoubtedly colourful, God the new arrivals, with their peculiar, spicy food, chose to pray to. Their lesser value system and culture could never effect Queen and Country after all.

One day, Yvonne from one of the other Year 10 classes, came in with her hair in braids. The bead colours caused a stir and at lunchtime the canteen came to a standstill, Our year gathered around her, shoving each other for a look at the blue and yellow plastic orbs. These were the colours of our unfortunate school uniform. Yvonne was part of a quiet revolution, after the only other pupil of West Indian heritage in that year had been sent home for sporting the same hairstyle. When asked why she was being dismissed from schools was told it was for a uniform infraction as the beads were not 'in the school colours'. To cheers of support, Yvonne, in her braids tipped by school colours, made her way to the deputy principal's office. She was not at school for a week after. Raised voices had been heard and rumours emerged that Mrs H (the Dragonesque Deputy Head) had been heard shouting:

'School colours or not, we will not tolerate any of that foreign culture here!'

***

My father's accident hit me hard. I went from an exam average topping 93 per cent to failing in many subjects. Nobody noticed. I found that my ability to put on accents and to mimic teachers reduced the amount of bullying significantly. I developed quite a repertoire of impersonations as a result; Mavis from Corrie, Kermit the Frog, and even Mrs Thatcher found their way into my break time act. Sometimes I smoked with the older girls in the utterly putrid wood and stone toilet block. It was clear to me that playing a role in certain groups of people could be a convenient way of getting by. Little did the fifth-year punks know that all alone on the walk home by the glorious Heath, I would skip and recite poetry, talking to the trees and asking them how their day was, noting every seasonal change and relishing every note change in the flavour of the air around me. And sometimes, sometimes I would speak to God and thank Him for nature.

Dad had moved back 'up North' to start yet another stage of his life. Only he wasn't stuck at his mother's house like he said. Pat Phoenix, a successful soap star of the time, nurtured him back to health in her pretty country home, Sunny Place Cottage, near Stockport. They had met decades earlier as young stars on a film set, though despite an attraction nothing had happened. Pat was a wonderful, earthy woman with star quality in every pore. My sister and I would spend glorious summers at her house or on tour with them both in the plays they staged together.

Dad and Pat would love each other joyfully until she died of cancer, six years later.

Despite my emotional setback after the accident, I somehow managed to scrape five GCSEs and two A Levels (pretty good for those times). Ignoring my grandmother's appeals to go to secretarial college I entered a small drama school, the London Academy of Performing Arts, and studied Shakespearean language, movement and improvisation, plus modern and tap- dance for two years. It felt like heaven on earth.

Leaving an unsubstantial drama school with an 'Acting Diploma' not worth the paper it was printed on, the reality of seeking an acting career struck home. By 1989, the throb of money 'talking' and compassion 'walking' was spreading its icy fingers into all our lives. Just a decade earlier, cafés, Post Offices and even (say it in a whisper) banks had been places where lonely pensioners could easily find compassionate people to chat with about the benefits of woollen underwear on breezy days. In Thatcher's Britain, they became places of 'commerce' amid a brutal rebranding of 'business'.

'There but for the grace of God go I,' I said, dropping some small change into one of the many sleeping bag homes cropping up across London. I worked in various bars and restaurants to pay for the room I was renting in a family home in Highbury. My breath tasted of tar and liquor when I closed my eyes to sleep, and my principles of fair play were being eroded by male attention. I dished out beer in place of kindness to the elderly, the frail and the poor, until they could no longer remember their misery and turned the key in their own lonely locks, falling unconscious. We were the same in many ways.

One night, ten hours into a double shift at the Steam Rock Cafe, Old Norm, the impoverished rocker, swayed at the bar. Two pence pieces were scattered on the sticky mahogany as he tried to make sense of the numbers.

'Sarah, love, is that forty pence or twenty or ...'

My manager came over, shouting into Norm's face with no hint of irony:

'No more for you tonight! You're drunk and we can't sell alcohol to drunks. So go home!'

***

Not long after leaving drama school, I set off around the world with my boyfriend. We kicked off the adventure in America where I spent three months working as a Summer Camp Counsellor in Vermont. In New York, we stayed with a millionaire actor called Missy, from drama school, before driving a car to Florida for payment. In Miami, I waited yet more tables, this time for gangsters from New York who ran a Steak House. I disliked the experience, America seemed crass. There were restaurants called 'Hooters' where teenage girls in micro shorts and skin tight t-shirts roller-skated pitchers of beer to tables of leering men who looked between their legs when they bent over. I sat on South Beach, a short walk from the bedsit we shared with a Serbian backpacker, where men in thongs paraded up and down. I would bury my head in a book and I told my boyfriend: 'If Australia is like this, I'm going home.'

The second we set foot in Sydney airport I was in love. The culture was manly and misogynistic, but the utter lack of snobbery was a refreshing change from London's 'hyper' atmosphere, and after Florida's flashy commercialism, the rugged blokes in the Greenwood Tree Pub where we worked were earthier. We stayed in Sydney for a year before setting off up the Gold Coast, turning inwards on the dusty road towards the Red Centre, driving thousands of kilometres in an aged Datsun 180b. When there were no trees to string up our hammocks, we slept in the back of the car.

It was in the Outback that I learnt a vital life lesson. We had a budget of five dollars a day, with this we brought packets of instant pasta and water, plus the occasional slice of kangaroo or camel meat from the fly-blown bush towns we passed through. We were young and madly in love, and the outdoors suited us. For the first month of our travels I would marvel at the star-packed skies. Before then, being a city kid, I had actually thought that the sky was naturally orange at night.

Waking before dawn, I climbed out of the back of the car, where we had accidentally parked in a dry river bed, 100 kilometres from Alice Springs. We'd need a tow to move on and had waited for two days, but no car had turned off the main route so far and we were getting low on water. I stood on the red sand, stretched and sniffed the air. A huge smile spread across my sun-tanned face as I bent down and blew new life into the embers of the previous night's fire. From a side pouch of my backpack I pulled out two tea bags, and using the army tins we ate and drank from began to brew up. The sun's first rays turned the horizon into a cradle of red and gold. This was being alive!

Our three month Outback odyssey ended in Darwin, capital of the Northern Territories. A steamy area where locals are famous for irrational behaviour nicknamed 'Going Troppo' as they link it to the tropical climate. We pulled up exhausted after our twelfth consecutive day driving. At dusk, the city centre car park was sweltering and my body pulsated with the adrenaline of travel. I was twenty-one years old, tanned, fit and unafraid. Even being broke, having lived in that state since childhood, held no fear. I emptied my pockets onto the dashboard and my boyfriend did the same. Then we rifled through every pocket in both of our army-style backpacks.

'Five dollars,' I said. We had to make a choice. We could either buy two cold beers and go to bed hungry, or we could use the money to buy a couple of burgers to eat, before settling down to sleep in the car, yet again. We headed to the nearest bar.

In khaki shorts, army jungle boots and a pink tank top with a knife attached to my belt buckle, I placed our precious five dollars onto the bar. Looking around, I noted sawdust on the floor, a usual presence in bars where blood was regularly spilled through fighting. At the base of the bar was the metal guttering I recognised from time serving beer in Sydney. It worked as an impromptu urinal or a place to vomit for men too drunk to make it to the bathroom. This was a venue for bikers who enjoyed violence and heavy metal. As we finished our single beer and prepared to go, a man in his thirties with a handlebar moustache offered us another. His name was Mitch. He was an office worker, who seeing two dusty travellers in his home town took pity on us. A tray of burgers arrived and Mitch invited us to spend our last week in Australia in his home.

As the place filled up, our table was joined by a biker with a long beard and leather jacket. He was trying to draw me into a conversation across the table, I could hardly hear him over the loud music.

'What?' I said again. 'Sorry? I can't hear you!'

I pulled out a Marlboro cigarette and asked the guy for a light.

'You shouldn't smoke girly,' he said.

'Yeah well I do, so you got a light?' I retorted.

'If you were my woman, you wouldn't smoke,' he snarled.

'Well that's never gonna happen, so just give me a light, ok?' I stared into his beery eyes unafraid of confrontation. I was invincible.

The biker leaned across the table and raised his voice, calling my bluff. 'Light that cigarette and I'll knock it from yer mouth.'

My boyfriend looked up from the jukebox and headed over. 'Listen mate, I wouldn't mess with her if I were you okay? She's her own woman ...'

'She your bit?' Asked the biker.

'Like I said,' my boyfriend said, seeking to calm things down, 'I wouldn't mess with her if I were you.'

Meanwhile, I was still hollering across the table for a light. I was passed a BIC lighter, which I used to casually, slowly, light my cigarette. Before I could inhale, the biker came round the table, bent down and smacked the cigarette from my lips. The shock sent adrenaline pumping through my veins. I leapt up, automatically unclipping my knife from its sheath with my right hand. With my left, I grabbed the biker's hair and pulled his head towards mine. I held the sharpened knife to his throat.

'Don't F- about. Understand?' I hissed.

Like in the movies, a sudden glimmer of respect – mingled with fear – crossed his face. He stammered: 'Alright, alright love, leave it out, no great shakes okay? Just having a laugh weren't we?'

People were looking at the posh-speaking 'Pom' with the quick draw. I was Wonder Woman. I had no limits and no one could, or did, try to tell me what to do. I had been a feral teen, free to do what I wanted, when I wanted, now I was an undercover feral adult. The normal rules of society didn't concern me at all. Principles and rules were for those without the guts to challenge them.

Returning to the UK, I worked full-time in the acting profession for around two of the next seven years. The rest of the time, I made ends meet in a series of part-time jobs. The most enjoyable of these being my time as a children's entertainer. Yes, I literally was a professional clown. I was signed to a posh Chelsea agency who provided entertainers for the amusement of children of the super-rich. My character, 'Marley Marvo', was a girl with freckles and bunches, who wore oversized dungarees. Marley became a presence, you could say, on the birthday party scene, which consisted of some of Britain's top celebrity families. Bob Geldof and Paula Yates held a party for Peaches in a West London church hall when she was five years old. Leading the fun – me! Michael Hutchence was in the back kitchen when I went to grab some paper cups. He was wearing rock star glasses with thick black frames, which his cheekbones somehow made trendy. It's strange to think that all three of them: Peaches, Paula Yates and Hutchence are all dead now. Victims of the modern celebrity cocktail of alcohol and drugs. Where too few friends will tell you what a vain, self-defeating fool you are being. A reality which pushes bodies and souls to the outer limits of hope and sensibility.

Billy Connolly and Pamela Stephenson's little daughters were a dream. I remember the Big Yin (as he was famously known) breezing in. 'How do you work the stereo, Mr Connolly,' I asked in awe of the famous comic talent before me.

He guided me to a long, flat, black table, with the vague instruction to: 'Just wave your hands over it! An amazing thing truly, it will play whatever you like!' For 15 minutes I flapped my hands over and around the coffee table. I finally figured out I had been pranked and that the coffee table was not actually some ahead-of-its-time high-tech sound system. Despite this setback, his daughters and I spent a wonderful, music-free afternoon putting on a play about fairies for the delighted parents.

I loved the work. I was aware that every week of 'clowning around' was another nail in the coffin of my dream to be a Hollywood actress, but at the same time I'd been taught to be grateful and to plough on with whatever life dished out. The pay was brilliant by the standards of the time, a whopping £25 an hour, less petrol. I had money to spend and weekdays off to write angry letters to theatre directors, berating them for not making the effort to witness my incredible talent.

There was some serious work too. In 1995, I played the lead role in a ten month tour of Austria with Vienna's English Theatre. And the years between the vanity of drama school and the reality of life as a children's entertainer and bit-part actress wore on. Waiting for phone calls from directors became a challenge even to my optimistic nature.

The future stretched out in front of me, an endless waiting room of auditions and 'no thank you' letters.

CHAPTER 5
LAUGHING FOR LABOUR

'Making mistakes is how you learn.'

Tony Benn

During my twenties I was busy tweaking my acting 'look'. From 'alluring secretary' to 'comely girl-next-door'. At auditions, I would suck in my cheeks and smile demurely. I perfected a sweet 'happy-to-see-ya!' tone to cover the desperate edge creeping into my voice.

At the same time I changed my name. All actors – who wanted credibility – had to sign up with the acting union, Equity. I was shocked to learn that my name, 'Sarah Booth', was already in use by another actor of the same age. At the other end of the phone, the Equity official impatiently waited to register me. As with all important decisions, I chose my new name impulsively: 'Sarah Booth's gone has it? Okay then, well …'. I was never going to change my surname. Dad had drummed it into me that as he had no sons his girls were his legacy and we must keep his name even after marriage – which many of us would. 'Well then, okay … Lauren! Yes, Lauren Booth, has a nice ring to it.' And there it was, my new name, my new identity. A blank canvas to play with.

I was being offered the full range of characters on offer to a young female actor and I received a phone call telling me I had passed an audition and had a role in a melodrama. A six month contract for a cast of three to tour colleges and village halls across France.

Despite the high jinks of touring with fabulously talented and amusing actors yet again, it was a rude awakening that at twenty-eight I was already too old for Hollywood. In fact, even a soap opera like *EastEnders* was out of my reach. My father had drilled into me that acting was not for the faint-hearted. He always used to say: 'Acting is a vocation not a vacation. The second you are not willing to starve in a garret for your art, get out and make way for the actors who love it more than you.' I didn't want my brain to turn to mush waiting for a single line on a TV drama, so in February 1997, I left the tour three months early and began two courses: One in touch typing (how proud my Nan would have been at this common sense!), the other a night- school course in journalism at Birkbeck College, London.

Having split from my boyfriend of seven years, I was back living with my mother in her small, modern apartment in north London. We would watch the nightly news, increasingly thrilled with the growing interest in my brother-in-law. After the unexpected death of the Labour party leader, John Smith, three years earlier, I watched 'our Tony' climb from the seemingly unwilling leader of a politically stagnant Labour Party to the bright young thing of British politics; the man on whom the hopes of a nation rested. He was quite simply amazing, a hero.

Whenever I met Tony he was kind and distracted, like a youthful professor contemplating a mathematical equation that would always be beyond my intellect. Tony and Cherie had taken on an elder sibling's role since I had been at drama school.

After Cherie had looked after me as a child, it was a pleasure to look after my adorable baby nephews, and cute niece Kathryn; although they would later recount tales of my ripe language and bizarre story telling. I'll never forget the first time I looked inside the Blair's fridge at their Highbury home; at that time I had been living largely on Rice Krispies, trying to eke out my education grant money from term to term. Cherie had invited me to dinner; a young barrister with two toddlers, she was always busy and rushing between childcare and professional work. I stood shyly in the hallway of the three-storey town house. It was grander than anywhere I had visited that wasn't under the auspices of the National Trust. Not that it was flashy, or even plush by today's luxurious standards, it was just a matter of perspective. To me it said something more significant than wealth, it smacked of security. Here was a professional couple in their early thirties who had plans that were practical and 'happening'. Meanwhile, I was floating about dreaming of being a theatre and film star whilst eating cereal in a room which was once a maid's quarters.

Cherie padded upstairs, flicking a hand towards the kitchen: 'Help yourself, down soon.'

The fridge was huge, I opened one of its white doors. Was that angels I could hear? The first thing that struck me was the smell. There wasn't one. It was as pristine as if it had been bought that very day. At eye level there were mini yoghurts, Italian cheeses, artisan relishes. I picked up one whose label read 'caramelised onion chutney'. I'd never heard of such a thing but just from the packaging I guessed it would cost most of my weekly food budget. Tears pricked my eyes. One day, maybe, just maybe, I could have a fridge with toffee vegetables in jars and Waitrose dairy products.

I became energised by the most dynamic election in a generation. I volunteered with Arts for Labour and was posted to a small office in the Labour HQ near Waterloo. Victoria, the strict head of the department, was suspicious of me and there were whispers I was spying for Millbank, the beating heart of the New Labour machine. The suits, the movers and shakers who governed the mysterious science of 'messaging', were based there and when Millbank rang the entire room was shushed, as if we were taking a call from Her Majesty.

I was given a dedicated phone line and the task of calling comedians and 'luvvies' from the entertainment industry to invite them to endorse Tony and 'New' Labour. I had a radio segment on LBC, reviewing theatre and comedy shows, which had brought me into contact with a number of celebrities and my rolodex of contacts was growing. I was convinced I had a pivotal role in a potential Labour victory, but in actual fact phoning radical left-wing comedians (who already hated and distrusted Tony for his jettisoning of traditional policies) was a job no one else particularly wanted. It was a way of giving me a back room role and keeping me out of the way at the same time. My usual phone call went something like this: 'Hi, is that [insert name of popular left-wing comic here]? My name is Lauren Booth and I am working for Arts for Labour. We are hosting several events in the coming weeks and would love you to take part. As you know, this is a monumental opportunity for Labour to finally win an ... New Labour? Well, ye- es, I am from 'New' Labour, but it really is just Labour, isn't it? I mean ... You think Blair's a Thatcherite tool who'll give money to the rich and leave the poor worse off? Well I ... Actually I went to state school! No, I don't think *The Sun* will be the paper of government if we win ... Hey, there's no need to be rude!' I did manage to persuade a number of reluctant comedians and stage stars to either stay with Labour or to join the campaign in earnest. Not on a 'pro-Tony' ticket by any means, but on the far more persuasive 'anyone-but-the-Tories' strategy we had to fall back on.

Two weeks before the election, Arts for Labour held a fundraiser in Bristol. I (an excited puppy let off the lead for the first time) played a small role in helping to organize the show. William Waldegrave, the Tory MP in the Bristol West constituency, had been linked to the sale of arms to various world hot spots and not surprisingly local voters who were sick of 'Tory Sleaze' packed the venue, though the sum raised made as much impact on the party's campaign coffers as Nick Clegg at a meeting of the Socialist Workers Party.

Then, at last came election night. Our family gathered at Tony and Cherie's Sedgefield home. The atmosphere was abuzz – hope tinged with anxiety. Every instinct, every conversation I'd had in the previous month said this would be a landslide removal of the Dark Forces of Conservatism. But what if we were all wrong, as we had been before? The spectre of the Kinnock debacle five years earlier fluttered in the back of my mind. Dad, sisters, Tony, Cherie, parents and children travelled in a convoy from the house to the count at the city centre Town Hall. Flashguns blinded us as we ducked into the pristine fleet of cars. Dad nodded at me and then towards the secret service agents speaking to their wrists. His nod said, 'be careful what you smoke tonight kid, people are watching'. My nod in return said the same to him.

The family's concerns, muttered en route, were not about the election of a relative. We desperately wanted change for the country. The Tories had run a course of boom and bust economics for two decades. Greed had become good and poverty was not a thing to be cured, but an identity to be mocked and loathed. All of the Booths had grown up in working class environments of one kind or another. We knew the monthly panic of our parents as they struggled to pay bills. We wanted a fair start for every child.

At the count, we gathered in the upstairs bar area, the floor sticky with ale. Tony was still an upstart kid, he wasn't PM ... yet. I caught up with him as he craned his neck beneath a mounted TV showing the first BBC exit polls.

'You'll never guess what!?' I gushed. My heart was beating fast with the conviction that somehow I was a pivotal part of whatever victory would take place for the Party and the nation. Tony turned his charming, always-smiling eyes towards me. Dual beams of benevolence and authority: 'Yes Sarah, what have you been up to now?'

'Arts for Labour, well we raised five THOUSAND pounds for the Party at our event in Bristol West, isn't it am-a-zing?'

A fleeting look of confusion crossed his immaculately-shaved expression. Then it cleared so the legendary earnestness could return.

'Right, well, yes, that's great. Well done to all of you down there.'

Alastair Campbell, chief press officer, jogged over, flicked his gaze across me, deemed me beneath a greeting and briskly led Tony away. They were about to win power, how measly a few thousand pounds made by some unwilling comics (who would turn on him at the first opportunity) must have seemed. At 9 pm events took a sudden turn and there were gasps, shouts of joy, and hugs as over the next three hours town after town and city by city the blue map of Britain turned Labour red. Cherie was tearful when her childhood constituency returned to Labour with a huge swing.

Suddenly, Tony and Cherie were gone. It was after 2 am in the morning and my Dad, sisters and I were driven at speed to a nearby airport. We were led onto a small jet and flown to London. Dad was delirious, hilarious. The pilot was told to play BBC radio for us, 'or we're not getting on board.' There were constant shouts of 'yes!' and 'shush, so we can hear!' Then Dad jumped from his seat and ran up and down the aisle, punching the air with glee.

'Up yours Portillo! Yes, yes, yessssss! Bloody hell, Portillo's gone!' The plane rocked with the mania as everyone joined him, standing up from our seats, hugging and crying, until the pilot threatened to land the plane in Birmingham if there wasn't calm on board and Labour wonks giddily wrestled Dad back into his seat.

There was just time for a single glass of champagne with party members at the London celebration before Tony's acceptance speech – as Prime Minister. He climbed onto the stage in the early light of a clear morning. He held out his hand and Cherie stepped up to take it. Tony Blair is undoubtedly one of the greatest, most convincing orators of the modern political age. In the coming years, I would sit in the press box at Labour conferences alongside the likes of Peter Riddell, Peter Hitchens and

Peter Oborne (someone really needs to research into the inherent sarcasm of men with that name), all ready to loathe the heavily-scripted words Tony was about to 'perform'. We planned on making edgy notes on the crafted music selection used by the New Labour apparatchiks to build up the audience before his entrance. The music would change tone, an edgy guitar swelling to hope-filled chords, and a hush would fall over the crowd, as if we were waiting for the Rolling Stones. Then – TONY!

In the press box an irritated yet reverential hush would fall, and pens poised and eyebrows skywards we would wait for the charm to be cast. He'd get us every time, at least temporarily.

I saw blue bloods who had cursed Tony to hell the night before at the Conference bar shaking their balding heads in wonder before his second, perfectly scripted one-liner. I choked up every single time. I wanted Tony to be great. I had the kind of innocent starry-eyed adoration for him that a younger sister has for a heroic, distant older brother. Tony at home was chilled and adorable, Tony outside was magnificent with that knack that cult leaders have of focusing on one person at a time. I wanted to believe he was something great for humanity. The people needed him, we needed hope.

To a crowd of thousands, not only party workers but members of the general public who had flocked to central London to see him, Tony announced to rapturous cheers: 'A new dawn has broken, has it not?' The tide had turned and in what became the modern symbol of the political phrase 'landslide victory', the great British revolt of the age took place. In a single day and night, the Tories reign of tyranny ended. The national turnout was 71 per cent and it would be nineteen years and an EU referendum before the country would mobilise in such numbers again.

After 1 May 1997, things were unexpectedly different for me as well. I didn't have a PR person when the Blair's became global figures. I didn't have an agent, I didn't have a 'plan' or a clue for that matter. These days, the sisters and brothers of superstars have their own PR 'people' before they leave school, to manage disastrous or disastrous-yet-lucrative moments in the outer celebrity solar system. I was a fledgling journalist in a short skirt and high boots with a double Jack Daniel's in one hand, a Marlboro Light in the other and the words 'political liability', visible only to Fleet Street editors, etched onto my forehead.

One day after the election I was inundated with invitations to jazzy lunches at Kensington bistros with Fleet Street editors in less time than it takes to say, 'Blair's sister-in-law'. From then on, the late 90s became a period of adaptation. A time to jump on board what the anarchy-supporting band Chumbawamba called 'the good ship lifestyle'. Jack f

A decade earlier, I had watched sunrises from a hammock in the outback of Australia, happy on just a diet of dried pasta boiled over a fire in the middle of nowhere. By thirty-three I was a fully-fledged career rat, with a grown-up mortgage, home repairs to pay for and a baby on the way. Life was suddenly happening *to* me and it was a bit of a shock. I ran after new jobs with the urgency of a rodent in a scientist's maze. Whoosh, a door opens, and in I would rush with my high heels and skin-tight jeans (no matter the baby bump!) It was exciting but psychologically draining work, trotting out sarcastic comments stretched over a thousand words for a living. In amongst the madness, a blindness developed to the beauty which travels silently alongside us every day. The dreamy child became a spiritually moribund adult. Showing off and being witty was the recompense for my loss of wonder in being alive. It had sneaked in, the need for others' approval. Coupled with the pressures of providing for my family, bad decisions were being made. The connection between the world of the body and the thriving life inside, with universal experiences, is veiled to the one who lurches between thrill seeking and insecurity. I lived with immense wealth compared to the majority of people around the world, yet inside I was starving, living a spiritual existence that was hand to mouth.

My boyfriend and I reunited. On 10 June 2000, we married in the Unitarian Church on Rosslyn Hill, Hampstead. Fashion designer Elizabeth Emanuel, best known for designing Princess Diana's wedding gown, designed my dress. This was not easy as I was four months pregnant. Liz cheerfully added extra panels to increase the waist circumference. Twice. *Hello!* magazine agreed to pay for the entire bash in return for the rights to publish photographs taken on the day and on the glamorous and free honeymoon they'd funded. A pretty good deal, we figured which would have cost us more than 50k.

I had worked for both *Hello!* and *OK!* magazines, interviewing celebrities and writing short political comment pieces. By now my income had skyrocketed and I was in demand, writing columns for several publications and co-hosting TV and radio programmes. The contents of my fridge no longer spoke of part-time jobs and pub working hours. Posh miniature yoghurts with French names chilled alongside Waitrose brand fishy dips. The kind of posh stuff I'd always dreamed of having – not so much for the taste but to enjoy the look of aka *North London fridge dressing.*

Whenever I opened the pristine door, the innards told me:

'You've arrived!'

Our honeymoon was on the private resort island of Canouan, in the Grenadines. It was low season and there were only two other guests poolside on our first morning. The man had silver grey hair and I watched from the comfort of my sun longer as he jogged back and forth along the short stretch of beach before his breakfast. His wife studiously ignored everyone except him. She had swirling black hair and a chic way of sitting delicately on a pool chair, as if ready to be waited on by an array of willing men. It turned out he was Sven- Göran Eriksson, the then-manager of Italian football team, Lazio, and the silent glamour-puss his girlfriend, Nancy Dell'Olio.

One afternoon, my husband and I were asked to pose together in the main swimming pool by the laddish, friendly, *Hello!* photographer sent to do our photo shoot. Large lights were set up next to the crystal blue water of was metres away from a sublime blue seascape, and work. The photographer directed my husband and I: 'Smile!' We looked towards him, swam about and posed in snorkelling gear. 'Smile!' He shouted for the thousandth time. Suddenly, as he moved left to get the shot he wanted, his foot caught in the lead of one of the huge lights, which lurched, slow motion, towards where we were floating in the warm water. I used my legs to push my husband and I backwards as dozens of bulbs plunged towards us!

There was a splash inches from my legs and I closed my eyes and held my breath. This was it! Death! So unexpected, so sudden. Shouldn't I have done more? Done more what, even? Crazy thoughts ran through my head as I waited helplessly for the pain of the electric charge as it surged through the water. The more chemicals there are in water, such as cleaners or salt, the more conductive to electricity it becomes. Most cases of so-called 'pool electrocutions' involve touching or handling an electrical device while in or near the water. The swimming pool we were in, between the restaurant and the seashore, was highly conductive salt water.

There was silence. All I could hear were the waves stroking the shore and the trilling of an exotic bird. My husband's arms were very still. Was I dead? Was he? I opened my eyes. Soca music played over a mocked the frozen scene with around me. The pool barman was a gaping waxwork clutching a tipped jug. A waiter, who had been bringing our lunch on a silver tray, was hand-to-lips, stifling a silent scream. The photographer was hunched in the position he had been in when trying to catch, then missing, the lighting rig.

Then everyone moved at once, as if unfrozen from the movie still we had been trapped in. The waiter shouted, 'Are you okay,

Madame, are you okay, sir?' I was immediately shaking in the sunshine. The photographer, finally recovering his senses, unplugged the lights muttering, 'How, how, how? Sorry, sorry, so stupid!'

I was lifted out of the pool by waiters, as my legs were trembling too much to hold me, and towels were put around us. My

We were fine. Why were we fine? That night, on the far side of a bed the size of a small room with waves singing their lullaby, a thought wouldn't leave my mind. If I'd died in the pool, it would have been without really knowing why I'd been alive in the first place.

CHAPTER 6
JUST BREATHE

We have a secret in our culture, and it's not that birth is painful. It's that women are strong.

Laura Stavoe Harm

Five months to the day, barefoot in the hallway at 4 am, my waters broke with a satisfyingly dramatic, 'pop'. When the contractions came every four to five minutes, I rang the hospital. The Irish midwife at the Royal Free in Belsize Park, North London, was brisk: 'Come in and stop being brave, before you have this baby at home.'

It was 8 am on a crisp and clear north London morning and the roads were quiet. Gulping cool air, I watched, thrilled, as my husband awkwardly tried to strap the baby seat into the back of the car. Soon, our black second-hand Rover chugged along the early quietness of Willesden Road. 'This is it!' Said my husband, reaching past the gearstick and giving my hand a squeeze. My response was a series of heavy pants – another contraction.

'This is the moment I've been waiting for!' He said. I turned to him, as best I could around the convulsing bump on my lap. I was relishing the sweetness of the man about to become father to my child. How adorable that this moment was as special to him as it was to me. How amazing to think that ... he suddenly interrupted my train of thought.

'It's legal to drive as fast as I want and the police can't say a single thing because we are literally about to give birth! Brilliant!' (Note: Never ask a man, 'what are you thinking right now?' It's always a disappointment and never what you hope to hear.)

Hubby slammed the car into gear, screeching to the end of our avenue. Thrown back into my seat I made an involuntary 'oof' tight. Cricklewood raced by in a blur of grey, the lordly stone empires of Frognal were soon behind us and we hit the lights at Whitestone Pond at almost 70 mph.

'Stop!' I shouted.

'Stop?' My husband was confused. 'Are you crazy, you are about to give birth. If we don't hurry ...' He screeched through the lights, boy-racing towards the hospital, where presumably he had dreamt of pulling up in a tyre-blackening skid.

I was conscious of my lungs moving in and out, jagged, rasping. My heart was thudding in my chest with hidden exertions of which I was not even fully aware. I couldn't finish the swear word I'd started. 'Slow ... down,' I puffed.

Reluctantly the car slowed to a crawl down the empty hill.

I remember the view. A vista I had walked across hundreds of times since childhood, a green field swooping down into a valley, the small cottages of the Vale of Health – so named because the Plague in the seventeenth century had never reached it – the long stone pathways leading into woods, where ancient royals once hunted deer with their well-loved, slavering hounds. Today, it was new to my eyes and life was so beautiful, all of it. Everything. The fact that the sun had risen over the heath, heating the water on the blades of grass and fern fronds just enough that they turned to mist. Miracles upon miracles upon mercies.

Inside me, a child wanted to be born. My body wasn't a 'theme park' (as my favourite t- shirt said) after all. It was a blessing, a shrine to creation. A complex mass of unimaginable processes brought together in perfect order to put blood, bones, flesh, and skin on a tiny human inside me. A life about to be released in an ancient act, to be experienced only once or twice in a (western) lifetime. And only by women.

How had I ignored on all my journeys up and down East Heath Road the magnificence of the oak and elm trees thrusting towards the sky? The abundant gift of air-giving nature rolled out before me until I began to whisper, 'Thank you. Thank you. Thank you.'

'Waddling' doesn't begin to describe the bizarre, knee-locked swaying with which I entered the main doors of the Royal Free. As my husband ran off in search of some help and a much need-ed wheelchair, I stood blushing at the obviousness of my state and at the curious stares of the patients smoking in the door-way. I was wheeled up to the maternity ward, where the sweet-ly-brusque young midwives took one look at me and said, 'In the room, strip and straight onto the bed for doctor.'

I would love to tell all mum's-to-be listening to or reading this that the next three hours passed in a wave of transcenden-tal glory, but I won't lie. During the 'transition' stage, when the process steps up from speeding around Brands Hatch to racing towards a precipice of agony, I yelled blue murder over the spe-cially prepared CD by the acid-trance band, *Air*. Gone was that brief moment of beauty. I grabbed my husband's arm, panting in this face: 'Can you see it? Can you see the waves on the beach, the waves, Oh my God the waves!'

'No,' he said, looking at the midwife, fearing I had lost my mind.

I gripped his arm until I knew it hurt: 'Can you see the WAVES AND THE FOREST AND THE TREES? TELL ME YOU SEE THEM!'

My husband said he could see them.

Another hour later, I was a foul-mouthed Liverpool dock-worker, screaming a colourful array of expletives loud enough for the entire ward – and beyond – to hear. Sunday was, unfortunately, the day when expectant mums' were given a guided tour of the maternity facilities. As I screamed ever louder, 'Nooo … Oh Gooood … Aggghhhhh', my younger sister sat outside with couples seeking their choice of birthing facilities. She told me later that most of the mums *and* the dads went pale at the sounds coming from my room. While one poor couple got up and left with the mum-to-be in tears.

For all that agony, it was the most beautiful experience of my life. A vital physical and spiritual coming of age event that I felt pretty pleased (and surprised) to have managed without medical support. Or a cocktail of pain relief. Cradled in my arms, Alexandra had a thick mop of chestnut brown hair and brown eyes from day one. Forget what the doctors say about all babies eyes being blue, hers were brown – always.

As soon as the baby slept for the first time after breastfeeding, I had my first sip of champagne. For months I had considered myself to be subsisting patiently on the occasional glass of wine and just four cigarettes a week. This had felt like an inhumane, enforced, fast and to sip from a glass of champagne was a welcome release. It was to be short-lived.

'Now, now, what's this?' said the Indian nurse as she came into the room to check my recovery. 'You can't be drinking that, you know.' She eyed me and I looked back. I suspected she was trying to force some of her alien culture (or worse, religion) onto me at this joyous moment of unity between myself and my fizz.

'And why NOT?' I replied. My husband and my sister Emma, who had both just been through quite an ordeal themselves, looked nervous.

'Because, my dear, the bubbles will upset your baby's stomach.'

I paused, with the glass at my lips. 'You are kidding! Okay, how long will that last? I mean how long before I can drink again and it won't upset the baby's stomach?'

'Oh as long as you breastfeed you shouldn't drink at all,' came the reply. So this, I thought was how grown-ups live.

Not even the news of weeks or months of further sobriety could dampen my moments with baby Alex. She was an incredibly 'there' baby, as my American friend Cher would say in her Chicago drawl: 'She is ON the planet!'

The next day, I sat down to feed Alex on our old sofa with the news on the TV. It was the usual array of murder and misery, complemented by a weather report of rain and cloud. The international segment included a report which was about Israel/Palestine. Just hearing the word 'Palestine' made me look for the remote control. 'No thanks Mr News, not today'. I was about to flick channels when a photo flashed up onto the screen for fifteen seconds, maybe less. It showed a boy, wearing dark jeans and a blue jumper, holding something in his right hand, raised behind him and above his head. Just feet from where the lad stood, a battalion of tanks and armed soldiers were bearing down upon him. The whole scene was oppressive and horrifying, yet bland, all at once. It looked so normal, that level of violence in that rubble-strewn environment. Another foreign child standing before the machinery of globally-funded murder. The new mother in me shouted inside, 'run boy, run'. I would discover the boy's name only years later: Faris Odeh. Four days before my daughter's birth, Faris had been shot in the neck by an Israeli sniper. He bled out on the dusty ground, denied an ambulance for an hour by the soldiers. Without knowing the full story until much later, the photo would nevertheless have a long-term effect on me.

At birth, we are shocked by the loss of safety, the loss of connection with the mother's beating heart, the warmth. We move from timelessness to now-ness. Then there is first love, and I'm not talking about a crush but the actualisation of a transcending union with another human being. When their breath is so sweet you want to drink it, bathe in it, taste it. When their smell is the flight of a lifetime through blue mountains, fresh with snow.

Near death experiences: To stand in a swimming pool as a giant lighting rig falls into the water and realise with utter clarity that I will die and be gone. As happened on the *Hello!* photo shoot during our honeymoon; to realise that the universe does not in fact hinge on our own being, or survival. It was there before us and will continue after, without pausing to wish us bon voyage.

Giving birth struck me with joy and confusion. I had spent half a decade building up a largely fictional ladette character known as 'Lauren'. This outer shell had been living in a body that she treated as a theme park. It had certainly been 'fun', but now what? Now what?

Our birth;

first love;

near death experiences; giving birth; and

breaking new

Less than a year later, I was at home watching a breaking story that would change the world. Like millions across the globe I watched, transfixed, as two planes hit the North and South Towers of the World Trade Center, New York. Like a real-life disaster movie, horror upon horror unrolled in real time. I picked up the phone, trying desperately to get hold of my younger sister who had called me the day before to say she was visiting the same area of New York that morning. The line wouldn't connect and I sat and I watched, unable to move, as the towers came down, one after the other. My husband was home too, we were renovating the flat we were living in before it went on the market, and we sat silently for a long time. Eventually, I turned to him and said: 'I wonder which poor country is going to get smashed apart for this?'

On 19 January 2003, I was standing before a small pool in a room about to give birth for the second time. I felt utterly enormous and was in the midst of the pant, gasp, groan routine of the penultimate stage. I heard voices behind me in the doorway.

'Can I ask her or should I wait?' whispered a woman's voice. I heard my midwife invite them to approach me. I looked up from my squatting position at a young nurse. 'Should we expect a visit from Mr Blair soon?' she asked.

I turned my neck slowly, feeling the hysteria rise in my throat. Of all the things I could want to visualise whilst at my most vulnerable and animalistic, a visit from the Prime Minister was not one of them. I gave the nurse this message in somewhat blunt language. She left.

A little while later, a baby slipped into what was now a cold-water, pool. 'Is she alive?' I gasped. A scream was rising in my throat. The midwife stood next to my husband and then they both laughed. 'You've got a chilled one there! She's fast asleep. By the way it's a girl.'

Her eyes were bright blue and her mop of hair had a delightful reddish hue, a tribute to an earlier generation and perhaps my great grandma, Tilly Macnamara. We called her Holly, and she was full of fun and cheekiness from the start.

Just weeks after Holly's birth, I bundled both new-born and toddler into full winter wear and caught the Underground to central London. I had spoken to Alexandra in a grown up manner, as I always did, about why we would be spending the day shouting slogans and walking in the cold: 'It's important to care about other babies and mummies and people. Do you understand, Alex?'

She nodded with the serious brown eyes of a Victorian teddy bear.

'It will be cold and it will *not* be fun, do you understand? But we are going to try and stop a war.' Hundreds of thousands of people were mobilised, taking to the streets of London to voice their opposition to military action against Iraq. The slowly unfolding plot of a war film was taking place on our news bulletins and Tony appeared to have been seduced by the trappings of power and feted by US president, George W Bush. His views – which had resonated with the population in 1997 – were now equally out of step. The arguments for a full-on invasion of Iraq, preceded by an airborne bombing campaign of civilian cities, were weak to say the least. The public simply did not believe that Saddam Hussein had the capability to bomb Britain in '45 minutes', as was being claimed. Our media went to sleep on duty, swallowing ministerial soundbites without due diligence. Police later said it was the UK's biggest ever demonstration, with at least 750,000 people taking part. Organisers put the figure closer to two million.

Marching, shouting and carrying placards had re-entered my life as suddenly and with as much importance and fervour as it had as a teenager. Tony Blair had radicalised me again, but bigger. I watched between my fingers as he completely missed the political moment to make history and stand with the international community against the ill thought out, vengeful US-led war in the Middle East. I mused over the coverage showing my brother-in-law simpering before men in uniform and looking faint with fawning around the idiotic President Bush. Perhaps my own uncertain childhood had given me a painful greater empathy with the underdog, but no argument I heard then or since will ever explain or excuse the agony which would be wreaked upon the people of Iraq.

On the journey into central London, the train carriage was standing room only. The train on the way to Marble Arch was not filled with the usual heavy booted and crop-haired brothers and sisters of previous anti-war demos. The demographic that day was far more diverse. Tony Blair had done what no one since the Peasants Revolt had managed to do quite so well – woken up well-to-do society against the nation's leaders. Long before an Arabian Prophet would touch my heart and reach my soul, Tony Blair was part of the process which reopened my mind to thoughts and beliefs beyond the mainstream body politic. I clung to Holly, who was getting warm in her new-born's snowsuit.

Alex slipped from my grasp to stand up in her seat. Her flat side-parting and blue jacket made her look like a little boy. In a high clear voice, with one tiny hand in the air she made an announcement: 'No attack Iraq, 'kay? Bombs bad, 'kay?' Faces young and old turned to look at the youngest protestor in the carriage. Alex repeated more loudly, 'No 'tack Iraq, no 'tack Iraq'.

The ladies around me did the thing women do whenever we hear or see something unbelievably cute. They bent their heads towards their right shoulders and made a chorus of: 'Aw, cute!'

At the double doors, a man in a suit wore one of the Blair Scare masks which were such a feature of the day. I watched him reach a hand beneath the mask and make a wiping gesture. I wondered if that was the first and only time Tony's face would leak for the horrors about to be inflicted upon millions of innocent people.

Alex was not done with her sudden, attentive fan club. Not lowering her voice, she turned to me and said in a stage whisper of which my father would have been proud: 'Momma, why does Unca Tony like Bad Bush? Why does he have tea with him? Why?'

I yanked her into a sitting position as a blush hit my cheeks. Fifty heads turned my way. Uncle Tony with 'Bad Bush'? I feared we might be lynched for being related to the hate figure of the moment, the British Prime Minister. Instead there was a pause, then a Mexican wave of applause travelled from seat to seat. 'That's whatshername isn't it – Cherie Blair's sister. Wow, here with us ...' People grinned at us and Alex was delighted with her impact and tried to stand and give another speech. I held onto her arm, you never know what kids will come out with once they start.

An elderly man with a walking stick came over and ruffled Alex's hair. 'No 'tack Iraq.' He smiled.

Walking along the Thames Embankment, snowflakes landed on my nose and our breaths came out in icy plumes. A mile behind and a mile ahead of us a sea of white banners read 'Don't

Bomb Iraq' and 'Bush and Blair Terrorists'. The bridge overhead was jammed with another mile of people, like us marching in near silence, pensive, wondering how they might feel if the tables were turned and it was our homes and towns facing ruin. Someone shouted, 'The BBC report police figures of 20,000 people here.' There was a chorus of boos from the half a million strong crowd around me.

I remember the rest of that day in mind pops, still images appearing in my mind's eye. Flash! Pushing Alexandra in her chair, with baby Holly held one-handed under my coat feeding. Flash! Walking past Downing Street, as if in a black and white film where we step in time past a dictator. On cue all heads turn to the black gates on right and a cacophony of boos and whistles fills the freezing air. Someone shouts, 'You won't send your sons to war will you, Tony?' On 20 March 2003, Blair and Bush took the world to war and the Iraqi people experienced the 'Shock and Awe' inflicted upon them.

CHAPTER 7
ARABOPHOBIA

'The tormenting dilemma of the Middle East is this:
either we have one people too many, or one state too few.'

Afif Safieh

My disappointment at the direction of the Labour Government had become a simmering fury. I had been distracted from politics by wealth, but it's fair to say that Tony Blair radicalised me. In 2004, troops from the Black Watch in the British army were sent from Basra to the Baghdad region to assist the US in their mission of civilian annihilation. The phrase 'collateral damage' was applied again and again to Middle Eastern women and children as if mass murder was okay so long as you had the right soundbite in place. I met with Stop The War activists and attended conferences where talk was of the carving up the Middle East to serve a deadly western neo- colonialist agenda. I remembered the boy with the stone standing defiantly in front of the tanks and began asking questions about the Israeli Occupation of Palestine. As Jesus said, 'seek and ye shall find.'

Six months after Holly was born, we moved from the small flat in North London to a beautiful, 100-year-old farmhouse in the rolling hills of south west France. I would work my visits to London around scheduled talks by Palestinian speakers and activists, especially the Palestine Solidarity Campaign (PSC). In December 2004, I approached my editor with the idea of visiting Palestine in order to cover the elections, secretly hoping he would dismiss the idea as 'ridiculous.' I was afraid to go, but something was niggling inside. An internal itch, an invisible hand on the small of my back, propelled me towards a land I knew little to nothing about.

As I didn't speak Arabic and had no training or experience in Middle Eastern reporting, it was peculiar to be selected for such a sensitive assignment. However, Peter Wright, my champion and the ebullient and imaginative editor of the *Mail on Sunday*, was mischievous in his decision. By sending Blair's sister-in-law to cover such a sensitive subject, Peter saw a chance to embarrass the prime minister, who was roundly loathed by Associated Newspapers. Whatever the reason, I was now expected to use my one and only regional contact to accomplish the Holy Grail of the moment: an interview with the man tipped to be the first ever leader of the Palestinian Authority (PA), Mahmoud Abbas.

On 6 January 2005, I arrived at Tel Aviv airport. 'Why are you coming to Isra-el?' The girl, much younger than myself, looked bored as she swayed to and fro on her seat inside her raised bulletproof box. Behind me, a queue of tired passengers were starting to tut at the delay and by my inability to answer even simple questions satisfactorily.

'I am here to cover the Palestinian elections in the West Bank. I will be getting my media credentials from your Prime Minister's office tomorrow.' I repeated for the fourth time.

The customs officer looked at her computer screen, looked at my passport photo, then eyed me suspiciously. Silently, I cursed my decision to dye my hair from blonde to brown just two days earlier. Apart from the fact that on being shown the 'big reveal' all my friends had said the same word, 'ageing', my passport photo now looked like someone else. The apparent disguise was clearly going to be a problem as I needed to negotiate my way through a region of military occupation and checkpoints.

'Rookie mistake,' I muttered to myself.

'I beg your pardon, what did you call me?' Things were getting out of control and I hadn't even left the airport yet.

'You are pretty' I said, floundering.

Unimpressed with my lame effort at charm, the girl in the uniform went to grab the entry stamp. I recalled the advice given to me by activist friends: 'never allow the Israeli authorities to stamp your passport'.

'Please don't stamp my passport' I stammered. In the customs queue behind me came Hebraic sounds of annoyance. The girl narrowed her eyes, then pulled out a piece of paper, stamped it, and shaking her head slid it into my passport.

'Next!'

I could hardly believe I was in the Holy Land. My stomach had butterflies which were only partly to do with my assignment and the potential risks which came with it. I was in the place where Jesus himself had actually walked and breathed! It meant everything to my Christianity that I was here. I had wanted to visit Jerusalem since the fervent faith of my childhood. Awareness of the Occupation and its cruelty had put that out of my mind, yet somehow, miraculously, here I was anyway. It felt like a great gift had been given to me by an unseen benefactor.

I had no idea what to do next. Not knowing anyone locally had made pre-planning difficult. How did you get from 'Israel' to 'Palestine' anyway? I didn't know, as carousel, but my naivety would be the route to accessing heart-breaking narratives beyond the reach – or interest – of many better prepared and experienced correspondents.

I had a vague idea what I would do in the coming days. After securing an (extremely unlikely) interview with Abbas, I would visit refugee camp projects run by the British charity Interpal, make a short film of the work they are doing, and write a report about what I witnessed.

All of which (besides the Abbas interview) sounded simple enough. An hour later, my brief euphoria at getting through customs had faded leaving me with my first tinge of anxiety. My luggage had still not emerged onto the belt and I stood in the chilly customs area with a middle- aged Belgian feminist who had taken me under her wing. Her luggage had also vanished.

'The Israelis always pull this stunt' she sighed.

We were sent to an office at the far end of Tel Aviv terminal to retrieve a ticket which guaranteed our luggage would arrive 'in three days. Maybe.'

Bagless, we made our way towards the hazy winter light outside. I rifled through my laptop case to find the business card of my single Palestinian connection, 'Afif Safieh, Palestinian General Delegate to the UK and the Holy See'. I had heard the ambassador speak eruditely on the plight of Palestine months earlier, with natural warmth, at a meeting in a London theatre. After his presentation, I had approached him to ask how I could find out more about the reality on the ground and if there were anything I could do to support the cries for justice.

'My dear Lauren' He had said, in his trademark, rolling drawl, 'You must go to Palestine and see for yourself. It is the only way.'

My stomach had lurched at the thought of going to a place which seemed on the television to be in a state of constant turmoil, with suicide bombings and religious extremism on all sides. 'Surely there is something else I can do ... from the UK,' I stammered. Afif was firm, no one should take a stance on a situation without first having the good manners and humility to visit and see the actuality first hand. He had a point.

On the back of his card, he had written two names and numbers saying: 'Call them on arrival in Ramallah my dear, not before. Everything for you will be sorted out.'

Shuffling from foot to foot outside Tel Aviv airport, I was too nervous even to approach a cab. I was going to the 'Palestinian zones' and I had to be careful who took me there. How to be 'careful' and what exactly was the risk if I weren't, I had no idea. It was like being told that a snake was venomous but wouldn't bite 'unless you annoyed it'.

'Hello. Do you need a taxi Ma'am?' A Palestinian, with the rolling 'r's and the same native Jerusalemite accent as Afif, took his hands out of the pockets of beige slacks and held the door of a taxi open. He was wearing a cream, immaculately pressed, Fred Perry t-shirt. Perhaps it was the very English shirt, perhaps it was something more. I climbed into the passenger seat where I was met with a barrage of questions.

'Where did you just come from? Where do you want to go? How long are you staying? Do you want the scenic or the quick route?' I pulled out a rumpled yellow post it note with the name of the hotel booked by the newspaper's travel agency.

'I am a journalist and I'd like to go to the Grand Park Hotel, Ramallah, please.'

'*Tafaddal*, welcome. A journalist, very good, I had a writer from the *New York Times* here last week. By the way, my name is Jamal. But you can call me Jimmy.'

The airport was militarised on the fringes and armed soldiers patrolled the terminal inside and out. Barbed wire braced the highway's edge, a cut throat, ugly beading. We rolled over pristine, modern flyovers beneath grey skies. The road signs, always such a clue to the state of a country, were notably precise, central to the lanes and easy to follow. The language at the top of each of the square signs was sloping Hebrew text, beneath it was English, which told me were heading down Avalon South, Lod Road. The blue signs rushed past, as the clouds drew brightness from the emerging yellow hillside. It was much greener than I had expected. I had an image in my head of Moses dragging his irascible people through endless desert, of Arabs on camels. This was no desert. And there was not a Bedouin in sight. Unbeknownst to me at the time, buried beneath the tidy flyovers, deep under the layers of cement upon which sat the red- roofed housing estates of illegal Israeli settlement communities, lay a hidden history of Arab Muslims and Christians.

In the caramel hills I began to play with the small silver cross I had been wearing since my children were born. Existence is more than politics, and this trip was more than a job for me. It was a pilgrimage, one that I had dreamt of taking since childhood. God sent prophets to these same hills, and taking photos through the car window I was aware of travelling at the heels of Moses, Abraham and Jesus. My mind wandered back in time to the white and the green of those hills at the time of Christ. I was staggered to think that a grain of sand which had been blowing around for two millennia might land on my skin through the open window. I hoped the visit would guide me further towards the Christian faith.

Jamal, my driver, continued being an unwanted tour guide. His family were locals, going back many centuries, with a four-storey building in the Palestinian suburb of Silwan, his parents having refused to leave in the invasion of the Palestinian city by Israeli forces in 1967. At the Kalandia checkpoint there was a long traffic jam, and I struggled to understand why that was as not that far back a road across the hillside travelling in our direction had been empty. A toll road perhaps?

'Jamal, I don't mean to tell you your job or anything' I said, completely willing to tell any taxi drive in any city in the world their job. 'I thought I spotted a better route a while back we could have taken?'

Jamal looked amused.

'Are you sure you are really a journalist?' He asked, 'Because you don't seem to know much about this area ...'

'Yes, I am. I have a Press card to prove it' I laughed awkwardly. How quickly I had been found out as a newbie in this region.

'Look then,' Jamal continued. 'I teach you something. The road you saw was for settlers only. Jewish people, understand? If an

Arab, Palestinian, Muslim, like me, drives there we are shot for sure in ... six minutes? You want we try?' He began to turn the steering wheel to turn round.

'No!' I shouted. 'Thank you!'

With a sigh he continued, 'And the joke is really on us as being Jerusalemite my taxes go towards the road system which I am killed for trying to use ...'

An American voice interrupted our talk. We had reached the front of the queue at the Ramallah checkpoint. An Israeli soldier in a green beret casually pushed a gun towards Jamal through the open window. He was no older than nineteen, with a thick Brooklyn accent. Snatching Jamal's papers, he looked them over with barely concealed disgust.

'You!' the soldier turned to me. 'Where are you from?'

'I'm from Britain' I added, then without thinking: 'Where are *you* from?'

The soldier turned my passport over in his hands. 'I'm Israeli.' He said.

'No, I mean where were you born. Where are your parents from?' There was an ugly pause. I glanced at Jamal in the driver's seat, his eyes made a silent appeal for me to shut up.

'I was born in New York,' shrugged the soldier. Then he grinned. 'Wow, Britain. We love you guys.'

The Grand Park Hotel Ramallah was the remnant of someone's business dream. Grand indeed at first glance, a closer inspection revealed plug sockets that hung from the wall, unrepaired, hidden behind chairs in the foyer. Under the night lighting I could tell it was partially finished and guessed it would never be filled to capacity. After checking in and heading to my room, I finally staggered towards the bed and called my husband in tears. Suddenly experiencing Israeli occupation through eyes which enjoyed casual freedom, it didn't take much to raise the fire of indignation. Waiting at checkpoints, a gun pointed into your face by a child of western immigrants already seemed like a dystopian nightmare. Yet what I had really seen, just one check-point and an apartheid road system? It wouldn't take long to discover that was as good as it would get for four million people.

*****

I awoke to a cement grey and sand yellow city abuzz with the politics of this significant day. It was the day of the Palestinian elections, and no longer could their legendary former leader, Yas-ser Arafat, be named as the outstanding obstacle to a yearned-for peace, it was a new dawn of democracy and hope in the West Bank and Gaza strip and I was there to cover it for the *Mail on Sunday*. Driven to my first meeting of the day, I photographed the spray painted graffiti yelling political slogans from every inch of wall space.

Outside a high school polling station near the famous Birzeit University, interviewed a 20-year-old student in the queue for voting, stretching into the faculty car park. Hanin Yousef wore heavy, glamorous make up, which surprised me as I had been expecting scrubbed faced, religious women. In her bright pink tracksuit she could have passed for a teenager in Manchester or Liverpool. We chatted in the cold about her aspirations on this 'historic' day. Hanin loved her studies in English translation and had proudly placed her vote for Mahmoud Abbas.

'I hope for a stronger government and an end to violence,' she said. She didn't mean the Palestinian violence which featured on the news in the UK. This student was talking about her violated life under occupation, the near constant Israeli incursions, daily infringements into her peace of mind.

'We need peace,' she said, as she jogged away arm-in-arm with her friends, a chorus of 'ciao' thrown back as they went.

Wrapping up my vox pops, a large 4x4 with darkened win-dows screeched to a standstill nearby. The crowd of voters looked over curiously as men in black suits and black coats sprinted my way: 'Hurry, Lauren Booth! We must go now!'

Amid Al Zuhieri, from the PA foreign ministry, and Muhanned Hammouri, from the Protocol Department, both Fatah men, were my chaperones and new best friends. I had called the numbers on the card given to me by Afif Safieh that morning over an Arabic breakfast of coffee, boiled egg and flat bread. The call had paid off, just as promised, and after just one brief phone conversation Amid and Muhanned took it upon themselves to introduce me to everyone they knew. And they knew everyone. Feeling a little like I was being kidnapped, I was bundled into their bulletproof car and we screeched off to an unknown destination.

Amid and Muhanned were upbeat as we squealed through the busy streets. So long as their leader, the 'moderate' candidate Mahmoud Abbas, won this election everything was going to be fine – at last, after a bleak six decades of Occupation. They seemed certain both Bush and Blair would support a viable Palestinian State, after all the Palestinians had kept their side of the bargain – they were now a democracy, just like Israel.

It was only 2 pm on my first day in the West Bank, yet my nerves were already frazzled. The pace in Ramallah was one of jarring, stop-start uncertainty. Who would be where and when was dependent on checkpoints, travel papers and army road-blocks. My hosts had confirmed that I would be granted an inter-view with the Presidential favourite, but after forty minutes skid-ding around corners I was told the venue had been changed yet again for 'security reasons'. The ministerial 4x4 careered through Ramallah's main streets with no thought for pedestrians, making U-turns at seemingly random places. We crossed back on our-selves three times, did an emergency stop outside a chemist, re-versed the wrong way up a main street amidst blaring horns, then pulled up in a parking lot.

'Are we avoiding a tail?' I asked Muhanned, breathlessly. He somehow heard me despite having a mobile phone jammed to each ear.

'No, Lauren,' he yelled into the back seat, 'the driver is just lost.'

I clung to the headrest of the seat in front as we set off again, swerving up a rickety side street. We ignored another red traffic light and following a route apparently dictated by piles of stones. There were no streets signs, but there was plenty of rubble.

After almost an hour, and by now suffering from motion sickness, the brakes squealed as we came to a halt outside a building decorated in the local flavour; bullet holes. We jogged around the back of the tall administrative building. Guarding the steel door stood a giant Arab dressed like Keanu Reeves in the *The Matrix* – dark sunglasses and a long overcoat. He held out a large hand, his other other held an even larger gun, and told us to stand still. Believe me, I wasn't going to move without his permission. The Israeli soldiers at the airports and checkpoints all had guns, but it was the first time I'd ever been that close to one and somehow it this one in particular, held at that moment by an Arab hand, bothered me more.

'Lauren Booth, Al Zuhieri, Hammouri,' he said into a walkie-talkie. After a moment he nodded at us, 'Hurry.'

We set off at a jog through the doors and into a stone basement. More security men with earpieces and guns. Fast Arabic was snarled into the Palestinian security forces' walkie-talkies and a steely glance was thrown my way. I tried to look cool, but my mind was pushing unwanted thoughts forward. Was I going to die here, right now, in this basement? Ushered virtually at gunpoint into a lift, I felt myself to be in a Hollywood movie, a feeling I'd had once before but under remarkably different circumstances. Fourteen years earlier I had stood at the base of the Empire State Building. The police sirens echoing around the buildings brought back memories of *Cagney and Lacey, Starsky and Hutch, King Kong,* and *Ghostbusters.* Everything there had seemed romantic and edgy in a 'cool' way, but this was different and as I stood in the lift sneaking glances up at the face of the security agent on my right I imagined he probably longed to shove a gun in my mouth and pull the trigger a dozen times. Surrounded by high-ranking Fatah militiamen I had a poorly timed awakening: I was scared to death of Arabs, especially Palestinians.

The state room in which Mahmoud Abbas sat was white, with rugs and chairs the size of thrones. Vast portraits of Yasser Arafat were on every wall and it was time for the interview of a lifetime, the one my editor had trusted me alone to secure. It turned out to be a mundane chitchat of clichés: 'if only we had more time,' sighed Abbas, defeated even on the day of his victory, 'when the time is right'. The passion expressed by the people hadn't penetrated the thick walls protecting the autocrats in that room. I was fed regurgitated soundbites until I stifled a yawn and looked and looked at my watch. I couldn't wait to get back outside, where hope ricocheted like bullets and young and old alike bounced to the beat of optimism. With a sense of dissatisfaction I wrapped up the interview, convinced Abbas was working for interests beyond – or perhaps outside – those of the Palestinian people. His rehearsed drone left me feeling that if he were the best option for the Palestinians, they were in deeper trouble than they already knew.

Heading back to the hotel, I received a call from Matthew Kalman, a British journalist living in Jerusalem. He has an Israeli passport (as a British Jew who moved there) and he's a top-notch journalist who would become my guide on the trip. He was assigned to me by the *Mail on Sunday* as a regional 'fixer' and he suggested that we head to Muqata to sample the atmosphere there and to visit Yasser Arafat's mausoleum.

'Relax,' he said, noting my jitters as we met before the guarded, white stone compound. I can only wonder at his casual confidence. He strolled at ease around the West Bank, greeting Arabs with a warmth which was returned.

A steady stream of visitors – official and unofficial – filed though the large gates to pay homage at Arafat's final resting place, and the Perspex-enclosed tomb was covered with dozens of wreaths left by visiting dignitaries. It's a regal place, French in its minimalist feel, and I was nervous and unsure how to act. How do you pay your respects to a man labelled a 'terrorist'? Bowing too low would make me look like a terror sympathiser when the photo was released. Not bowing at all? Well, that would be bloody rude. In the end, the decision on precisely how much to incline my neck was made for me. Matthew, standing behind me, whispered as I made my approach: 'They brought the soil here from Israel. So that even though he lies here, Arafat is really buried in Jerusalem.'

My head dropped thoughtfully. I imagined the clandestine mission to smuggle soil from one part of this old land to another. Was it done in suitcases? No, it would have been brought in on the back of a lorry. Poked at, inspected by soldiers who considered themselves this man's enemy. Arafat, ordering the dirt for his own burial, began to put something in place in my understanding of the dispersion of the Palestinian people from the land of their ancestors. My moment was interrupted by a commotion from a far corner of the compound. I looked over to where a group of male Arab voters were crowding around three figures in black making an announcement. I couldn't believe my eyes, was I back at my mum's home in Golders Green, watching the Sabbath journeying of Orthodox Jews from home to Temple? Or were there actually Rabbis here in Ramallah?

One of the men was shouting in American English: 'Hundreds of thousands of Jews do not believe Jews should be here. They believe this to be Palestinian land.' The announcement was made again by the eldest of the three rabbis to the crowd of dubious Arab men, this time in Arabic.

'We're very disappointed that they (Israeli authorities) don't let us to participate. However, we accept the Palestinian rules because we consider the Palestinian parliament as our leaders and our parliament,' said the leader.

The group were Neturei Karta, founded in Jerusalem in 1938. A highly religious Jewish organisation, their ethos is to adhere strictly to the teaching of the Torah, including that a Jewish State cannot and must not be forced into creation by mankind. Rabbis against Israel believe that the

Jews will have a homeland only when the Messiah comes and these rabbis had attempted to register as legitimate voters in the

PA elections in Jerusalem. The whole thing seemed so utterly bonkers, I started to giggle. One of the rabbis began to quote from the Torah and Palestinian voters listened politely to the religious text. Except for some teenagers at the back. Arms crossed, head tilted to one side, one of them muttered 'Yehud' (Jew) under his breath and found himself cuffed across the head for impudence by an older Palestinian 'uncle' and given the kind of stare that doesn't invite cheek.

I'd had enough for one day and I needed to get away from the mixed messages, the politicking, the desperate hopefulness. I was backing down the steps of the polling station, ready for an hour in my hotel room, when the back of my legs connected with something solid. I stumbled, falling into the lap of a man in a wheelchair. An embarrassing scramble ensued as I quickly removed myself from the man's thighs. My ability to garner some relief from the fact that at least he didn't seem to be an Islamic cleric was ruined by Matthew's ever cool voice in my ear: 'Introduce yourself, Lauren, quick. He's the founder of the Al Aqsa Martyrs' Brigade.'

For the previous five years, 34-year-old Khaled Al Shawish had been evading arrest by Israeli security forces. He was one of the Brigade's most highly respected fighters and leaders. One of an elite group who had barricaded themselves inside the Mukataa compound in March 2002 as Israel launched the largest offensive in the West Bank since 1967. I was silent with embarrassment, having sat in the lap of the disabled stranger in combat clothes, but Matthew stepped in and made an introduction he knew would have impact:

'This is Lauren Booth, sister-in-law of British prime minister, Tony Blair. She is a writer and would like to interview you.'

The winter sun flirted with the mortar damage of the walls and I wondered if being linked to a world leader had just made me a tasty kidnap victim. I was broadly aware that Palestinian resistance groups were not al-Qaida and I knew that Ramallah was not, for example, Kabul or Fallujah. But if asked to define the differing convictions of the various armed factions from these regions I would have fallen back on a single hopeful idea: that not being an Israeli soldier meant I was safe.

Polling day crowds wandered past, towards Minara Square for a celebratory Coca-Cola or perhaps to smoke shisha, and Matthew and I waited for Shawish to cast his vote. The name of the man in the wheelchair was already a jumble in my mind. Arabic is a swift, loud language, the volume not making the rolling sounds any easier to decipher to the untrained European ear. I wandered around outside muttering under my breath; 'Khaled Ali Shwishm? No, Khalili Amin Showeeeri?'

Matthew helpfully alerted me to the fact that the day before there had been reports of two Spanish journalists being kidnapped by Shawish's organisation. The whole thing is ridiculous, I thought, a writer of articles about buying a house in the Dordogne has no place being here. I took a mental inventory of what made me in any way fit to report on the 'most wanted man in the West Bank'. I had Ken Livingstone's Dictaphone from the GLC days, a pretty pink notepad, and the feeling in the pit of my stomach that if I didn't get back to my comfortable hotel room and out of this madness right away I might actually start to cry.

Matthew, David – the Jewish photographer with us – and I followed Shawish and his foot soldiers through a huge, rusted metal door which slammed ominously shut behind us. I didn't want to go up the narrow stairs into a building so heavily bombed it seemed against the laws of physics to be still standing. Between the polling booth and the winding staircase where I stood dithering, the men around us had suddenly acquired some serious weaponry. I had no choice but to carry on climbing and my breath was shorter than the exertion demanded. Beneath my borrowed coat, my knees were shaking. This, I realised, was what trembling with fear actually felt like. We headed down a corridor with more bullet holes in the walls than plaster, then through a doorway on the right. We entered a tiny room, not unlike a cell. Dominated by a single scruffy bed, the small gas-burning fire did little to dispel the approaching chill of the evening. It was little more than a squat.

The man in the wheelchair was lifted lovingly onto the bed by two comrades. He arranged himself painfully into a sitting position, with cushions placed behind his back by a boy of around nine years old who seemed to have raided a military dressing-up box. He was in head-to-toe khaki, just like the men. Without making eye contact, Shawish motioned for me to sit opposite him in a plastic garden chair. At that moment, an M16 automatic rifle was put into his hands and I felt another sensation I had only read about, the feeling of blood draining from my face. I felt it happen in a detached daze, leaving my head and neck strangely cold. Nobody spoke as I waited for the long black barrel to be turned towards my face, as it surely would be.

The room was clean yet desperate, and Shawish took a long while to settle. Whatever his injuries were they clearly caused him discomfort. Just above my left ear a canary swayed silently in a tiny cage. The boy in army fatigues scowled at me from the corner and sweat gathered in the small of my back. I summoned up a question, perhaps *the* question every foreigner feels compelled to ask: 'I wonder if, with all the killing, you hate Jews?'

Shawish still didn't make eye contact with any of us visitors as he thoughtfully began to answer. 'I have Israeli friends. I have Jewish friends,' he said evenly.

He told me his story. Originally from Jenin, as a young man he went to a high school in Acre where he fell in love with a Jewish girl, Hava. 'We even wanted to get married,' he said. This was a shock. The Brigades were infamous for suicide bombs targeting Israeli civilians. An act of religious hatred, surely?

He carried on in his sad monotone, his words translated by Matthew. When it became harder for Palestinians to move from town to town he could no longer see Hava. They were both heartbroken: 'My Israeli friends are aware of our suffering. I don't have contact with them now as they could be arrested.'

His words had the detachment of a stranger talking about a young man who has long since died. I no longer felt afraid, my instinct told me there was no immediate risk. My body, however, treacherously continued to jerk and visibly tremble, from time to time in reaction to the guns all around. Guns held by Arabs.

Shawish was wounded in a shootout with IDF troops during an arrest attempt in 2001, from which he managed to escape. He had nine bullets lodged inside him, those injuries rendering him handicapped. As I took notes it became clear to both of us that not only were my knees shaking, my hands were too. I couldn't help it. Shawish sat with the M16 lolling across his legs, perhaps for comfort, and I felt faint when I looked at it. There was a pause while I gathered my thoughts for the next questions. Suddenly this man, the head of the notorious Al Aqsa Martyrs' Brigade, looked at me fully for the first time. He was dark-skinned with heavy black brows. His eyes were bright and lucid and he looked a lot like Al Pacino. He had an air of controlled energy and his lips flickered slightly in the midst of a smile. In Arabic he offered coffee, 'and perhaps,' with a sympathetic nod at me, 'a cigarette?'

As he leant forward to light one for me, my hand trembled so badly his son laughed, the sullen boy had moved from the corner to stand with one hand proudly (protectively) on his father's right shoulder. As we waited for the coffee to brew somewhere along the blighted corridors, I began to swap kid stories. I brought my mobile phone out, pointing at photos, and he shuffled along the mattress for me to join him on the metal prison-style bed. He cooed and clucked over my family, far away in the green fields of the south of France.

The man (now 'Khaled' in my mind) explained his family situation. Since the shootout with Israeli soldiers in Ramallah three years earlier he rarely, if ever, left the compound. He would never again share a home with his wife or his kids, as he was targeted by Israel for assassination. The only contact he had with his wife and children was when they were brought there to see him, one or two family members at a time, and only when his intelligence contacts told him it was (relatively) safe to do so.

The coffee in the plastic cup was bitter. It went perfectly with the third harsh Egyptian cigarette I was chain-smoking. The coffee singed the taste buds and the smoke scraped my throat, and it took my mind off the fact I was with a wanted terrorist. Or freedom fighter? Khaled dismissed the Spanish abduction story as nonsense. To what possible end, to what possible good was capturing journalists, he asked? The story was later proven to be false, the inference from Khaled, which brought nods of agreement from his men in the doorway, was that some writers actually come to Palestine just to pretend to get captured. They briefly interview fighters like Khaled at their hideout, then afterwards send texts saying they were held against their will for hours.

'Why?' I asked.

'In order to get a bigger scoop.' Did I wish to be captured for a big story, he asked? He said he liked me and was more than happy to boost my career with a kidnap scoop, if I liked. I couldn't help but laugh.

'No thanks,' I said, 'maybe next time.'

He posed for photographs with his trusty M16 and I was invited to dine with his wife and children at their home. The address would be communicated the next day in a phone call. I asked why he would risk giving me his home address. 'Because you have come here to find out the truth. And we thank you for that,' he said. My assignment was to cover the first presidential election, but I was already starting to feel the tug of something more.

'I am the most wanted man in the West Bank,' said Shawish as I gathered my things to leave. 'I have influence over all the men in the Al Aqsa Brigades. I tell them we want peace.'

He got a comrade to print out a letter pledging allegiance to Abbas, who in a matter of hours would indeed be the first elected president of the new Palestinian Authority. Ceremonially, Khaled

Al Shawish stamped the letter with his official seal. I left him in that mournful room, in the gloomy, bombed out place of siege and suffering.

As Matthew left me at my hotel he gave me a serious piece of advice: 'Don't think about wandering off on your own, Lauren. You don't know this place. Everyone seems, and yes most people are, very nice to be with. But things happen here that defy logic – all the time. So if you want to go out somewhere call me and I will try to get you to the interview you want. OK?'

It was excellent advice. Advice I would completely ignore.

***

A year later, in January 2006, I successfully urged Peter to send me back to the West Bank asking the question: a year on from elections to write a follow up article – what's changed?

After the first trip I had told my whole family about the Palestinian families I visited, but my words in no way did justice to the loss of farming land, the restricted freedom of movement, to the incarceration of three-quarters of the men at some point in their lives. More than all of that, I hadn't found the courage to share the feeling that Christianity was not the main story of the Holy Land after all.

Matthew had again agreed to be my guide, and looking for stories and people of interest he introduced me to 'Amin' a well-connected, middle ranking member of Fatah security. Amin was over six feet tall and gangster-rolled when he walked. His moustache was cropped, like a 1970s Arab movie idol, and the gun on his hip, barely hidden beneath a light leather jacket, was removed from its holster at regular intervals and waved around with calculated threat at anyone the least bit annoying. This was especially useful for crossing the road, where a firearm was much more effective at stopping unwilling drivers than a traffic light.

Walking to a shisha restaurant between appointments, a car careered towards us in the barely-controlled way of all the vehicles in the West Bank. Amin pulled out his gun, turned and flicked the barrel towards the driver. The car screeched to a halt. He sauntered over shouting something loudly in Arabic to the driver, clearly meaning, 'make my day, punk'. The apology was rapid and Amin amicably waved the driver on, ambling back towards me with his affable, nothing-to-see-here, grin. He was funny, likeable and protective of my safety. But the CV I imagined for him would tell a different story: 'High ranking security expert based in the Middle East. Special skills: Spying and torture techniques. If I tell you more, I will have to kill you.'

Matthew and I sat down to a meal cooked by Amin's 20-year-old cousin-wife. Maryam was sweet and clever with reddish hair and a cheeky smile. She had single-handedly cooked a lavish, homemade feast of regional delicacies. Forget *MasterChef*, every mother and wife I met should have been awarded a Michelin Star, just for their weekday lunch menu.

'Where is your husband,' she asked, heaping charred aubergines known as Baba Ganoush onto my plate. It was so incredible it removed my long held loathing of the vegetable. 'Is he in Filistin (Palestine) with you? How are your children coping without you? It must be hard for them?'

Over my heaped plate I watched the new baby being passed from one adoring family member to the next. What interested me was that this was a weekday not a weekend. The capitalist structure of neglecting loved ones in favour of work five days a week didn't exist in that environment. Every day was family day. In the West Bank, it was common for Palestinian families to own or to rent an entire small apartment building. Elderly parents lived on the ground floor, their adult, married children on the floors above. They take from each other's fridges without having to ask. The sharing ethos is as natural as waking up in the morning. The people I was meeting knew each other's challenges and needs without having to make a phone call, much less book an appointment or a time to see one another when it's 'convenient', as we did in London. They were deeply, immovably embedded 'in' one another's lives.

I considered my own, fairly typical 'modern' marriage. I had been conditioned by society to believe in the ability of coping alone. Relying on others was dangerous and it made human beings weak. Certainly, I could cope without a man. Perish the thought of feeling vulnerable in life without one. I watched Amin's wife bring tray after tray of food with a smile on her face. Imagine the washing up afterwards, I reminded myself. Since I had walked out on my first live-in relationship aged 18, I had felt in many ways superior to men. I didn't need or value them the way the women I met in traditional homes in the Holy Land did. Was it because women there didn't know 'freedom'? Was it because the men were controlling, withholding funds and stopping wives and sisters leaving their homes? Or was it me who was disconnected and detached from any other version of family life. What was illegitimate about a unit of interdependent elements, each protected and valued?

Over the next week, I came face to face with the fact that I had always, unknowingly, been an orientalist. The academic Edward Said coined the term, defining it as a person who imagines, emphasises, and distorts differences of Arab peoples and cultures when compared to that of Europe and the US. From the moment I had landed at Tel Aviv and travelled to the West Bank a year earlier, I certainly fell into that category. I may not have liked the fact that Americans with Israeli passports routinely pointed guns at me and at the indigenous people they subjugated, but the effect it had on me had been markedly different to that of meeting Arab men holding the same weapons. Even as I walked through the markets of Ramallah, it was impossible to deny that Alan Whicker was the internal voiceover to the everyday life I saw around me: 'Here, in the wilds of the West Bank, these exotic, charming people hunt for mint to spice their sweet tea, as the nearby mosque echoes its ancient tones for worshippers of the One they call "Allah".' I was facing my inability to accept other ways of life as equally valid to my western experience and choices.

What unsettled me was the question raised about my version of motherhood as being of a lower status than that of a career – any career. Doing housework was a chore to be escaped, but could it also be an act of love? Of achievement? In Palestine, the mothers I was meeting had absolute commitment to something far more permanent than any job: a family. And in old age, the return for their sacrifice was clear in the way old women were revered. I saw gnarled hands kissed. I had never kissed my Nan's hands, or my own mother's. The needs of the elderly were met by teenage boys, the runners of the household, whose fitness was used to run every kind of errand. The love and affection between the generations was so natural, I envied them.

Four days after Amin's invitation, the whole region was shutting down for the Muslim holiday festival of 'Eid'. Luckily Natalie, a twenty-something staffer at the Palestinian Authority, invited me to share in her family celebrations in Jenin. We set off early in a car driven by her colleague and Natalie rang her parents: 'Yes, Mamma, see you tonight, *insha'Allah*, don't worry. Yes, I have blankets and extra food. Yes, I will be careful. Love you too. *Fi amanillah*.'

I wondered how far we would be travelling, considering the need for emergency supplies. 'How far is Jenin from Ramallah?' I asked as we weaved our way up the first of the rolling hills.

'Thirty-nine miles. Around ... sixty kilometres.'

'But that's not far at all! How long will it take us?'

'Well it should be two or three hours because of the bad roads, traffic and also the hills. But ...'. There was always a 'but' if Palestinians tried to move for work, funerals or family visits between towns and cities in their land. 'But ... on special times it can take from five hours to ... the next morning. Are you okay with that, dear?'

The reason for the delays would soon become clear. After 45 minutes, the driver groaned to a halt behind a long queue of traffic on the hillside. He turned the engine off and walked to the car in front. Natalie shrugged. '*Insha'Allah* (God willing),' she said.

Our driver smoked a cigarette, sharing a joke with the man in the car ahead of us. He stubbed it out underfoot and ambled back. Natalie climbed out to speak to him and there was nodding, shrugging, sighs. Then he pointed over the precipice and down the rock-covered hillside, which made me nervous.

'Okay,' she said, coming over to where I sat on the back seat. 'It's not just a checkpoint, it's a block. We won't get to Jenin this way. But ...' Again? 'But the good news is that Mustafa knows a way. It will be really bumpy. Are you okay with that?' My excitement at continuing our journey off-road was somewhat tempered by the fact we were in a VW Golf and not a Range Rover.

'Sure ...' I replied.

Mustafa steered us towards the road's edge. The slope was steep but not impassable. Gripping the door handle, prepared to leap should things go wrong, I held my breath as the tyres pounded us down the ravine.

'Will we get shot at by the IDF doing this?' I asked. Natalie's juddering answer as we bounced along was the usual Palestinian shrug - which translated as, 'who knows, what can we do, let's try?'

We heaved across the uneven landscape for half an hour before reaching another road. It was coming up to noon by now and after two hours we had travelled just ten miles. The new road was free from traffic, which I took as a good sign. I was wrong. Another five miles along there was a checkpoint manned by soldiers. Behind them, the road was blocked by a tank. Guns were pointed at the windscreen as we approached and the palms of outstretched hands ordered us to stop at a distance.

'Let's back up and find another way,' I suggested to Mustafa. He shook his head.

'This is one of the bad ones, don't move too much and I must turn the engine off. Sorry for your trouble.'

We sat very still as the soldiers pointedly ignored us for 15, 20 then 30 minutes. We couldn't eat, it was too risky to reach into a bag, and we couldn't call anyone to ask about alternative routes, as using our arms could be perceived as a threat. A hail of bullets could result in any suspicious-looking movement. No wonder the road had been so clear, word had got out on the drivers' grapevine. Before long a 'checkpoint app' would be available, easing the horrors for Palestinian drivers – slightly. Finally, two of the soldiers walked over, their guns waving us out of the car. Food bags and bedding, clothes and gifts were searched and pushed about with army boots.

'Go back,' said one of them, an armed teenager with a French accent. He gestured generally to the countryside behind us.

It was the equivalent of Christmas Eve for the Muslims and they just wanted to get home, have dinner with parents or grandchildren, hug nephews and nieces, joke together, and pray together. We drove back the way we had come, all the time Natalie taking phone calls from other drivers similarly negotiating the cement blocks, checkpoints and tanks en route. The endless jolting made me nauseous and I climbed out of the car and vomited, twice. It was now 3 pm and we were back on a real road fifteen miles from where we had started almost six hours earlier. Our next traffic jam was met with less optimism and I wound down my window to take in the scene. Men and women, young and old, were unloading cars and word reached us that the army had completely blocked most routes towards Jenin. An elderly lady was loading her husband's back with bedding rolls, handing him plastic bag after plastic bag of food. On arthritic legs, they skidded into the crowds of families all heading down to the distant buses waiting at the bottom of the slope. Those without money for bus fare or who were too old or unwell to risk the scramble had two choices: They could sleep in their cars and try to travel on Eid day, Israeli army permitting; or they could go back home and abandon the two-day religious holiday with their family altogether. We arrived in Jenin after 8 pm.

'You're early,' clapped Natalie's mother joyfully. Eleven hours for a trip of less than forty miles was considered fairly good going on Holy holidays.

Natalie introduced me to her nine brothers and sisters. Some were married, some still at primary school. She gave me her bed and slept on the sofa, it was inconceivable a guest would have anything less than the best room in the house. My last thought was one of gratitude, I had slept on a lot of lousy sofas back in the UK and it was the first time someone had given up their own bed for me.

The next morning I woke up to my favourite smell in the world, roasting lamb. Looking at my phone my mind was confused, 9 am was too early for meat surely? My stomach growled a different opinion. Still in pyjamas, I sought for the source of the gorgeous smell and climbed through a window onto the flat roof of the cement home. The father, Hussam, a taxi driver, was alone in the bright morning chill. He was carefully turning skewers of spiced lamb on a small tin barbeque. We greeted each other and I took in the view. The dusty road rolled into the green hills that had tormented us the day before. I glimpsed hints of the former beauty of a region once known as the 'Garden of Palestine' for its fertility. Gardens and courtyards below were lush with tomatoes and the flowers of the 'majnoun' (crazy) plant. But here too, decades of Israeli occupation and violent military incursion had disrupted the beauty. Nature was punctuated by crumbling brickwork and its commas were bullet holes.

The first batch of luscious meat ready, I offered to take the five sticks to 'Mamma', who was downstairs in the kitchen, working since 6 am on the rest of the day's food.

'No,' laughed Hussam, 'All these are you for you, our guest.'

I laughed too at the crazy generosity. A little nervous at the idea that I was expected to eat so much meat whilst still barely awake. The kebabs were succulent, sweet and spiced to perfection and the last luscious cube fell into my mouth ten minutes later. I was unable to move and ashamed to admit to myself I could have eaten more. 'Thank you so much,' I said.

'Don't thank me, thank God' Hussam replied. 'Anyway, here is more,' and he piled my plate again and laughed as I began eating.

'Is no one else hungry or awake yet?' I asked.

'Yes ... But you are our guest and no one will eat until you have blessed us by being content.'

I was content to bursting.

That night, the youngest nephew, aged nine, listened along with the extended family of 15 as I told the story of my travels across the West Bank so far. 'I can't physically fight for your rights,' I finished, 'But I can write what I see happening to you and your people.'

The little boy left the room and returned a few minutes later with a large red object in the shape of shield. A gasp escaped some of the older aunties when they saw what it was. Solemnly, the boy walked to where I sat and in shy, broken English said: 'Please take this. I love you for the sake of Allah. You ... good berson. Sanks for being with us in our pain.'

There was a long silence and I held up the handmade object. Two identical cardboard shield shapes had been cut from thick cardboard then glued together using long pieces of card to form a solid shape. On the back it was covered with silver foil and the front and edges were glitter pen covered by glued designs on red felt. On the front, a shaky hand had written words in Arabic in silver glue-pen. Beneath the writing I recognised an attempt to recreate Al Aqsa Mosque in Jerusalem, loved and revered by Muslims for a reason I didn't understand but which I realised had great significance. The quiet was becoming unnerving. The many gifts I'd received before from Palestinians had been given with shouting, clapping, smiling and with barely a break in conversation. This was different.

'Did he ...?' I turned to the lad's mother, a slender lady in a black abaya and matching hijab. 'Did he make this?' His mother shook her head and looked down at her hands. The matriarch of the house, the grandmother, began to speak in broken English. She held a tissue to her nose as she was weeping. Standing up she pulled the boy to face her. She spoke in Arabic to him, but the meaning was clear.

'Are you sure, are you certain you want to part with this?' The boy nodded twice, his short black hair bobbing. Released by her oak-coloured hands, he came over to me again, waiting for my response.

Then the grandmother spoke: 'What you hold was made by his father, my son ...'. Her voice broke, 'Salim has never met his father. He was taken from us by Yehudi (Jewish troops) almost ten years ago. He has been in prison ever since ... He made this and had it smuggled to us. To keep us ... strong.' Other women relatives were now openly sobbing. Tears pricked behind my eyes.

'I can't take it,' I stammered. I gently tried to hand it back. The boy's deep brown eyes met mine. He stood upright and held a palm towards me.

'La (no),' he said.

A lump was rising in my throat. How could I take this child's one gift from a father who had been tortured and incarcerated by their Occupier? Was there a likelihood that in my culture a traveller, passing through lives for a couple of days, would be given anything so precious? I couldn't imagine it for a second.

'Why would you give this to me?' I asked.

The boy's mother took my hand in hers. 'You came in peace to us. Our God tells us in the Holy Qur'an to give the best things to the family, the neighbour, the poor and the traveller. This ...' she pointed a shaky finger at the precious object, made by a husband imprisoned for life, 'This is the most special thing we have. May God accept it for you and may He accept it from us.'

The women engulfed me in hugs, with their foreign clothing, foreign language and this alien love.

CHAPTER 8
JERUSALEM SYNDROME

'The revolution will not be televised...
The revolution will be live.'

Gill Scott-Heron

I had wondered if I would find religion when I visited the West Bank and Gaza, spending time with a people who still believed in God enough to pray regularly. Instead, I was finding anger – my own, not theirs – and the more the people I met at checkpoints told me to be 'patient' or to see 'a blessed future', the more rage bubbled inside me like Old Faithful in Yosemite Park. I was ready to go toe-to-toe with every gun-toting kid claiming his 'right' to patrol the land for the 'Jewish State'.

After Jenin, I went to Bethlehem. I was taken up cement stairs to a family whose walls were scarred enough to bring back memories of Mukataa and Al Shawish. The 50-year-old father's eyes rarely left the floor during my interview. Sipping tea, Ali told me the family's story: At approximately 2 am on 2nd April 2002, Israeli occupation forces invaded Bethlehem, Beit Jala and Beit Sahour. The siege of Bethlehem by Israeli forces lasted 39 days and according to the Palestine Centre for Human Rights, seven Palestinians were killed and at least 40 injured by Israeli snipers. The family's home had been shelled and the windows burst by bullets from Israeli sniper fire. As I sat making notes, his striking 15-year-old daughter brought us a tray of snacks, then left without a word. 'My beautiful daughter is double incontinent with emotional and psychological problems from that time,' said Ali.

Everywhere I went businesses were failing because of the growing number of checkpoints. I met children whose education and future were damaged as a direct result of Occupation policies and violence. One afternoon, I took a taxi to the hillside city of Nablus to meet faculty members at the famous university campus. The Dean greeted me with sweets and tea in the boardroom. Local papers featured my visit, curious as to why the British prime minister's sister-in-law was seen here and there. Was it an unofficial (yet official) visit by the British PM's family? Was it a behind the scenes show of support from Tony Blair? Hopes were raised, which I extinguished with brutal honesty. Blair didn't speak to me, I told hopeful dignitaries, as I had campaigned for his removal from office. Arab men in grey suits, faces etched with a lifetime of difficult decisions, shifted in their seats. Disappointment was never allowed to break the code of hospitality. My lack of political clout was not a problem, I was assured, far too often for it to be true.

In the Dean's office we talked about children and family. He told me without a trace of visible emotion that the car his wife and three children had been in was forced off a hillside road six years earlier by a violent Jewish settler. The extremist had been responsible for the death and injury of other Arab women and children and was known to the Israeli authorities and the army. All of the Dean's family had died in the attack. 'And so it goes,' he said simply.

After lunch on campus and a tour of impressive new buildings, a university driver took me back towards the notorious Nablus checkpoint. As expected, the line of vehicles waiting to be systemic searched, of drivers and passengers awaiting systemic humiliation, was at least an hour long.

'You have a British passport?' asked the driver. I nodded. He turned his engine back on and turned the steering wheel right, intending to drive out of the standstill lane and to overtake the Palestinian drivers.

'What are you doing?' I asked.

'You are a British traveller here. You have greater rights than us locals. I can drive you right up to the checkpoint, there's no need to wait.'

I told him to stay where we were. I felt ashamed of the 'white privilege' which would allow a visitor like myself to queue-jump local people. The driver looked at me intently, checking I was serious. After a while he started to cry silently at the tiny act of solidarity.

'I pray you come to Islam, Madame. May God the All Merciful bless you always.'

Back at the Grand Park Hotel in Ramallah, I rang London from the basement office, bizarrely the only area that had internet. The editorial team at the *Mail on Sunday* were 'pleased' with the first draft of my second piece from Palestine. It would run the following weekend as a double-page spread.

The day of my Tel Aviv flight to Paris, Jamal, by now a trusted friend, drove through the hectic streets of East Jerusalem dropping me alongside Jewish soldiers, at the Lions' Gate entrance to the Old City. I felt the anger again and wondered what would happen if I gave one of them a brisk kick in the shins. Jamal, protective and sensing my mood, shouted back at me as he drove away: 'Just go shopping Laureen. Blease.'

I had just over 40 minutes to buy my family and friends souvenirs from a place it was unlikely they would ever dare visit. A light drizzle fell on the ancient cobbles which slipped under my heeled suede boots. Overhead was the gate's crest of four leopards (mistaken for lions and the reason for its local name, Lions' Gate). The Christians knew the entry as St Stephens' Gate. All around me were signs of ancient victories and the melding of beliefs into uneasy stonework. The lions/leopards had been put there to honour Sulayman the Magnificent, after the Ottoman defeat of the Mamluks in 1517. It was the same spot where the 55th Israeli Paratroopers Brigade had entered the Old City during the Six-Day War in 1967, unfurling their blue and white flag over East Jerusalem.

Amongst the tourist-empty market stalls, I pulled a shopping list from the pocket of my jeans. My husband and children had asked for a couple of things: He wanted a ceremonial Arab knife to add to the weapons collection he had started as a teenager; my daughters, who were easy to buy for, would be getting toy camels. What else would English toddlers expect from an Arab world consistently painted as an uninhabitable desert wasteland? For friends I'd buy Palestinian scarves, the black and white tartan worn by anti-war protesters in London. For my Mum and other Christian friends, I had already brought wooden crosses made from Holy Land olive wood. At the bottom of my shopping list, dashed off as a quick afterthought, were the words 'Quran in English'. Buying the book was an act of curiosity, not conversion, I told myself. I had seen enough of the Palestinian way of life to know that I could never be a Muslim wife. I mean, those women seemed to sew their own clothes, cook feasts at the drop of a hat, have spotless homes, a dozen children and still look tidy and excited when guests came over. I had yet to meet the other sectors of female society – that would happen on later visits. There were women with multiple bachelor's degrees in charge of university departments, government ministries and global businesses. I thanked God my own husband had no idea what women were actually capable of.

I was never going to change my faith. I didn't need to. Christianity suited me and God was in His heaven. He was there if I needed to cry or let off steam, like a divine Spotify account; silent until I switched Him on. Distant enough to expect nothing tangible, yet close enough to hear my occasional prayers. Wandering the streets of Al Quds, I was greeted again with kind glances and this big smiles. I had never experienced love between people like I had seen on my visit to shattered, scarred land. The brightness of the faces as I walked through their midst made my own grin feel haggard by materialism. Who were these people and what made them so special? In European markets, the stallholders show casual disdain toward customers. We are made to feel that spending money on their products is a great piece of luck. Market stallholders at Islington Market would yell, 'Two for a tenner! Come on love, it's your lucky day, get your money out! These won't last long!' In Palestine, markets were places of yelling and pleading. 'If you don't enter my stall my wife and children will starve,' an obese man shouted as he ate a sandwich.

Beside him in the next stall, selling plastic toys, another old man offered me sweets. I shook my head. He switched his offer, 'rugs, mugs, keyrings, anything!'

A young man in his late teens fell into step besides me. 'Marhaba,' he said. This meant 'hi' in the local dialect. He was rangy, lean like all the shabab (Palestinian youth) I'd seen. Compared to his western peers, the teenage boys here always appeared underfed. He wore faded tight jeans and trainers, his red collared t-shirt tucked beneath a brown leather jacket, mitigating the persistent afternoon rain. I wasn't in the mood for a 'marhaba' sales ploy, I was in a rush. I'd yet to be tricked in Palestine, but I guessed that if that were to happen then a major tourist market like this one would be the venue. I turned to the young guy, a curt 'no thank you' ready on my lips. But my inner voice told me not to brush him off so quickly. I remembered the kindness I'd been shown by his people and I wanted to learn from the experience. To change, to improve myself. No one had so much as asked for sympathy from me (even in the worst of situations) and in the small Gazan towns I had been fed and given gifts by families with nothing to spare. With these thoughts in mind I forced myself to return the greeting. As if thrilled to hear me talk, the young man jumped from foot to foot. He asked my name.

'What can I assist with you today, Madame? Lauren, yes?'

His smile was beautiful and simple, emitting a bright energy that was infectious. I handed him my shopping list rather than explaining what I needed.

'Can you show me where to buy these? I've got half an hour before I have to go the airport.'

'This is GREAT news, Madame Lauren, all of these men here are my uncles.' He waved his arms at the middle-aged and elderly gentlemen sitting or standing amidst coloured scarves, oil lamps and the bric-a-brac of Palestine, old and new. 'Let us begin.'

Jerusalem was not named by the Hebrews, as is often supposed. It was a thriving Canaanite town from the early Bronze Age, one of the oldest cities in the world. As far back as 1330 BCE it was known as Ursalim, and its sand gold walls wind protectively around the plateau central to the three Abrahamic faiths; Judaism, Christianity and Islam. No Taj Mahal, Eiffel Tower, no pyramid, strikes as deeply at the faithful heart. How the greenery and yellow sandstone, offset by the grey stones of the Holy sites, intertwine. Jerusalem climbs the hillside in distance. It overlooks mankind's joys and its miseries, silently accepting the prayers and the pleadings of ages. The first Biblical mention of the city is in Genesis, when the Prophet Abraham meets the king of Salem and priest of El Elyon, Melchizedek. El Elyon refers to the Most High God and later appears as Elohim in Psalms. The Arabic name for the city is Al Quds or Bayt al-Maqdis, from the verb *qadusa* meaning to be holy or pure. People go mad setting foot on the cobbled stones of Old Jerusalem. Its wide pathways have remained largely unchanged since the time of Jesus and Caliph 'Umar Ibn al-Khattab. Except now there is a new kind of soldier on the streets. I wanted to stand still and take it all in. I remembered reading the Bible during my school break times and I wanted to visit the Church of the Holy Sepulchre. It would be wonderful to sink to my knees there, in that holy place of Christianity, and ask for forgiveness for the sin of being a selfish 'prat' my entire adult life.

The young man was making introductions to the first 'uncle' stall holder: 'This is my special uncle, Hamid. His wife has how many ... fifteen ... no eighteen children, *masha'Allah*.' We had wandered into a covered area of the market. Gigantic bedspreads of red, green, even gold hung behind tabla drums, bangles and wooden donkeys. Stubbing out his cigarette, 'uncle' Hamid ushered me onto a plastic chair.

'Chai,' he shouted. A young boy sprinted off to fetch some. 'What brings you to our country my dearrrrr? Travel, work perhaps, charity?'

He can't figure me out. Neither can I. It's my second visit to Palestine in my capacity as a journalist, but I've lost my bearings this time round. I had arrived a year earlier as a curious writer, seeking a bit of adventure and a scoop. But I had never been a war correspondent, nor a beyond news hack. That battle-hardened breed lived above the normal threshold of pain or feeling. They forced themselves into emotional immunity in order to deliver news that fell within their publication's editorial narrative. I had begun to feel more inclined towards Archbishop Desmond Tutu's view on the subject of being 'unbiased': 'If you are neutral in situations of injustice, you have chosen the side of the oppressor. If an elephant has its foot on the tail of a mouse and you say that you are neutral, the mouse will not appreciate your neutrality.'

Who could be 'neutral' in Palestine? To be unmoved by the gross injustice was itself an act of barbarity which made us all a party to the oppression we reported. I had ignored my Israeli handler's advice, which had been to stay at the hotel in Ramallah, to carry out organised interviews then leave. Instead, I had thumbed lifts between cities, slept in stone-empty rooms in refugee camps, seen first-hand the agonising detail of occupation and trauma.

'I came as a journalist but now I'm ...'. In the dusty shop I felt tears prick my eyes when I thought of what I knew, what I had seen. 'Now, I want to use my words to ... to help ...' Embarrassingly, droplets began to flow from my eyes. Having Scouse roots has its downside, I thought, irritated by the constant eye leakage. All I could do was sit and sniffle as my cheeks then my collar got damp.

The shopkeeper was distressed. 'Quick tea! Yassine! Where is that boy? He is so slow! For goodness sake stop crying in my shop? Please, my dear, stop. Listen to me. We are O-Kay. We know that our God — I think you are Christian yes? Well our God, same as yours, but called Allah. We know He takes care of everything.

Nothing bad, only 'qadr'. That means ...' he searched in his pockets as if the word was in there. He pulled out an unsatisfactory tissue, then put it back.

'Please get our exceptional guest a tissue – quickly! Tears in my shop from a guest – never – I won't allow it.'

He turned to me, finding his earlier train of thought: 'The word I think is 'fate' the meaning is that all this is written, by God. The good, the bad of things, the in-between.' He tried to catch my eye.

'The love, the children ... the grumpy husbands. Yes?' There was a flicker around my mouth.

Yassine, the boy who had run for chai, handed me a glass cup filled with the dark brown, sickly-sweet mint tea. I had tried to come to love it, but I just couldn't.

'Mmmm, lovely,' I said quietly.

After more gentle cajoling, we were back on track with our salesman and customer relationship. Toy camels were pulled from dusty shelves. Much fuss was made about the names of my children. A prayer in Arabic was offered by both men in the store for the girls' 'happy, blessed lives'.

Other bits were tugged from neat piles, or pulled from cardboard boxes; a shawl in painstaking red embroidery, key rings which read 'Jerusalem Capital of Palestine'. I was fascinated by the extraordinary knick-knacks which bore the name of a country being erased from geography books. Everything was lovingly placed into plastic bags. I reached for my wallet. My bank card was waved away. 'Pay when you finish shopping,' said Hamid tapping numbers into a calculator from Roman times. No amount for the bill was given. I was expected to trust I would not be ripped off.

An almost identical scene (even my embarrassing tears) took place in five other souk stalls which the young man led me into. The pain I'd witnessed, the bravery, was mixed with a desperate need to see my own children. Beneath it all, the pain of leaving Palestine took my breath away. It was there, waiting to be acknowledged beneath the shopping, the tea, the laughter. In thirty minutes, we somehow completed all my shopping. In each store I felt compelled to drink mint tea with five heaped teaspoons of sugar in each (not optional). Amounting to at least twenty-five teaspoons in a short time. How I never succumbed to diabetes whilst in Palestine was a miracle. Finally, the young man and I were standing near Damascus Gate, where Jamal had promised to meet me in the gloomy, late afternoon drizzle. Around my feet a dozen bags warned I had overspent on my souvenir budget.

One item was missing. I mentioned it to the young man, looking at my watch anxiously. He immediately sprinted off, zig zagging through the market shouting *'al-Qur'an - Engleezi'* (The Qur'an in English)?' I checked my watch again, what awaited me at Tel Aviv airport could only be guessed. Out of breath the young man, soaked for his efforts, put a green and gold embossed book into my hands. It was huge, six hundred pages.

'Quran ... in ... Ingleeesh, Madame Lauren. Especially from God to you.'

Out of respect, I put the Qur'an into my shoulder bag rather than on the ground, wondering if I would ever even open its cover.

It was time for wrangling. I'd always loved bartering and had earned a reputation for ruthlessness during my travels in my twenties. I looked now at the empty shops around us knowing that trying to win shekels off the already impoverished owners would be a sin in any faith. 'How much do I owe you, brother?' I asked. Rain dripped off my nose, there was a pause.

The young man's black curls clung to his skull, droplets gathered on his leather collar. He put his head to one side as if hearing something. Then he shrugged.

'You don't owe me anything. Please take these small things to your family with *salaam* from Al Quds.'

I disagreed, there was around £100 worth of gifts, more than 600 shekels, in the bags. I knew the shops here could ill afford such losses. He held a hand up to quieten me. Unblinking, he looked me in the eyes: 'Just one thing I ask from you, that's all. Don't forget Palestine when you go home. Remember us. Please.'

His words entered my heart and twin rivulets began to weave their familiar route beneath my eyelashes. The lad was suddenly tearful too. How, why could an hours' shopping feel like a lifetime of friendship? Embarrassed by the emotion he jogged away, turning to give me a final wave. Then he vanished into the network of ancient cobbles and striped awnings. That was how I received my first copy of the Holy Qur'an. As a gift from the people of Jerusalem, Palestine, asking not to be forgotten.

I ran to Jamal's car and we sped towards Tel Aviv airport. There was no time for a meaningful farewell outside the terminal as having unpacked my cases and gift bags from the boot of his taxi, Jamal was waved away at gunpoint. I was partly relieved, I couldn't have withstood another teary goodbye. At the first baggage check inside the departure terminal, the contents of my case drew some concern. Out came the souvenirs, one by one, and too late it occurred to me that perhaps I should have reconsidered my purchases. There was a mother of pearl embossed portrait of Yasser Arafat, my husband's gift of an Arabic-style knife ('on a flight?'), followed by the shield, made by the father of the young boy in Jenin with words in Arabic like 'freedom' and 'victory'. Finally, pulled out from my hand luggage with a plastic- gloved flourish and a knowing nod from the security officer, the translation of the Holy Qur'an. This, as they say in the US, was going to be epic.

The armed Israeli security man now barked orders: 'Grab your things! Over there! Move faster!'

Stage training doesn't have to useful only in the theatre and I decided to use my acting to slow things down. My militarised personal guards (there were suddenly two of them) snapped at me in an accent reminiscent of a war film: 'Move! There! Faster!'

I began to hobble a bit, as if I had a bad case of sciatica. I focused not on the situation but remembering the feeling down my spine and through my left hip which I'd endured at the end of my second pregnancy. Twinge, wince, twinge, wince, I limped towards my bags on the belt. I looked over bravely at the security, wincing again. They wanted me to remove my ten-tonne case from the conveyor belt by myself. At Tel Aviv, once something Palestinian is found the option of 'innocent' is removed. You are either guilty or complicit of something. Ten days of clothes, gifts and dozens of books had made the case well over thirty kilos in weight. I made a grab at the handle: 'Ow, Oh no, my back! Sorry ...' and slowly began to inch the case off the edge. I let it fall, with a thud. Security looked furious.

'Urrry Upp!' I took 30 seconds to bend down and another 20 to stand the case on its side.

'I'm so sorry sir, my back you see, not as young as I look.' I gave what I hoped was a charming, smile. We were heading to 'a private area for checking'. I had no idea what that meant but I was in no hurry to find out. In disgust, the guard took hold of the handle and dragged my pink suitcase to the airport's farthest corner. It was a small victory, which I internally, invisibly relished, limping all the while.

I was shown into a small white cubicle. Two young women in uniform told me to remove my bra from beneath my shirt after the security 'wand' beeped when it was waved there. 'Under wiring', I thought. The wand was waved down my trouser legs. Another beep. It was the end of a long trip and my hectic schedule had not allowed for the hand basin washing of underwear. As a result, by this time I wasn't wearing any. If I removed my trousers I'd be nude from the waist down. Not that I cared particularly, shame was something so out of fashion it had almost ceased to exist in my friendship group to allow outdated feelings such as dishonour or impropriety to impact on our choices. But I wouldn't give them even the perception that they controlled me.

I would be as difficult and as awkward as possible. I refused to drop my trousers, 'unless you bring me a towel to cover myself'. There was talk between the women in Hebrew and one left. After a few moments, she returned with a single sheet of toilet paper. Touché, I thought. Note to self: the mind games had started. One of the soldiers held the single sheet of toilet paper to my nakedness as the other scanned for the hidden weapons they knew perfectly well did not exist inside my womb.

Zero internalised weaponry found, I dressed and was shown into a bland space with two chairs, a desk and another long table. In the corner was a coffee machine. I was told by the departing women my luggage had been taken off my flight to Paris. I leaned against the desk table, dreaming of the hot coffee I was missing in the business lounge. On a long table a few feet away, everything in my luggage was being removed by a group of armed Israeli security officers. Make-up, the girls' presents and coffee grains were all meticulously examined. After a while, a short man with a large air of self-importance opened another door to the room and strolled in with his hands in the pockets of his suit.

'Do you have your press pass?' I handed him the pass I had been issued by Ariel Sharon's office, valid until February 2006.

'What was the purpose of your visit?'

'My work agenda was to test the political water of the elections for the PA.'

The election had been contested chiefly between Fatah, the 'establishment' party founded by Yasser Arafat, now led by Mahmoud Abbas, and Hamas, a movement regarded by western politicians as a terrorist organisation bent on the destruction of Israel. In Palestine and other parts of the world they are viewed as a political party of resistance. In the elections, Hamas had virtually swept the board. It was the year after western leaders, including Tony Blair, had failed to make good on promises that if the Palestinian people 'democratised' they would find support for their economic, security and social needs. Now there was grassroots anger at the never-ending and unproductive 'peace process talks' between Israel and PA leaders. Talks my friend Afif pithily summarised as: 'plenty of process with no peace.'

In between researching for my piece and carrying out interviews with members of the two main parties, I had travelled across the West Bank and Gaza to find out whether life had improved since my first visit. Everywhere the situation was worse, as a result of the increased illegal Jewish settlement building.

'Why did you go the West Bank?' Asked the man pretending his name was 'Yanni'. He reminded me of Captain Mainwaring from the 1970s sitcom *Dad's Army*: all pomp and no circumstance.

'I went to the West Bank, to several cities. I was there as a journalist, covering the Palestinian elections.'

I was told I was in trouble. As far as I could understand from the veiled language used, I was being questioned because despite obeying Israel's 'laws' I had disrespected some of its authoritarian, unwritten, 'rules'. After days of witnessing the awfulness of daily life under occupatiosn, I now had a front row seat to the theatre of apartheid rule: the Shin Bet security apparatus. The man questioning me was a member of Shin Bet, better known as Shabak in Hebrew and Arabic, one of three branches of the Israeli General Security Service. Barak Ben-Zur, the former special assistant to the Shin Bet director from 1996–2007, gave an interview to Al Jazeera describing some of the agencies working practices: 'Shin Bet is no different from the other security divisions in Israel. They all started as secretive organisations that preceded the state. The intelligence body of the Haganah army was the seed that created Shin Bet', he said.[1]

Haganah, the terror organisation used by Israel's first prime minister, David Ben-Gurion, and namesake of the airport whose interrogation cells in which I was detained. Haganah was created

---

[1]   Al Jazeera World, 'Inside Shin Bet: An investigation into the methods used by Israel's controversial internal security service' (Al Jazeera, 24 October 2013).

to sow fear and confusion amongst the British forces and the indigenous Palestinian people, both of whom the Jewish Zionists sought to remove. Documents from British records made during the period reveal that more than 500 terrorist incidents against Palestinians and the British occupation occurred between 1939 and 1948. These included (but were not limited to) bombings, booby traps, landmines, kidnappings, torture of prisoners, bank robberies, the murder of Arab civilians, and the assassination of police and British officials. With this in mind, the chance of my missing my flight if I didn't 'co-operate', as threatened by Yanni, faded somewhat into insignificance. I would get home. Unlike the hundreds of thousands of Palestinians who had passed, and continued to pass, through similar cells at every major crossing in and out of their homeland.

Before travelling, I had researched could reverse the control dynamic in an interrogation scenario. I combined these with role play from 'status' workshops I'd taught since drama school. Rule number one in an interrogation scenario: Appear unbothered and relaxed. Two: Stay in a higher physical position than the questioner. This shifts the sense of superiority. The Israelis had mistakenly sent a man of five-foot one to question me. I strolled the room, at five-feet eleven, towering over my inquisitor. At times, I perched on the end of a table, in my mind playing the part of a secretary who was patronising a boss about to be made redundant because of anger issues. My relaxed attitude was making 'Yanni' irritable.

'Do sit down, Miss Booth,' he gave a thin lipped impression of a smile.

'No thanks Yanni, I prefer to stand. Does this coffee machine work? Does it need change? Perhaps you could lend me some coins, because errm ...' I waved towards the armed men, smashing and methodically destroying the gifts and souvenirs from my travels. His politeness was a thin veneer, but necessary. I was a British citizen not a 15-year-old Arab whose family could be threatened with home demolition or worse. I knew for certain that after they had had their fun with me, I would return home. Still, the scene made my nerve endings twitch with nervous energy. I continued to glue on a smile which said Yanni and I were having a good old chinwag. Just two old friends catching up over a coffee. Which, by the way, Yanni had failed to buy me from the machine.

'You appear very relaxed,' he observed an hour into the game.

'You guys are nice people just doing your job. Why wouldn't I be relaxed?'

'You are not behaving like others in your position. Why?'

'What position do you mean? I'm just waiting for my flight, chatting to you.'

He stood very still and stared at me. He looked as if he wanted to slam the table, make me jump, bring out some pleasing semblance of fear. Something was stopping him. Was it because I was Tony's sister-in-law? I wasn't sure that would be a bonus. In fact, I suspected Tony had given the nod for me to get a proper going over. Such was his clear political alignment with the Zionist project of expansionism and domination of Arab lands.

'We don't like how you are behaving. Do you understand? We are watching you. We know everything. We have ways of getting information.'

I grew up when repeats of black and white movies about Nazis were the highlight of Sunday lunchtimes. I was now pretending to be John Mills in *The Colditz Story*. Stiff upper lip, old chap. Or was I more William Holden in *Stalag 17*, sarcastic and unafraid? The parallel to the scenes of that era were impossible to ignore. How was it, I wondered, watching this man try to intimidate a western journalist, that the Jewish grandchildren of the Holocaust could behave like this? In disgust, I dropped out of character for a moment: 'Do you know what you sound like? Do you ...?'

The staring contest that followed lasted a long time. It went on until I felt sweat on my spine. No doubt his people had a reach beyond Tel Aviv. His look was silently telling me that I had triggered future interference in my professional and possibly my private life. Yanni eventually looked away. I was British, white. There was only so far he could go without revealing that what was really happening was the attempt to stifle writings which ran counter to Israeli messaging. After two hours' detention, I was asked to write down details of my mobile phone number, my address and all my emails.

'Yanni dear, you have all that stuff anyway. As you said, you know everything about me.'

He actually flushed with anger, which I found very pleasing indeed. 'What if we want to follow up this meeting?' He demanded.

'You are more than welcome to leave me a message at the *Mail on Sunday*,' I replied. He looked at me and curtly responded: 'Leave now'.

I made my flight to Paris at a sprint, out of breath and with an armed escort that raised the eyebrows of my fellow passengers. I half expected to be handcuffed to the arm of the seat but I wasn't. I was going home to my family. I was escaping a brutal, insane mess. I would focus on my kids, swim in our pool, bake cakes. Be normal. I would go out of my way to make my family feel special for the worry I'd caused. I would do all these things to the best of my ability. And I would never forget the promise made to that young man on the rainy streets of Al Quds, the City of 'Salaam'. I would not forget the people of Palestine or their struggle for freedom, liberty and justice.

CHAPTER 9
HYPOCRISY TO HOPE

'Ladies and Gentlemen, we are floating in Space.'

Spiritualized

Back home in the South of France, my daughters and I were attending the traditional grey stone church at the top of the hill in Limeuil Haut at least once a month. It was an Anglican congregation of retired middle-class immigrants from cities and shires across the UK. There were other younger families like mine, whose children would chirrup away in 'Franglaise' in the sunshine outside the quiet, cool chapel.

My main reason for taking them was so they would have an inkling that there was more to life than materialism. It wasn't really working. The more we went, the more I became aware of my own doubts. During the services I had had started to mumble through bits of the Apostles' Creed in which I didn't believe. My recitation from the pew began well:

'I *believe* in God, the Father Almighty,

Creator of heaven and earth.

I believe in Jesus Christ ...'

Then when the son and Lord part came I just mumbled under my breath. At the end I would mumble the whole section before saying out loud:

'... the forgiveness of sins, the resurrection of the body, and the life everlasting. Amen.'

Trying to understand more about God I felt as if I were chasing a rainbow. Who was the Creator? What did He want with me or from me? If He was so beautiful, as I had once felt, why was there pain, murder, torture? The more I tried to connect with the Unseen via church services, the further away I felt from the Divine. I sat on a wooden pew in that stone church staring at a bleeding man on a cross and it made me sad and confused. The Gospels told us of Jesus' agony, hanging for days with nails in his hands and feet before finally dying. I didn't want him to have suffered for my sins. How ungodlike was his humiliation, how strange for a man-deity to expire between a robber and a murderer. Was this what forgiveness looked like?

As the sermon droned on I would consider the unfairness of Jesus dying on the cross. On the one hand God was all forgiving, on the other He extracted a terrible retribution on Himself (?) for all the sins human beings commit. Forgiveness cannot come *after* punishment, it only exists without punishment not instead of it. If Jesus were God incarnate, why did He punish himself as an example? My daughters, of course, were masters of these questions, spotting gaps right away and seeking along with me a faith that gave guidance by making sense. I persevered with the churchgoing because when I sat there, quietly holding those two little hands, I felt so grateful for the period of blessing we were in and I knew no other way of communicating that to God.

One afternoon, a month after returning from Palestine, the children were at their little l'Ecole Maternelle (nursery school) in the local village. I walked into the tiled coolness of our living room, where the front door was wide open – as always on a warm day. Beside the short gravel driveway to the quiet road, a peach tree was attached to the wall of our barn and the first buds peeped between the leaves. In a matter of weeks the tree would burst with pale blossom. I glimpsed a head bobbing above our eight-foot hedge. 'Salut,' I shouted, no longer surprised at the unusual sight. The first time I saw Pierre my heart had skipped a beat. He was our local extreme sports competitor and he often bounded past the house on stilts, pounding the hilly roads, training for an alpine race he claimed (and we doubted) took place.

I heard the springs of the specialised leg extensions pop popping past and smiled. People did incredible, pointless things when they set their minds to it. I tried to think of something more useful to do than the washing up. I remembered the Qur'an. On my return from the West Bank I'd wedged it between a water-damaged fifteenth century King James Bible in Latin (a prop from a play I'd stage managed which I'd retrieved it from a skip when the run ended) and on the other side was an eighteenth century Bible featuring terrifying graphic plates of scenes of death and vengeance. My mother had picked it up from a second-hand store in the 1970s.

I decided it was time to take a look at the Muslim book, so I washed my hands and sat on the sofa, placing the Qur'an in front of me. I turned the book over gingerly, front, back, back, front, figuring out which direction it was meant to be read. The chapters were helpfully numbered. *Al-Fatihah*, translated as 'The Opening', turned out to be at the front of this edition. I started to read:

Praise be to God, the Lord of the entire Universe, the Most Merciful, the Most Compassionate; the Master of the day of Recompense. You alone do we worship and You alone do we turn to for help. Direct us on to the Straight Way, the way of those who You have favoured, who did not incur Your wrath, who are not astray.

The 'Opening' sounded a bit like the Lord's Prayer. There was nothing too scary or different from the Christian New Testament in that chapter anyway, I thought. As the February sun sauntered through the open door and enthusiastic bees, awoken from sleep by the unseasonable heat, looked for willing buds to feed from, my mind put the words into easier language to try and decipher the simplest meaning: Love God alone. He is the Master of Creation. Ask Him for help when in trouble. Keep away from sin and protect us from hanging out with or following other sinners who have already made God angry.

God introduced Himself in the book as the 'Lord of the entire Universe'. I didn't know it, but the more common translation is 'Lord of the Worlds', in plural. I wanted to read more. I turned to the next page and a new chapter. It was called *al-Baqarah*, 'The Cow', and began the same as the first: '*In the name of Allah, the Most Merciful, the Most Compassionate*', then came three random-seeming letters from the Arabic alphabet, '*Alif, Lam, Mim*.' Odd.

Beneath was a short explanation. It said that scholars had not been able to agree on the meanings of the letters but grasping the meanings of the Qur'an didn't hinge on them. They were a mystery known only to God. Page two and 'mysteries' already. I looked at my watch, wondering about the school run, but I wanted to read more.

This is the book of God, there is no doubt in it; it is a guidance for the pious, for those who believe in the existence of that which is beyond the reach of perception, who establish prayer and spend out of what We have provided them, who believe in what has been revealed to you and what was revealed before you and have firm faith in the Hereafter.

Whoah. Four lines of 69 words, packed with meaning. In two pages, it struck me as amazing that I had clearly been told God was the Transcendent, Creator. Happy if we did not sin, angry if we did. That was followed by the command to 'establish prayer'. I didn't like that bit very much, didn't it mean that I was already on the wrong side of the fence – my spiritual 'strike one'? Unless the God of the Muslims accepted the church visits the girls and I made, I had failed to be a 'good' worshipper by page two of the Qur'an. I turned back to the first page. There it said God was 'the All Merciful and All Compassionate'. I plunged on to the next verse, number eight: '*There are some who say; "We believe in God and in the Last Day," while in fact they do not believe*'.

I sank back into the cream leather sofa. How come the book was speaking straight to me? Had I been pretending at faith? I'd taken my girls to church not out of worship or an overwhelming belief in an Almighty, but seeking some kind of hippy counterbalance to the wonderful (too good to be true) way of life they had been blessed with. They attended a charming European kindergarten where the chef (chef!) served them four course lunches, for crying out loud! The only thing missing for my kids was a glass of Chablis after the cheese course. Having grown up with relatively little, I was disturbed by the risk of my own children being utterly unaware (and therefore unconcerned) about others' hardship.

What I didn't know that warm February morning was that our time of great plenty was almost over. Hardship was just around a bend on the hill between the village and our peaceful cottage. My heart was beating loudly in my ears:

In their hearts is a disease which Allah has increased all the more and a painful doom is in store for them for the lie they utter. Whenever it is said to them, 'Do not spread disorder on the earth', their reply is, 'We only seek to put things aright'. Beware, they only spread disorder but they do not realise it. And when it is said to them, 'Believe sincerely as the other people have believed' they reply, 'Should we believe as fools have believed?' Beware, they themselves are the fools, but they do not know it. When they meet those who believe, they say, 'We, too, are believers', but when they privately meet their evil companions, they say, 'Indeed, we are with you: we are only mocking these other people'. [Little do they know that] Allah is mocking them. He gives them rope enough, and they wander on and on blindly in their mischief and rebellion. (Qur'an 2: 9–15)

I had been going to church simply to assuage my middle class-guilt at having success so easily given to me whilst others went through so much suffering. It was little more than an insecurity linked to my childhood. My faith, such as it was, had been social conscience, not submission to the divine at all. I was a faith-faker.

And that fakery was written as clear as day on the second page of the Qur'an sitting right on my coffee table. I closed it in case the words had the power to leap off the page and devour me, like the spectral light at the end of an Indiana Jones movie. Terror was welling up inside me; I had a diseased heart. How else could you describe going to church and muttering half of the Creed, then swearing and partying at weekends? I said I was a 'believer', then temptation came and my moral compass lost its magnetic North immediately. I was in rebellion against good sense and God himself. Shaking, I carried the Qur'an to the wooden hallway between the living room and bedroom. On tiptoe, I pushed it into the farthest corner of the wooden shelves. Hopefully, I would never *ever* have to glimpse it again. But I knew it was there, and while I would never consider throwing it away, I felt its deep presence every time I passed it by.

CHAPTER 10
WELCOME TO THE JUNGLE

'You can taste the bright lights but
you won't get there for free...'

Guns N Roses

'Oh my God!' I gasped, 'I can't go on the show. No way! They are going to make me bungee jump! Please promise me, swear you'll phone in the morning and call it off.'

Half asleep, my husband shushed me: 'The show is about living in the jungle with insects. Spiders are what you should be worried about. Go back to sleep!'

It was the end of October 2006, just ten days before I was to fly to Brisbane, Australia, to take part on the reality show *I'm A Celebrity Get Me Out of Here*. I was one of ten celebrities (of varying degrees of fame) who would be dumped into the Australian jungle for the new series. There we would be made to do challenges in order to feed ourselves and our camp mates. Pushing aside serious arachnophobia, I had accepted the offer to appear in the series after months of pleading from TV executives. On top of a large fee and a wonderful free holiday for my family, my part in the show would raise a minimum of £15,000 for a charity of my choice. Even if I came last. I chose Interpal, as I had seen their work supporting refugees and Palestinian infrastructure projects first-hand on my regional visits. The deal was agreed and the contract signed. My husband soothed my nerves and I was ready for the challenge and looking forward to it. There had never been a bungee jump in the previous five series.

On the first day of filming, I stood in a suite at a five-star hotel on the Gold Coast of Queensland, Australia. A female runner from ITV told me to change into my jungle costume; red canvas trousers, a khaki shirt and a cowboy-style hat. On the floor were a pair of army boots, almost identical to the ones I had worn to travel around the outback a decade earlier, which was reassuring. I could do this! I tightened the laces in anticipation. I was given a backpack to carry into camp, containing bug repellent wristbands, extra socks, khaki shorts, a blue shirt, a t-shirt, and a wash kit. For my 'personal item' I'd chosen a plastic photo cube. I felt pretty clever getting six photos of my family into the camp in one item. My smugness was instantly deflated on seeing another contestant who had chosen to bring a pillow with a family photo printed on the cover. I would enviously watch him snuggle into it at night as I put my photo cube on the ground next to me, resting my head on smoke-smelling clothes.

Arriving on a patio surrounded by a camera crew, David Gest, best known at the time for having been married to the musical actress Liza Minnelli, was dressed all in black with a huge cross hanging on a chain around his neck. I was ushered towards David by a producer and without missing a beat he looked at me and said, 'Hello, Cherie.'

'Okay, David. Good one,' I said, 'My name's Lauren. Nice to meet you.'

The camera moved on to the other newcomers: Myleene Klass, Jason Donovan, Toby Anstis, Phina Oruche, Faith Brown, Scott Henshall, Jan Leeming, and Matt Willis.

We were introduced over five-star nibbles on the terrace, which was to be our last decent meal for weeks, then we were split into two groups. Half of us were taken for a hair-raising thirty minute helicopter ride that ended in a clearing far away in the middle of the Australian Bush. When the helicopter landed I felt exhilarated, I was back in a world of excitement and – better yet – was with Jason Donovan! I'd had a crush on Jason since I was thirteen years old and he had been the blonde heartthrob in the Aussie soap, *Neighbours*. I imagined days in the open air with my teen dream and was grinning away in the warm sunshine when the production's health officer, Bob, came towards us. A lovely older chap with a white beard who I'd get to know quite well in the coming days.

'We'll be taking you in the BK 117 helicopter in a moment over the Australian bush.' Okay, I thought, back in a helicopter. No big deal.

'Once there, we will stay at a thousand foot hover. And then ... you'll be entering the location by bungee.' There was a moment of absolute silence.

Suddenly, pop star and classical pianist Myleene burst out laughing. I blurted a stream of words that were bleeped from the television transmission and Matt, from the boyband Busted, just looked shocked.

The jump was managed by giant South African mercenary types. One of them stepped in as our group fell apart: 'The only thing to fear is fear itself,' he shouted.

'Yeah,' Matt yelled back, 'but fear is pretty effing scary'.

We were told only a handful of people in the world had ever done what we were about to attempt, and the others had been bungee experts with dozens of jumps to their credit – we were 'first timers'. Jason Donovan, true to the role I had assigned him in my mind, was chuckling and reassuring everyone.

'I can't do this!' I told him.

'Don't worry, Lauren, jump – you might fly!'

I was petrified, but I was not a quitter. That meant the only option was to bungee jump on TV from a helicopter at a thousand feet. I walked away from the group, remembering the visualisations I'd done during childbirth. Back then I'd focused on waves on a beach, and that had helped me to have a drug-free birth.

'You'll be in free fall for a maximum of six seconds,' said the ex-army brute, roughly putting on my harness. Being a thrill seeker, during my travels I had ridden some of America's largest rollercoasters at Six Flags theme park in Los Angeles. I recalled they were around 180 seconds long and this jump, well this fall, would last only six seconds. I climbed into the helicopter without a word and kept my eyes closed, ignoring the deliberate goading of the film crew attempting to get the best shots of each contestant's frightened faces.

'Have a look at the great view, Lauren,' said the cameraman when we reached 500 feet. 'Are you scared right now?' He asked a little while later.

Of course I was bloody well scared! I clammed up, focusing on my birth breathing, quietly muttering my mantra over and over again: 'I love rollercoasters, I love rollercoasters, I love rollercoasters ...' The next thing I knew, I could feel the wind on my face, my feet on the runners beneath the helicopter: 'I love rollercoasters, I love rollercoasters ...'

I heard a voice say, 'Three, two, one, bungee,' and I pushed myself backwards into thin air. We had been told not to push back, which was exactly what I did, and as a result instead of falling straight down I went horizontal for an instant which allowed the bungee cord to wrap around my upper arm. I had three seconds to unloop it or the force of my weight would snap the bones, or worse. Panicking, I spun my arm round in a wide loop, just as the bungee went taut. It slid, razor sharp, along the skin of my upper arm then fell loose. I was falling head over heels, shouting family names and letting go of my fear.

Have you ever noticed how letting go is a relief? When you are stuck in traffic, instead of stabbing at the phone to call someone to let them know the 'disaster' that you are in the middle of and making them anxious too, just saying: 'Here I am, there's nothing I can do. Better make the most of it.' That moment feels like a mini-break for the heart. It's madness to expect everything to go well, to plan every day when all previous life experience has taught us this is not how life works. We don't even have control of our own bodies. Try and tell your heart to beat a single pulse beyond its given time. Try to tell your lungs to breath if they collapse. We make all kinds of plans for tomorrow, next week and next year. Yet, we can never know about the fishbone that gets trapped in the throat or the motorbike accident waiting to happen. Letting go gives us a break from thinking we are running our own universe. It is a relief to acknowledge our lack of control. Even for six short seconds.

'Whoooooh! Yeah, I love you Alex, Holly, Granddad!' My family would be watching back home and I was yelling to them, shouting at the blue sky, swinging under the helicopter. I'd done it! The bungee jump that had woken me from a nightmare weeks earlier was over. Everything else would be easy.

I ended up sleeping in the bunk directly next to Jason Donovan at the top level of the camp and waking up inches from him for fifteen days.

One afternoon, model-turned-actress Phina, fashion designer Scott, soap actor Dean Gaffney and I were called for a 'group trial'. We trekked for 40 minutes, accompanied at a distance by members of the New Zealand Special Forces. They weren't allowed to speak or communicate with us though I'd made eye contact with one of them, who knowing I was the least fit, hissed out of pity: 'Keep going, Lauren, just 100 metres and you're there.'

The show's presenters, the popular British television duo Ant and Dec, were waiting when we reached the clearing. Bob, the health and safety guy, approached us. In his hands he was holding something, a set of harnesses. It couldn't be, I thought, there was no way that what he was holding were bungee harnesses? Not Again?

'Today you will all be doing two bungee jumps ...' he began.

Once rigged up, I stood on the top of scaffolding 250 foot above ground level. I looked straight ahead, at the top of the jungle canopy spreading endlessly into the distance. Tropical birds trilled, concerned by the unusual presence of metal and mankind in their environment. There was no breeze and sweat gathered along my spine.

Behind me a man attached the cord to my ankles: 'Put your toes over the edge, Lauren. You can do this.'

My heart was beating too hard, as if it had moved into my neck. My hands gripped the balloons filled with white paint and I looked down at the distant yellow star I was expected to hit with the balloons as I bounced back from the jump. The camera helmet I wore felt heavy on my neck. Was it even safe? Too late to ask now. Two men held my arms wide, speaking into walkie-talkies to the ground crew.

'Bungee ready. Lauren's ready. Counting down, five, four ...' I felt a gentle push on my arms and lurched forward. My eyes sealed themselves shut. As I felt the bungee jerk I released the two balloons and was yanked upwards with an audible 'ugh!' I let the nausea and an agonising headache overtake me.

Dizzy, on the ground I heard Ant say from a distance: 'Well done, Lauren, that's two stars and two meals for the Camp.' I struggled up with help from the crew and walked over to the presenters for a brief interview before going back up the scaffold for my second jump. The heat of the Australian jungle was pounding, we had been out in it for almost two hours, and my ears were ringing. I forced my lips to keep smiling when they wanted to tremble. Back at the top of the scaffold, I shuffled my toes over the edge, my eyes drinking in the birds, the beautiful blue sky, and the treetops.

'I am *not* going to bungee, I am going to move forward into the beautiful green and smell their exotic fragrances,' I told my mind, but my mind wasn't listening that time.

'Counting down to bungee: five, four, three ...' This time I fell forward without hands needing to push me and my skull smashed against the camera helmet. Then someone turned the lights out and I fainted.

I found myself on the ground again, then using all my acting skills managed to walk cheerily over to Ant and Dec, who stood with the other two contestants for the debrief. 'I'm just going to sit for a minute,' I heard someone say. It sounded like me, but I wasn't sure. After that there was an oxygen mask, a heart monitor and some blessed shade from the sun. My heart was pounding far too fast, our Bush doctor told me, and there was brief talk of a hospital.

'Breathe deeply and slowly with the mask on, don't fight it. You're okay it's all over.'

A day or so after the bungee horror, I was called to a wooden building fifty metres up a jungle track lit by cutesy electric hanging lanterns known as the 'Diary hut'. The disembodied voice we contestants were used to hearing give out daily instructions was not the same. It told me the charity I'd chosen had been deemed 'controversial' and that I would need to make another choice. All I had to do was to give the production company another charities name and I could go back to camp. I asked why Interpal was considered controversial. The confident voice faltered and I was asked to wait a minute. A new voice, older, less jolly, that of an executive, echoed round the small humid hut where I was sitting alone. It would be 'best all round' if a charity which operated somewhere else besides Palestine was chosen. The whole region was 'sensitive' and that word came up again: 'controversial'. Silently, I unclipped the lapel mic we had to wear at all times and unhooked the battery pack it was attached to from the back of my shorts.

'Now hold on Lauren, no need to ...'

I held the microphone to my mouth, looked straight into the camera hidden behind the screen and said, 'F. . . you'.

A new, more soothing female voice floated into the hut. She told me to be reasonable. They couldn't do anything about what the executives had decided and it would just be easier if I chose another charity. Why not one which worked in the UK?

'I signed a contract with ITV which clearly said, "Lauren Booth's accepted chosen charity is Interpal". Try to change this and you are in breach. I will walk. Then I will write far and wide about ITV's prejudice against the Palestinians. You have ten minutes to get an answer. And right now I don't care if I walk off this show, I am so disgusted with this whole thing.'

I had done a lot of studying since spending time in Palestine. I had discovered all kinds of modern historical facts that were never taught in schools or featured in mainstream documentaries. It was Moshe Dayan, for example, who famously said: 'Jewish villages were built in the place of Arab villages. You do not even know the names of these Arab villages, and I do not blame you because geography books no longer exist, not only do the books not exist, the Arab villages are not there either.'

The rugged wood of the cabin seat pressed against my trousers and my legs began to cramp as I waited for a TV executive in London to find a way to get out of a contract that promised funds to Palestinians in dire need through a registered British charity. I thought of the taxi driver, Jimmy/Jamal. In our last phone call, he had told me that his five-storey family home in Silwan, Jerusalem, was being threatened with demolition by the Israeli authorities under the pretext of 'planning permission'. I thought of the young man on the streets of Jerusalem who had refused to accept any money for the souvenirs in Al Quds. The way he had handed me the English version of the Qur'an with the words: 'Just don't forget us when you go.' Of the children made incontinent, terrorised by the armed incursions of troops into their towns, schools, homes, and bedrooms.

After twenty sweaty and claustrophobic minutes in the Bush Telegraph, a response came: 'OK, Lauren. Go back to camp.

The matter has been resolved. Interpal will remain your choice of charity.'

'And you'll honour paying them?' I caught the sound of an exaggerated sigh.

'You have our word.'

***

My heart began thumping hard in my ears. Sitting on my bunk, I realised I was high. I didn't want that feeling at all, being in the jungle had begun to bring me back to myself. Nature, not narcotics is the 'rush' human beings grow up with. My years of 'tuning out' and trying everything on offer had only created a void and a sense of insecurity about who I really was.

'Feel better now, don't you,' laughed David that evening. I wanted to tell him 'no' and 'I'm really angry with you right now', but the prescription narcotic had sealed a plastic grin on my lips. All I could do was jump around the campfire to an internal reggae channel, until the effects began to fade more than five hours later.

The next time I had a headache I upped my water intake instead.

On the 12th April 2016, almost ten years after his appearance on *I'm a Celebrity*, David was found dead in the Four Seasons Hotel suite where he was living in London. It seems he spent his last days alone and according to friends, 'strung out on sleeping pills.' He was a kind, humorous, man yet in the end celebrity did nothing for his loneliness and all his wealth couldn't extend his life by a single heartbeat.

CHAPTER 11
IN SEARCH OF MEANING

'Be detached from this world and then God will
love you and do not be attracted to what people
have and then the people will love you'.

Prophet Muhammad PBUH

A week after the jungle show wrap party, my family and I flew
to Egypt where we planned to spend Christmas and New Year
with a French couple and their two sons. Marc, our neighbour
in the village, had been a tour guide in several Muslim countries
in North Africa. He had hired a Bedouin guide, 'Swelem', to take
us across parts of the Western Desert in a large jeep. We would
sleep in tents and the aim was to remove the cloying materialism
of Christmas from our children and let them experience a way of
existing which was different from the 'brie and swimming pool'
lives they had been blessed with so far.

I strongly believed that the teachings of Christ had absolutely
nothing to do with the increasingly frenzied, materialistic mayhem celebrated in December. What had simplicity to do with
the massive amounts spent on throwaway gifts that would end
up a week later in a landfill? Like most parents, I had been dis-
mayed to have spent a hundred pounds or more on the latest
plastic-fantastic toy, only for my toddlers to delight in playing
with the giant cardboard box it came in, instead.

Dawn in the desert was a crisp array of gold and orange, and
on Christmas Day our two families awoke in sleeping bags in a

desert camp beneath one giant awning. Swelem muttered prayers under his breath then set about making traditional Bedouin bread on the fire. The children, already awake and shouting with excitement, had discovered their presents. Each one received a wooden musical instrument, an item of Egyptian-style clothing and a toy doll or plastic animal. I watched, smiling, as they made up stories together on a high mound of sand nearby. Later they would put on an unforgettable show using their costumes and instruments, which made zero sense but was cute beyond belief.

During those days we ate simply, slept on the ground, and shared stories. In the Australian jungle all uneaten food had to be burnt on the fire right away, otherwise the smell would draw rats and the smell of the rats urine would attract a far greater worry; snakes. The desert was different. I watched each evening as Swelem carefully collected our sand-crunchy plates of bread, soup, cheese and a little meat. He would scoop every last morsel of food onto a plastic lid and once the children were asleep he would slip away from the fire, placing the leftover titbits somewhere in the darkness.

'Why do you do that?' I asked one evening as the adults sat under the desert stars.

'As Bedouin, we know desert life is hard for humans like us. Sometimes we wonder if we can even survive. We know these creatures and they know us. We have to take care of them, it is our duty. They know this so they follow us, at a distance.'

As he spoke, I glimpsed over his shoulder two glittering orbs reflected in the fire's flames. Eyes! We were in the depths of one of the harshest desert areas in Egypt. On the day's drive to get here we hadn't seen another living thing, not even a bird of prey. Nothing could live in this bleakness.

'Swelem,' I gasped, 'An animal, behind you.' He nodded, his red kaffiyeh blowing in the name from a Palestinian activist – who knew someone, who had met someone from chill December air. 'What is it?' I asked.

Without turning around he said: 'It's a desert fox. He has been with us since yesterday, tracking us. We have an understanding, me and him, so don't be scared.'

I sat huddled in my sleeping bag, feeling certain existence had more to it than thrill-seeking and owning as much as possible before I died. Hard on the heels of forty, I was feeling nudges towards a new set of questions and a vastly different path than before. I had picked up the Qur'an, given to me by a young man in Jerusalem, read a couple of pages, found it scary and put it well out of sight. Yet each time I remembered its clear and certain tone and I knew I had missed something fundamental, a message others had access to, in those strange back-to-front Arabic words and their translated meanings.

***

Spring came and I was invited to London for a meeting with a new TV channel. On a rainy afternoon on Cleveland Street in the West End of London, Mohamed Ali, founder and managing director of the Islam Channel, showed me through the door of an Italian bistro.

War, address. Dressed in my interview outfit of tight jeans, pink shirt and high black boots, my blonde hair was cropped into the current pixie fashion. I had deliberately made no concession to the faith of the person I would meet. Why should I? Islam, I felt, was fair enough in the Middle East but in the UK it was like any private habit, best kept at home. Or at least out of sight.

When they arrived, my two hosts looked like something out of a spoof Tarantino film. The first was a giant of a man in a bespoke grey suit. Behind him a bearded man with an air of authority in a black suit, black tie and black shoes.

'I'm Carl,' purred the giant. Six-foot four, with white hair and the accent of an Oxbridge don.

'I am Mohamed Ali, Miss Booth, a pleasure to meet you.' The man had a chest-length beard and an accent. More the 'style' of person I had been expecting to meet from a Muslim channel.

The waiter asked about drinks. I hadn't had a business meeting without booze since, well, since I'd ever had business meetings. I asked for the wine list and Carl looked at his hands. Mohamed Ali didn't react at all. 'A bottle of house red, please.'

Carl, who was not Muslim, felt he had to speak out: 'Lauren, I won't be joining you and ...' he smiled towards Mr Ali, 'I know our CEO won't be drinking. So perhaps a bottle will be too much? I'm sure half a bottle, or perhaps a soft drink, would be better?'

I smiled internally. This was going to be dull. To show willing, I changed the order to a half bottle. There! That was concession enough for anyone's little sensitivities. I was now ordering a half a bottle of wine with teetotallers. My heart sank at the potential for boredom.

What was my fun-packed life coming to? As the drinks arrived, Mohamed Ali gently pushed back his chair and stood up.

'Dear Miss Booth, please enjoy your wine. However, as a Muslim I cannot stay whilst you drink it so sorry for that inconvenience. It also wouldn't be right for the Islam Channel to buy it but don't worry,' he gave Carl a look, 'My director of programmes will be happy to oblige. We can reconvene when you are done.' He left.

There was an awkward pause, which I covered by cheerfully pouring myself a large glass of red. 'So you're not Muslim then?' I said to Carl.

'No. They keep asking me if I want to join them but I haven't so far.' He smiled. 'Just not me, I guess. Nice people though, lovely in fact just ... well, wine could be one reason I suppose.'

I offered him a glass, he refused. As we chatted I could see Mr Ali taking calls on his mobile in the drizzle of the afternoon. Every so often he would glance over, then look quickly away as if not wanting to make me uncomfortable. I sipped the wine. A queasy feeling was developing in my stomach and a stinging sensation crept into my chest. I took another sip. My heart lurched disturbingly. Another attack of the palpitations I had been having for a while, I thought. No, this was something else. Watching the 'host' of this meeting walk outside in the cold whilst I drank alcohol, I had an inkling what my physical symptoms were related to. It was a long-forgotten ailment. A function related to the heart by an invisible series of interactions on a microcosmic level. I felt like the Grinch when his heart started to beat again. Except this feeling wasn't love. It was ... shame. I was feeling ashamed of myself.

Carl was talking about the opportunity for growth of the new channel in its first two years, the wonderful outlook for global expansion. I wasn't listening. I was taking an internal inventory for the first time in years. I was hearing a stifled inner voice telling me that I had fallen below acceptable standards of consideration for others. The chest pains were telling me that after a decade working with hacks, drinking with actors and giving in to virtually every whim of my ego, I had reached a new low. When had I become the sort of person who would make a believer in God go into the street so I could drink alcohol alone? Where was that little girl who had loved to pray? Where was that person who valued the rights of others? What a hateful, disrespectful act! The internal nausea was rising until I felt my cheeks and throat flush. I was selfish, disrespectful to someone who believed in God.

'Waiter, I'll leave the wine. There's something wrong with it. It's ... corked.'

I looked at the Tunisian man outside. He would sooner freeze than ask an English person not to drink in his company. Good manners, these Muslims, I thought.

On his return to the alcohol-free table, Mohamed Ali Harrath put his hands tidily in front of him. A Tunisian former activist, he had spent time in prison under the reign of the dictator Ben Ali. He spoke gently but firmly with no hint of taking in or being concerned (or interested) in how I was dressed or the way I looked. He asked if I would be interested in hosting a political flagship programme, interviewing figures from faith communities. What were the viewing figures for his channel, I asked? The men exchanged glances as if they had never been asked such a thing before. Inwardly, I sighed. A few hundred Muslim households, I thought. Their answer stunned me.

'Into the millions, worldwide,' said Ali. Millions? Did 'millions' of Muslims watch TV in English? Honestly, it had never occurred to me they might. Or that the numbers of Muslims who lived in Europe, Canada and America may seek out appropriate material in the English language.

Carl Arrindell and Mohamed Ali Harrath were talking between themselves, waiting for my answer.

'There are two things I need to have understood before we move forward,' I said, wondering if they had ever had a woman negotiate with them before. I would break down the walls for feminists to follow in my footsteps: 'Let's be clear from the start. I won't wear a scarf for this series. I don't believe in it and I will never, ever wear it.' The Islam Channel would have its own set of religious ethics, but if they wanted me on screen they would take me as I was.

'You are you. We respect your choices, Lauren. May I call you that?' asked Mohamed Ali. I nodded. 'You may do your show in the clothing you wish. Perhaps though we should at least agree to avoid, shall I say, low necklines.' He didn't look at my chest, which was mostly on display.

'Sure, agreed'.

'What is the second condition?' He asked.

How could I say what I needed to say without causing offence?

'Well the thing is ... Look. What I mean is ... Don't try to make me Muslim, okay? I like your people and everything. You have lovely manners and I will fight for the rights of Muslims to have their rights recognised to the best of my ability. Just don't try to make me become one. It's just not my ... thing.'

Carl was nodding vigorously on the other side of the table, but Mr Harrath was looking towards me thoughtfully: 'You don't know whether you will be Muslim or not, Ms Booth, only Allah knows what is written for you.'

'Let me stop you there. Allah has nothing to do with me. I'm sure He's very nice, but I know in my mind that I won't be Muslim, so.'

'God knows best, actually.'

'I know best for me.'

'Allah will decide.'

We could have gone on like that all day. 'Fine. Okay. Allah will decide. Just don't expect me to convert and don't try to change my faith. That's all I'm saying. Agreed?'

I was laying out my stall early. I liked alcohol, being free to dress as I liked: bacon, ham, roast pork. I didn't want to have to be bored by talk of faith all the time. Leave God out of the workplace. I was a political interviewer and that was it.

Mohamed Ali and Carl Arrindell stood up. Carl offered his hand and we shook on the deal. I offered my hand to Mr Harrath, who put his right hand to his chest.

I dropped mine awkwardly. Is my touch septic?

'I wish you peace,' he said quietly.

***

On Saturday 5th May 2008, I arrived at Copenhagen's Brøndby Whalen stadium for the Sixth Annual Palestinians in Europe conference to film interviews for my new show on the Islam Channel.

Men in shiny suits, women with baby buggies and curious teenagers with Palestinian black and white hair bands were smoking and calling to one another in Arabic.

I inhaled the heavy Arabic accents, the calls of 'marhaba' taking me back to Palestine. Mohamed Ali, resplendent in his long black robe, chest-length beard and matching skull cap, found me wandering around the first floor of the conference centre. He seemed pleased to see me in a calm, paternal way. Despite the fact he was just four years older than I was, we had fallen gently into the roles of prodigal daughter and patient mentor.

'I won't shake your hand,' I said, as he put his right hand automatically to his chest when I approached. I still hadn't quite been able to shake the habit of offering my hand, though.

One of the main speakers at the conference was a much adored leader of the Northern Branch of the Islamic Movement in Israel, Sheikh Raed Salah. In 2003, the spiritual leader whose special focus is the protection of Al Aqsa Mosque (the complex which includes the famous golden dome) had spent more than two years in an Israeli prison without charge. He had been accused of inciting racial hatred and tensions, and of encouraging violence inside Israel. He had not been convicted of these accusations and looking around me at the other conference-goers I suspected almost every man present would have been on one Shin Bet hate list or another.

The VIP lounge was an underwhelming, coarsely-lit room with no air-conditioning. 25 tables were laid out for the visitors' dinner. There was water on each table and not a drop of alcohol in sight. Aldo, the Italian director and producer working with the Islam Channel and my show, shared my longing for a double shot of 'anything'. We would have to get through our work as teetotallers yet again.

The Palestinians at the conference were a fairly even split of Christians and Muslims. Sipping water as I went over my notes, I noticed that the men in moustaches with a preference for black leather jackets despite the heat no longer made me nervous. They were individuals, friends, colleagues, dads, academics. How differently I felt in this crowd compared to the preconceptions with which I had arrived in Ramallah just three years earlier. Majid Azeer, director of the Palestine Return Centre in London and conference organiser, came over to our table and warmly greeted Mohamed Ali. Mohamed turned to me.

'This is Lauren Booth,' he said. 'Blame her for Palestine – she's English.' I tried to think of something really, truly rude to say about Muslim clerics, then thought better of it. The only joke I knew about them would be held back for a few months only to be blurted out at an even more inappropriate moment.

'Correct,' I said with a smile, 'In fact you can blame my whole family for all the woes in the Middle East, why not?'

'Precisely,' fired back Ali. 'Her brother-in-law is Tony Blair.'

There was nothing I could say to counter that.

Later, over platefuls of salmon, salad, breads and hummus, Mohamed and I talked about the Qur'an. What was relevant fourteen centuries ago may not make sense now, he said. Banning chess, for example, may have been important to one Islamic foundation in the Middle Ages when students were distracted by it, but did that mean it should still be 'haram' (forbidden) today when there were far more socially dangerous habits?

Carl talked about going to the Love Music, Hate Racism festival in Hackney the month before: 'We couldn't cover it for the Channel, unfortunately,' he sighed dramatically, 'Otherwise we'd have had to call it 'Hate Music, Hate Racism'. I forgot any pretence at polite protocol and fell about laughing. When I had calmed myself down enough to notice, I saw that Mohamed Ali had a straight face. There was an awkward silence. I asked if he was annoyed.

'No, Lauren,' he deadpanned, 'I've just heard it so many times before. Ha ha, Carl, very good.' Who knew Muslims had a sense of humour?

Over sticky Arabic cakes there was time to discuss the place of Jesus in Islam. Mohamed, now in scholarly mode (the equivalent of a trendy teacher), was in his comfort zone. He liked to smile, was friendly and not easy to offend (believe me, I tried). Yet, shortly after the conference, I would be shocked to see him on the front page of several UK newspapers, vilified as an extremist. So vast was the press vilification of him that he later joked: 'I have been called an extremist, an Islamist, a terrorist – all the "-ists"'. In 2017, he would be awarded £140,000 damages by a British court when the pro-Israel group Stand For Peace wrongfully labelled him a 'convicted terrorist'.

As jovial as Mohamed was, on clerical questions he would not joke. Nor did he insult the faith or culture of others. That was the central reason I kept working at the Islam Channel, despite the reservations of friends and family, and there were increasing struggles with relations over my work and my interest in the situation in Palestine. Most of my relatives had made up their minds that Muslims were mostly wife beaters. There was also an increasing concern that my humanitarian activism was taking precedence over my media career. 'No one gets rich making a fuss about Palestine,' my Mum would (correctly) tell me over and again.

By 11 pm, the women and children, full of sugar and having run them ragged, had left the conference as I dragged my suitcase towards a group of twenty or so Arab men in the foyer of the hotel attached to the conference centre. I was the only woman amongst a group of men who are now all Muslim and I felt oddly shy. As if amongst friendly older brothers I sat quietly, listening to the talk of PR men and Middle Eastern political movers and shakers, as I waited for their sheikh – Raed Salah – to finish a meeting. I still didn't understand the rules of social engagement and I wondered if smiling out of context could be taken as flirtation. Nursing a Pepsi I compared the scene before me with the Labour Party conference to which I my paper would send me every autumn. It was already 11:30 pm, and by that time of night the MPs and newspaper editors around me would have been flirting, shouting, and drunk. In Copenhagen there was a quiet sobriety, and I had received multiple offers from Muslim men to help with my case. In Brighton, at the Labour Party conference, I had once been left crying on a kerbside by attendees when heavily pregnant.

The Arab guys in Copenhagen were playing by a social code I was clueless of despite my travels. But the basis seemed to hinge on politely ignoring I was there at all. Which I found better to the forced flirtations or faux camaraderie of other male-dominated events I was used to attending.

Finally, Aldo set up our cameras and placed two chairs at forty-five degrees to each other on the mezzanine floor, overlooking the lobby. I moved my notes around, seeking a better light to read them by when I noticed my part-covered chest for the first time. 'Damn!' The buttons of my tight blouse ended well short of the throat and I had certainly breached the 'neckline' understanding agreed with Mohamed Ali. I tried to arrange my jacket so that the collars reached higher round my neck. As I was fussing, Sheikh Raed Salah arrived amidst a flurry of excited supporters. The man I recognised from news cuttings stood a few feet away in the melee. He was tall, with tanned skin, wearing a full length grey robe below a surprisingly quaint and pretty crocheted cream skull cap. I felt flustered and not just due to my outfit. I never got nervous before interviews. So why now?

Sheikh Salah came closer, bringing a soothing, gentle presence with him. He took the seat on the makeshift set silently, then quietly looked down at his hands as if meditating on a deep mystery. Checking my script, I briskly reminded myself this man was accused of raising millions of dollars for the feared Palestinian resistance group, Hamas. He was barred by Israel from travelling abroad (or visiting Al Aqsa Mosque). As part of my research I had found that many sources, including Jonathan Cook, author of *Blood and Religion*, didn't believe the Israeli accusations against Sheikh Salah. Cook wrote, 'the purpose of this persecution (of Salah and others) has been to neuter all manifestations of Palestinian consciousness among the minority (in Israel) – to transform it into a docile and anonymous grouping the state likes to call the "Israeli Arabs".'[2]

At last we were ready. The Sheikh met my eyes with his, which were sad and deep. He smiled, before nodding his head back towards the hands folded in his lap.

In the West we tend to label people with big mouths, loud laughs and plenty to say as 'charismatic'. Hollywood, soap stars and a thousand pointless reality shows have confused garrulous-ness and vanity with charisma. Sheikh Raed, on the other hand, was quietly, genuinely compelling. He didn't fling his personality or his views in my direction, like others I'd interviewed. Time and again I left my notes to study him instead. My mind was slow to understand what every instinct was telling me: That I was sitting with a spiritual person. It was if a sweet-smelling invisible mist surrounded him and it enveloped me too. My heart filled with uninvited joy being near him. I had to rearrange my facial expression to stop me looking like a star-struck gawping fan.

We used a translator, a young man from Palestine '48, and Salah answered my questions in an Arabic which sounded as warm and coaxing as English. His words flowed in a deep dar-buka rhythm, neither guttural snippets nor roaring authority but quiet, storytelling. I asked if he had 'run' money for Hamas.

The language of his answer belied the lullaby sound of his voice: 'If raising money for homeless, hungry children is an act of terror then this I am happy to be called.' He talked about the Palestinians right to resist the occupation of their land and at-tempts to 'squat' on their future. For reasons I could not fathom, he punctuated each sentence with 'Thanks be to Allah', and 'All praise is to Allah alone'. There seemed little in our conversation about the situation to make someone thankful. Who, I wondered, would be grateful for hardship?

---

[2] Jonathan Cook, 'Matrix reloaded – yet again' (Al-Ahram Weekly, 13 November 2003).

At almost midnight I wrapped up the interview, regretting the impending loss of Sheikh Raed's company. My low neckline had not for an instant drawn his eye, nor did I feel that my western feminist appearance had earned his dislike. Standing together by the stairs I said the words I'd picked up in the West Bank: 'Fi al-Quds'. It is a hopeful call to a freedom sometime in the future, meaning literally, 'In Jerusalem'. As I spoke, Sheikh Salah's dynamic eyes met mine and flickered with polite interest. As he looked at me I was swept away by the urge to shake his hand, to touch his robe, to meet him again, to know more about his hopes for Palestine – for the world. I wanted to speak to him about the human experience. About how difficult it was sometimes just to be alive, how conflicted I sometimes felt about what I should be doing and why I existed at all. He, I felt certain, had extraordinary answers.

He left as gently as he had arrived, the father of eight and a poet. I stood at the top of the stairs watching him leave. My heart had been deeply affected, changed by just an hour of his company. What was the cause of the peace I felt in his presence? Why did everyday life increasingly seem like a series of 'to do' lists with no ultimate purpose? Could it be Islam I was craving, the path that gave my new colleagues the peace they seemed to hold within them?

Weeks after the Danish conference, I met two converts to Islam at the helm of a fundraiser for a new charity, 'Help the Needy'. They called me to their offices beside a main road in West London. I was hungover from a movie premiere the night before and they looked surprised when I threw myself onto a chair, keeping my sunglasses on despite the rain outside. Their names were Yusuf Chambers and Abdur Raheem Green, and they appeared to me like modern curios. Green was tall, with a reddish beard that touched his chest, and Chambers had the look of a wild lake poet, with shoulder length hair, a shaggy beard and a mischievous glint. Green was politely cool during our conversation, Yusuf, of Irish heritage, was blunt and funny. He invited me to give a speech at the charity's launch event and I agreed.

On the night of the fundraiser, I arrived at the Marriott Hotel, St John's Wood, and sneaked to the bar to buy a vodka with lemonade in a tall glass. I would pretend it was a soft drink. The function was for Arabs and Pakistanis of a different faith to me, but it was held in a place I was familiar with from my 'real' life. Walking through the vast white foyer I remembered the last time I had been there; after a gig with friends from the 90s pop band, James. A group of us had spent until dawn upstairs in a suite, drinking and talking nonsense with the musicians. With my new friends, even one weak vodka felt naughty. I sat and drank in a quiet corner, then went to the ladies to rinse with mouthwash before retouching my makeup. The thought of being found with alcohol was too hideous to contemplate. I imagined a room full of swooning ladies and angry Arabic voices all shouting 'infidel!' at me and shaking their fists.

The women arrived in a cascade of shimmering scarves above glitzy yet modest evening dresses. Even my cleavage was covered for a change – can you 'catch' modesty, I wondered? The men, milling around, were a mix of full 'Osama beards' on the elders and Saddam-like moustaches amongst the younger crowd. I stood outside the hotel's main doors with the other European guest speakers, who were thankfully also smokers. Denis J Halliday was the United Nations Humanitarian Coordinator in Iraq from 1 September 1997 until 1998. A smiling Irish man with forty years' experience of UN humanitarian work, he was scathing about 'Blair's right to be walking free' and his dislike for 'patronising charities'. 'I hope this isn't one of them,' he sighed, holding my handbag so I could light up yet again. 'The last thing Iraqis want or need is another set of do-gooders telling them what needs to be done. Change needs to come from the ground up if it's going to work.'

With us stood Steve, a shy ex-soldier. He looked awkward in a houndstooth jacket and a bright green tie: 'It's my first speech,' he said nervously. He had written a brave memoir called *Squaddie*, 'But I'm not here to sell my book,' he said, 'I just want to help if I can ...' he looked down at his shoes and I wondered what he was like before he saw war.

Qatari Royals accompanied by other robed sheikhs arrived to a stir. Standing in the foyer, I watched them float past as if on a conveyor belt, their feet hidden by long robes, like Arabian actors off a George Clooney film set.

One of their entourage found me: 'Lauren Booth, we like your work very much. Would you like to come to Qatar?' I blustered a response, it was a strange invitation from people I'd never met.

The audience at the pristine white tables beneath glistening chandeliers was the Muslim elite in London. Backstage, I had a briefing with the comedian Jeff Mirza, my co-compere. We had met once before, in 2003 at the Labour Party conference in Bournemouth. Jeff had turned up as Saddam Hussein in full military regalia and fluffy black beard and he was greeted with great affection by the Labour delegates I had been with. One Ministerial advisor even laughed, drunkenly: 'I hope you've brought your WMDs with you mate ... or we're effed!' Never a truer word spoken in jest.

Clutching my notes, I looked across at a vast screen showing a fundraising film. My eyes froze on the most horrific clips I had ever seen. It was Iraq before, during and after the invasion. Grand stone works, giant monuments, happy stall owners. Then it cut to: missiles taking off, planes landing on US aircraft carriers, George W Bush declaring, 'historically invasions have been about conquest with the invaders competing for the spoils' the rest of his words were cut off by the screams of women on the streets of Baghdad. The sound of their cries made me look at the floor. Then the screens showed tiny limp broken babies pulled from beneath slabs of stone. A father's hands tenderly rubbed dust from the dead child he was clutching. Mothers were dying everywhere, there were more children. Tuts could be heard from the audience and I felt sick. Next to me, Jeff was not happy either. As the horror film ended he said: 'How do you combine humour with dead kids?'

I watched from the wings as he tried to get the crowd of royals and wealthy donors going with an opening gag: 'Lots of brothers here with beards! Wives, do you like your men with beards?' There was a smatter of agreement to a chorus of jangling jewellery. 'Husbands, clearly you like your women with beards!' Had there been tumbleweed it would have rolled across the stage. There was some embarrassed laughter.

During a break, Carl from the Islam channel arrived, mischief as usual written on his face: 'Ah, here we go, Muslim charities competing against one another. I know this routine so well, this should be good!'

It was time to introduce soldier Steve. He was very nervous, but the words 'British soldier' stopped the guests eating for a moment. Steve's notes were handwritten in schoolbook-style books. He ignored them completely: 'I was in the army, I knew the risks. I don't ask for sympathy, but the children, the women, they didn't sign up for this.' He looked around as if the thought had fully occurred to him for the first time. 'This is their life! And I want to say...' he swallowed, loud enough for the mike to pick it up. 'Blair and Brown, that lot, won't say it so I want to say, how sorry I am for what we've done ... what we're doing. We shouldn't have gone. We shouldn't be there, this should not be happening. All I can say is that me, I'm really sorry, really, really sorry ...'

He trailed off, looking down at his feet. Then the applause began, a thunderous and sustained respect. He ended saying: 'To Blair and Bush, I have been thinking of one thing I'd like to say to these false Christians. "What serves a man if he gains the whole world but loses his soul?" What does it serve a man to gain the world, if he loses his soul,' he repeated, quietly. Everyone was moved and Steve was applauded to his seat.

The night held meaning because it was an opportunity to spend time with two British men who had both changed their name to Yusuf after converting to Islam. Firstly, Yusuf Chambers, who had invited me to the event. He greeted me in a smart black suit beneath his long flowing hair. Then there was the person for whom the crowds were willing to pay extortionate amounts for their tickets: legendary folk singer, Cat Stevens. His chart success had been well before my time, but I remembered his spiritual hit 'Morning Has Broken' playing on the kitchen radio as a child. Now, Yusuf Islam had replaced Cat Stevens and he had become the most famous Muslim convert from the West. A star who had made the epic transformation from the music business to man of devout faith. After my experiences in the Middle East, I was curious and interested to hear to him speak.

The guests pulled out mobile phones and pointed the camera towards the shorter than expected Yusuf Islam. Wearing a long black shirt, with a shaved head a dark beard, he walked with calm grace onto the stage. 'As-salamu 'alaykum,' he said. I supposed this was his version of 'okay, London are you ready to rock?' The audience were ready to do whatever he told them. He talked in a pattern similar to the sheikhs I met, his speech broken up with references to 'the great and glorious Allah … Muhammad, peace be upon him.' He peppered his fund appeal with phrases such as: 'As the Prophet himself says' always followed by 'more peace be upon him.' I found it riveting, although I had no idea why he felt the need to talk about dead prophets so much.

Yusuf Chambers was more accessible to me; jaunty, jokey, his clothes, his chatter, and his humour were British, without a doubt. Yet clearly he was also a devout Muslim. Chambers introduced me to other guests as 'Sister Lauren …' which made me feel obscurely pleased and rather proud of the title. It felt as if I were being invited into an inner circle, how my grandfather perhaps felt when he was presented with a kukri knife in a Gurkha village in the 1940s.

As the desserts were served, I was taken by Chambers to the top table and introduced to Yusuf Islam. He shook my hand warmly, firmly. I had to do my job, of course, and requested an interview for the Islam Channel. He looked into my eyes with a soft curiousity. He was busy with a new musical, he said, but would try to come onto my series very soon. I had to crouch down to hear him better, so soft was his voice. He whispered to me: 'Your speech was the best, Lauren, keep it up ...'. It felt as if Sting had complimented me on my voice.

There was a final auction, where money was drawn from the audience with more pain than blood being pulled from a stone. I wrapped up my presenting by taking a tenner out of my pocket and telling the audience: 'You can all match that from your wallets, so ante-up!' I looked at the silent room, fearing I had pushed my unconventional directness to the limit. However, after I had clambered off the back of the stage and grabbed a bucket from a volunteer, going from table to table I was met with open wallets, big notes, several pledge cards, thanks and smiles. At 11:30 pm it was all over. Yusuf called me over to where he was chatting with a group of international Muslim guests: 'Well done, Lauren!' he beamed.

'Yeah,' I sighed dramatically. 'I do my best, but I still won't get into your heaven will I gents?'

Chambers looked hurt. 'Who has said that to you, has someone said that?' He had the manner of a big brother in a school yard. Scowling at his Gulf comrades he said, 'No one here can say they know what Allah's plan is for you, Lauren. Am I right gentlemen?' The Arab men nodded, enjoying the banter.

I shoved my hand forward for Yusuf to shake. He shook it automatically. Perhaps it was the residual shot of vodka, but I said in a loud voice: 'Ha! Now you're coming to hell with me! You're going to hell, Yusuf's going to hell!'

The three men in suits laughed out loud and joined the chant: 'Yusuf's going to he-ell!'

I headed off towards the hotel exit, wondering if I would meet Allah for my few good deeds. Getting my coat from the cloakroom, Mohamed Ali Harrath, resplendent in a black floor-length shirt, waved me over. He stood with a group of men from the Middle East.

'I have just got back from Riyadh and Makkah,' he told me. He introduced me to his friends: 'Have you met Lauren yet? She is a good person, but sadly will not be joining us in the glorious Afterlife in Paradise!' There is an accepted wisdom in Islamic tradition that urges those who wish to share their faith to speak to people of other beliefs and cultures in the way they understand. Mohamed Ali and I had been colleagues for long enough for him to know my sense of humour.

Yet his parting quip played on my mind, as it was meant to. I realised it bothered me, the idea of not being invited in to a heaven where Allah was the sole deity. In a way I was able to understand, I had just been reminded that I was far from being in a decent spiritual state required to earn a good Afterlife.

CHAPTER 12
WITHOUT A PADDLE

'When a man is denied the right to live the life he believes in, he has no choice but to become an outlaw.'

Nelson Mandela

Outside our stone farmhouse the peach tree was in full, sensual blossom and around the front door jasmine wound its way up the part-rotten beams of our little porch.

I sat at my desk in the renovated attic unable to tear my thoughts away from all that seemed 'wrong' with my life. Daily niggles, like unpaid bills, played on my mind day and night and even the merry noise of the children playing by the pool at the end of our vast garden was little more than a reminder of the hair washing I would need to do later. The beautiful moments in which I was unknowingly cocooned were being psychologically slept through.

Browsing through the emails on my desktop, I opened an unsolicited message which read simply: 'Would you like to go to Gaza by boat? If so, call "Osama" on the number below.' I laughed out loud. Go to Gaza by boat? Who on earth would be idiotic enough to try that? To get onto a boat, annoying the Israelis, and with someone called Osama? Surely it was a joke from one of my media friends. I scrolled up and down the message and checked the sender's details for clues. It wasn't from anybody I had ever heard of. Was it possible that a bunch of nutters were suggesting a boat trip towards a coast aggressively patrolled by one of the world's most highly armed militaries? I read the message for the tenth time: 'Would you like to go to Gaza by boat? If so, call "Osama" ...'

The illegal Israeli siege of Gaza was hurting the families I had met on my visit. The articles I'd pitched for months to features editors, travel editors and news editors on the mounting humanitarian crisis had been given the almost standard answer: 'Our readers are tired of the Middle East, they just aren't interested any more. It's been going on for so long ... both sides are to blame ... There's no answer. No thanks.' It was clear to me that Muslim lives did not matter to our leaders to the same degree as 'white' lives and I was becoming frustrated at the impotence of the shouting and banner waving outside Downing Street. I stared at the phone number at the foot of the email and had 'the feeling', a recognition that some things are simply going to happen no matter how much we resist. Whilst others, no matter how hard you push, are not destined.

Tony Blair had resigned as the British prime minister and was now in his new role as Middle East Envoy to the quartet of power brokers: the United Nations, US, the European Union, and Russia. I knew that as the media were by this time bored of stories from Gaza, a report of Blair's sister-in-law sailing to Gaza would certainly increase the chance of some coverage of this flotilla. So I dialled the number. The voice answering was blunt and rude with a heavy Palestinian accent: 'This is Osama, who is this?'

'My name is Lauren Booth, I'm a journalist.'

'We have journalists and the boats are full now. Goodbye.'

'Wait don't hang up!' The call was nearly over before it had started. 'Look, I think I can help, that maybe I can draw attention to your mission.' There was a pause. 'Your name again?'

'Lauren Booth.'

'Never heard of you.'

I didn't want to mention Tony's name at this stage. If it was destined to be then I would go as a writer, an observer, if not ...

The gruff voice was unconvinced: 'I'll put it to the committee. Don't get your hopes up. We might be in touch.'

The next morning, I called Peter Wright at the *Mail on Sunday*. He instantly agreed to a double-page spread and enthused that the story was a grand idea. It was instantly commissioned and expenses arranged. Two days later the call came back from the mysterious 'Free Gaza' group which no one at work had ever heard of – I was on board. That night I sat between my babies' beds, clutching one pudgy little hand and one skinny little one in my own. I told them it was a short trip and I talked to them about justice, equality and fairness.

Did European children matter more than African children? 'NO, mamma!'

Did Christian children matter more than Muslim children? 'NO, Mamma!'

I told them about the children being kept on the brink of hunger, denied decent schools and clean water or freedom of movement. I told them I wanted to help. Holly, then three, looked at me with her gorgeous, vast blue eyes: 'Mamma please go and help the Palace Indians.'

I didn't bother to correct her cute misunderstanding. If she cared about the needs of imagined people in a vast palace as much as her own that was good enough for the time being.

Alex, five, put her hands together as we did in church. She made a prayer: 'Dear God, please help the Palace Indians. Let them have nice homes, nice food and no wars. Let them have nice schools and always, always be happy. Look after Mummy too, please, we love her a lot God. Amen.'

I watched them until they fell asleep, and then for a long time afterwards. After that I packed my trusty pink suitcase and headed to the airport. It would be months before I saw them again.

***

On 1st August 2008, I arrived at Paphos International airport in Cyprus and from there I made my way, by bus, to a university in Nicosia. Osama, the Palestinian I'd talked with initially, had only briefly summarized a 'possible' timetable, despite much pushing on my part. As far as he knew, I would spend 'a couple of days' on campus in Nicosia before relocating to the boats. Although I was on board as a reporter, everyone would have crew duties, and everyone would be at equal risk of injury or death if the boats were sabotaged or attacked. In Nicosia there would be briefings about the mission, surviving gunshot wounds and more. I was part of the so-called 'land team', who would meet the 'boat team' in charge of bringing the ships from a hiding place to the port when everything was ready. The activists' aim was to highlight the illegitimacy of the land, air and sea blockade by the Israeli military. The sea blockade extended far beyond any agreements outlined in the Olso Accords, which were still meant to apply. The whole 'mission' would, he told me, mean I would be away from home for 'about a week'.

Blazing sunlight bounced off brown, flat-roofed buildings as I arrived at the campus gate. I was greeted by a crop-haired feminist in a khaki shirt covered by ink drawings. She gave me a brusque handshake: 'Lauren Boom? Never heard of ya,' she said in an irritated US drawl. 'Donna' grudgingly showed me towards a cement block; student dorms now being used for the activist sailors. As I looked for a room with a name card telling me it was mine, I was met by an older lady, also American, with glamorous hair. She was utterly charming.

'I'm Greta Berlin, honey. Welcome.'

Greta was a former oil company executive with a vibrant history of social activism. We walked down the detergent-smelling corridor to a tiny room.

'See you later for lectures on boat safety and triage in case of an attack on board.'

Training began the next morning and was pencilled in for the next four days. But in the background, elements which were being hidden from us were delaying our voyage. Every day for two weeks I sat in the same broiling classroom with talks which were now down to engine minutiae. For a change of scene, activists began painting banners for the side of what were alleged to be two ships, not just one. Where those mystery vessels were, or when they would arrive, no one but Greta seemed to have any idea. And Greta was clearly stonewalling all of us. A small 'need to know' enclave inside the main group were hiding information from Israeli spies, which meant keeping it from us passengers as well. It was a cat and mouse operation against Mossad, the Israeli secret service, and their motto: 'By way of deception, thou shalt do war' would summarize the experience of numerous attempts to sabotage the boats.

Meanwhile, far away in a variety of sea ports in the Aegean Sea, two dumpy Greek fishing boats were being tracked and monitored. Previous efforts to sail to Gaza via the Mediterranean had ended in murder. In the 1970s, Palestinians from the PLO tried to return home by sea. The men involved were murdered in a 'car accident' in Cyprus and their ship was blown up at a Cypriot port.

The days ticked by as we were fed story after story to try and keep us all patient. 'The boats will arrive in two days,' Greta told us for the fifth time, after I'd already been ten days in Nicosia. There was a near mutiny – the first of many – and the teachers, nurses and business people made it clear that everyone had jobs and families who needed them. We simply couldn't keep on waiting for a mission that never seemed to start. After weeks of fudges and half-truths, I had to tell Greta that without seeing the boats in twenty-four hours my newspapers said the story would be dropped.

Later that day, three of us were selected to fly to the ships' location for the first major press conference about the Free Gaza mission and its aims. I was delighted to get off campus and headed off to the picturesque Crete sea port of Chania to meet with the British journalist Yvonne Ridley and Jeff Halper. Jeff is an Israeli Jew who was nominated for the 2006 Nobel Peace Prize for setting up a human rights organisation inside Israel which opposed the state-sponsored demolition of Palestinian homes.

I had no idea about the dramas the 'on board' crew had been experiencing. All I knew was the group were finally ready to go public and I could actually start my work. First though, came a shock. Greta had shown the landlocked passengers in Nicosia photos of a pristine white boat rather like a small yacht. Just the thing, I thought to myself, for a merry jaunt into deadly waters. Still, it had looked rather pleasant and comfortable and if you are going to die, die in style, I mused. The evening I arrived in Chania, I was told to make my way to the chintzy, pretty port where one of the boats was due to dock. I arrived in darkness at the promenade of seaside tavernas and summer holidaymakers. Fellow journalist Yvonne met me with a scowl: 'Look at that!' She pointed into the near distance. The worst Greek fishing boat ever to stay afloat was floundering curiously. 'The *Liberty*,' said Yvonne, shaking her head and sighing. Jeff clearly didn't know quite whether to laugh or cry.

'We are all going to die, one way or another,' he said, 'probably by drowning.' A crowd of wealthy yacht owners had gathered on their highly-polished decks beneath the twinkling lights of nearby promenade tavernas. They were pointing at the spectacle of our boat, which was endlessly shunting backwards and forwards just eighteen yards from the dock. Jeff, Yvonne and I were supposed to sleep on board tonight. That looked unlikely, as the ship couldn't even make it into the dock. After more than an hour, ten bleary-eyed and extremely grungy people abandoned ship and a dinghy buzzed its way to the shore. Everyone was in a foul temper and not in the mood for introductions. Yvonne's cameraman was British singer and musician, Aki Nawaz, founder of the controversial band Fun-Da-Mental. I knew him already as we had appeared together on a talk radio series which, reminiscing on the dock, we remember ended badly. I had been given the sack from MP Edwina Currie's show for saying during an item on elderly people and physical relations: 'well you should know, Edwina, you're an OAP aren't you?' We weren't laughing now, as along with Yvonne and Jeff we had to find a hotel for the night, still in serious doubt that the boats were fit for purpose.

Over the coming days we finally joined the tired crew on board the *Liberty*. I was stunned that the unlikely band of well-meaning activists were rudderless and without a definite leader. How was this mission ever going to succeed? For every smile I have from that time, there is a sadness in my heart, too. A painful recognition that someone great was to be lost along the way. In dark situations there is always a person who raises the spirit of those around them. Besides Greta and the increasingly less sullen Osama, I made another great friend on board; an Italian writer and activist called 'Vik'. He is best described in Biblical terms as Samson, a vast real-life hero of tanned muscle and never-ending hope and good will. Once the problem with the steering had been corrected we set sail, though were told little about our direction except that 'soon' we would meet and collect the land crew in Nicosia and after that head to Gaza. When the sails needed hitching or heavy work needed doing, Vik was always there. He was always the first to volunteer and never the one to make difficulties – and we had those in abundance.

From 8th to 23rd August, when we finally left on our true mission, we were trailed by Mossad 'hippies' following us from port to port. The second ship, the *Free Gaza*, lost its US $60,000 sat-nav ability time after time, almost crashing into the rocks. At one port, helpful locals on jet skis guided us out of the bay, averting near catastrophe. Captains came and went and mutiny raged. The problem was that the male Greek communists who had arranged the boats and were in charge of the seaboard and port arrangements clashed with the ideals and working policies of the feminists in charge of the mi: , and any interactions which might occur with Israeli forces. I tried to keep out of the way, drinking raki with our Greek comrades and lending a sympathetic ear to the sisterhood.

Whatever the issues, one person always called all the mayhem to a halt; Vik: 'These-a people must not-a be allowed to win! Stop the fighting now – just get to Gaza and help-a people in trouble! Now stay human!' His uniform was a black sailor's cap, black t-shirt and a pipe. He wore a Palestinian keffiyeh scarf, either as a bandana or over his shoulders like a cape, and his image would become the stuff of legend. He always called to me the same way: '*Yalla* (come here), Miss Free Gaza, time to eat-a, drink-a.' In Gaza two years later he would be killed in the first ever murder of an international activist there. The men who killed him entered Gaza from Jordan using tunnels especially dug for the execution.

Meanwhile, beneath the smile I wore despite the infighting I started to have my own fears about the crazy task. On 7th August, before leaving Nicosia for the Larnaca press conference, I had made it into a local internet cafe to Skype home. It was weeks since I'd seen the girls but when the camera brought them into view, they could only sit still long enough to blow me kisses. Then they wriggled out of their dad's lap to play in the garden. When they had left, my husband stopped smiling and his tone changed: 'They've been calling the house, Sarah.' By 'they' he meant people paid money to threaten and intimidate activists, which it appeared I had become. A man with a Middle Eastern accent had called our unlisted, private landline number in France saying the boats would be blown up and that I must not be on board when they left Cyprus. The voice had told my husband I was in danger and that I should go home. The call ended asking if I could swim. 'I don't want you to worry, but I thought you should know', my husband said. Despite the cloying heat of a Nicosia afternoon, a chill crept up my spine.

There was more: the telecom box outside the house had been tampered with. Our dog had been barking at night (she never had before) at the front door near where the box was positioned. My husband believed, 'people have been paying us a visit.' Loudly, and to make me laugh, he quoted Shakespeare: 'And I'll make a ghost of him who follows.' He reminded me that he was military trained. However, just to be sure he was sleeping next to his gigantic Australian bush knife. We discussed the need for me to come home and that if there was any risk to our children we had to protect them. My husband was adamant: Bullies mustn't be allowed to win. Fascists are just 'bullies with armies'. Others on board had received similar threats, and the family members of Palestinians who were assisting the mission had been taken from West Bank streets and beaten up in 'mysterious' attacks. Hedy Epstein, who was in her eighties, was a gentle lady with a strong spirit for justice. Her parents had died in a concentration camp and she wanted to travel to Gaza to show her solidarity with their struggle, but she was enduring a torrent of online abuse and the day before we set sail she became ill due to stress. Doctors took the difficult decision and advised her not to sail.

The two weeks I spent on board were far from glamorous. Below deck, the single toilet had to be used by fifteen people and it quickly became full to the brim and stank. The 'cabins' were hard bunks, used only in emergencies by the Greek fishermen who had (surely laughing) sold the near-useless vessel to the activists. The cabins were stifling and sweat-pungent. When I tried to lie on one of the bunks the seasickness was instant. I opted instead to sleep on deck in a sleeping bag – like most of the crew.

We sailed through clear blue waters, docking at a number of small ports on tiny islands whose mayors were friendly to the Palestinian cause. At sea, we lived on tins of tuna, water biscuits and warm water. There was a twenty-four hour watch rota, which all passengers had to sign up to. After midnight, I checked the duty rota and saw I had been paired with the film- maker,

Osama. Aki, Yvonne and Huwaida Arraf, a Palestinian lawyer and an incredible rights activist, were catching a few hours' sleep on the slippery wooden benches behind us. Osama and I watched for the lights of any boats who had not alerted us to their presence via the onboard radio, a sea-going courtesy. We were also listening for underwater activity, which could indicate an attempt at sabotage. The hull rose and fell in choppy waters and for the first time I began to feel queasy on deck. To try and help get rid of my seasickness, Osama staggered down the deck to the single fridge in the Captain's steering room. He slipped back from port to starboard, reminding me of Manuel, the Spanish waiter from *Fawlty Towers*, making me laugh.

'Fruit and juice to make you feel better,' he said. Gratefully I took a sip of the juice. It was fizzy but off and I sprayed it out of my mouth, over the side. Next I took a bit of the fruit he had brought me. It tasted like cheese and I began to gag. By now Osama was laughing so hard there was a real risk he would fall overboard. I became hysterical, too. Luckily, we were strapped to the bow so as not to disappear over the side in rough seas. I unclipped myself, needing the toilet, just as the boat tilted and I sat, unceremoniously, on Huwaida's head. Osama was now screaming with laughter and woke everyone up. We were roundly told off and relieved of our night watch duty like naughty school kids. Never has such a risky mission been carried out by such good- humoured, ill-prepared, jokers.

Overnight, on course to reach Larnaca by mid-morning, we were chugging along at a pitiful 5 knots an hour. I was on the Captain's deck with 'O.J.', a sailor from England who was able to steer the ship. Even though O.J. was tiny and weighed 5-stone 'dripping wet', as my Nan would have said, she was made of steely stuff both physically and in her character. Like everyone on board the two ships, O.J. had signed a piece of paper saying she realized the risk of being shot, sunk or imprisoned by Israel. Like all of us, she believed that was a worthwhile risk if the plight of 1.8 million people could be eased as a result of our peaceful voyage. If things went well, our journey had already generated some international chatter about the possibility of a renewal of the ancient trade route from European to Palestinian shores.

At sea, there are certain radio channels for general conversation between vessels which can be picked up and followed or joined-in by fellow sailors. Communications between the SS *Free Gaza* and the SS *Liberty* did not use those channels, for obvious reasons, nor was anyone allowed a mobile phone, even at port. I had been assisting the Comms Team communicating via walkie-talkie with Osama, who had moved across to the other ship, and for the ships to remain in contact we had to keep the two ships close together. Standing alongside O.J. in the darkness, suddenly the ship's radio buzzed into life, making us both jump. A message was being transmitted over VHF channel 16, the channel monitored twenty-four hours a day by coastguards around the world and solely for maritime emergencies.

A sinister voice floated out of the speaker: 'Free Gaza, Free Gaza, Zis iz ze Israeli navy. Turn back now. We are warning you, turn back now.' The breath caught in my throat – this could be the moment we had trained for in Nicosia, when a threat to our life was to be ignored in favour of completing the mission to bring the world's media attention to the condition of the besieged people of Gaza.

As O.J. and I looked at each other, the Lord's Prayer automatically began to run through my mind; it had been a long time since I'd prayed. Then laughter filtered from the speaker and muttered words hissed through the radio, filling the Captain's deck with barely legible threats, then we heard more laughter and we realized it was bizarre Psy Ops, psychological operations, from the Israeli military intended to scare us and abandon the mission. Next Hebrew music was being cheerily piped into the cabin.

As O.J. and I looked at each other, astounded, I asked her: 'What do we do?'

'Well,' she said, 'there's only one thing to do. Dance!' And that's what we did. We danced as the music played for us as the *Free Gaza* chugged along, somewhere in the Mediterranean Sea. There was no turning back and I remembered gratefully that I could, indeed, swim.

At 8:30 am on 20 August, the *SS Free Gaza* and the *SS Liberty* rounded the final coastal corner of Cyprus, under escort from the Cypriot Coast Guard. We pulled into the Northern side of the commercial port in Larnaca where the land team, who had caught a coach from Nicosia to meet us, were waiting.

After a thorough inspection of both boats, the Port Authority allowed for final preparations and all 46 passengers were finally reunited. With everyone on board for the first time, it was evident how little space there was to move around, let alone sleep, during the thirty-six hours or more we would be spending at sea. The maximum legal quota for each boat was just twelve people, but there were twenty on board the *Liberty* and more of us on the *Free Gaza*. We faced the very real prospect of sinking en route. Meanwhile, the Israeli navy had announced that during the precise time of our sailing, they had decided to conduct 'military exercises in the area'. The perfect window for an 'accidental' attack on the ships. Then all of our communication systems failed – our single satellite phone link to the outside world was dead.

After eighteen hours on the choppy seas of the Mediterranean, many of the passengers were suffering from severe seasickness. An emergency meeting was held on each boat outlining the options. What would we do if: There were shots in the air; there were shots at the boat; the captain was shot? Despite so many of us down with seasickness, the vote was taken to sail on and to break the siege. No matter what fears we had that day, every single person overcame them for the sake of other human beings in desperate need of support. Morale was boosted in no small part by Jeff Halper: 'We've gotta go and push on and break the siege of Gaza!' he shouted to our cheers. It's not possible to go into full detail of the whole chaotic voyage. However, there was a book published on the mission called *Freedom Sailors*, edited by Greta Berlin and featuring first- hand accounts from some of the activists on board, and Yvonne Ridley and Aki Nawaz made their documentary, *To Gaza with Love*, which is freely available online.[3]

On 23 August 2008, around midday, our Irish skipper climbed the mast and shouted the most beautiful words I have ever heard besides, 'It's a girl' – 'Land ahoy! Land ahoy!' We were 6.5 miles from the shore when the Palestinian flag was raised on both vessels. Rising out of the Mediterranean in the distance, in a haze of summer sun, was Gaza city, a shimmering mirage of silvery high-rise buildings. Soon boats came towards us from the Gaza port, the first a yellow fishing vessel, whose hull was almost completely submerged as it held what looked like a hundred people. Three giant Palestinian flags were fluttering from its masts and the sound hit us; cheering, chanting 'Free Gaza, Free Palestine!' On board I started crying, without really knowing where the tears were coming from. I looked around and everyone else was crying too. The sound reaching us from what appeared to be every floating piece of wood in the region was a cacophony of joy: whistling; horns blowing; shouting. There were hundreds of children swimming out to greet us, others rowing boats and even people on surfboards coming to cheer us to their land.

Due to our patchy communications, we had no idea that for days hundreds of Palestinian men, women and children had been gathering on the beach waiting to see if we made it, praying for our safety. When an announcement was made on the news a few hours earlier that we were going to make it ashore, an estimated 30,000 people gathered to greet us. It was the greatest

---

[3]   Nawaz, A., To Gaza with Love, 2008, video recording, Vimeo, viewed 17 July 2017, <https://vimeo.com/9995669>.

moment of my life besides childbirth and I was born to be here, I thought, as we sailed into port. I was meant to reach Gaza, to stand shoulder to shoulder with people of another faith, another tribe, another land, as precious and full of hope, and with the same right to justice as anyone else. Greta and I had the presence of mind to apply some makeup to our weather-beaten faces before we were suddenly boarded by dozens of bearded men plus TV crews. We hugged: 'We did it Lauren, we actually did it!' She shouted. We were not commandos on a military invasion, we were piano tuners, teachers, nurses, journalists, lawyers. Even Anne Wright, a septuagenarian nun, was on board.

What I discovered that day was that love knows no race and recognises no border. The people I had been warned to fear differed in customs, but their faith would increase them in love and kindness as we joined together seeking justice for one, for all. The sound that transported me as we drew in to the dock was coming from 30,000 Muslims: 'Allahu Akbar! Allahu Akbar! Allahu Akbar!' God is Great, God is Great, God is Great!

Plans for what would happen if we made it to Gaza were handled by the organization, Popular Committee Against the Siege, headed by the ebullient Jamal al-Khodary. The group's main committee had been in touch with Free Gaza leaders for some months, including Paul Larudee, a piano tuner from Los Angeles. After our incredible reception at the port, we were led in something like delirium to rooms at the surprisingly beautiful Al-Deira Hotel, overlooking the seashore and (importantly) our boats. To take a shower and to lie on cotton sheets on an actual bed was a gift for all our travel-weary bodies. We now had six days to maximize press interest in the situation for the people of Gaza. My work and Free Gaza's real mission was just beginning.

I couldn't wait to walk the streets, eat a kerbside falafel, hug the children and greet the parents on my walkabout. However, as I headed nonchalantly towards the Hotel's exit after our first evening meal I was in for a surprise. I was met by a stern-looking young man with an automatic gun wearing the blue uniform of a Hamas civic soldier. His name was Hasan and he was blocking me from reaching the street. I went to the left and the right trying to dodge him. '*La* (no),' he said. We did the side-step several more times and each time he made it clear I was not going to get past him. News came that all forty-six of us were to travel in convoy at all times during our stay. This was primarily for the safety of the Palestinians. It is common policy for intelligence agents to use international convoys to smuggle themselves into territories like Gaza. As Tony Blair's sister-in-law, no one was going to trust me easily for a start. Wouldn't I be the perfect British government spy? I knew very well I would only be there by choice, but I respected the government's right to be cautious on behalf of the people they represented. Plus the siege within a siege we were placed under was also for our protection.

On 12th March 2007, the BBC correspondent Alan Johnston had been kidnapped by a gang known locally as criminals. Johnston was one of the last international journalists based full-time in Gaza, as most Western news agencies had deemed the area too dangerous. He was held captive for 114 days by the Dagmush clan, and his release was only secured once Hamas removed the power from other armed organisations on winning the election. Johnston had been rescued and released by the regional government on 4 July, a matter of weeks before our arrival. I backed down, to Hasan's clear relief, and contented myself with smoking shisha and watching a glorious sunset. After a refreshing nights' sleep, I had two wake-up calls. The first was the dawn call to prayer from the surrounding mosques, a deep-throated Islamic song of yearning that pulled me out of a dream. It was still dark when I got up to look outside and the surf crashed onto the beach as I heard Muslim men quietly chatting on their way to the mosque across the road. After the *adhan* ended and I was falling back to sleep I heard a distant rumble, like thunder; the Israeli army were firing at Gazan fishing boats.

At our first lunch on the peach-coloured Al-Deira terrace, passengers and crew held a major discussion. Paul Larudee, one of the organizers, told us to general gasps that: 'We have all been invited to have lunch at the home of Prime Minister, Ismail Haniyeh. The government here knows that this is a controversial invitation so we need to submit a list of those who would like to attend. There is no pressure on anyone to be there whatsoever.' Right away our Israeli comrade, Jeff Halper, sensibly opted out. He was already facing police action and pressure when he went back to Israel, so there was no sensible reason for him to attend. As a journalist still on commission with the *Mail on Sunday*, I knew I could not miss the chance for a potential interview with such a controversial political figure. The Islam Channel had also been in touch requesting me to interview the Prime Minister, if possible. I decided to go along for work reasons, but I would stay in the background just to be on the safe side.

We were taken by coach and dropped at the entrance to the outdoor 'dining area' at al- Shati, also known as Beach Refugee Camp, and I hopped in my sandals over dirty pools of water filling gaps in the broken paving. Once inside the main open air area I was surrounded by Haniyeh's special guards, boys who looked too young to be carrying such large guns. I was already used to the casual way guns were being carried by the police. I reminded myself of armed police in the City of London, or security at JFK for that matter. There was, I kept telling myself, nothing to fear but fear itself. The young policemen scowled at us, trying to portray, I thought, weighty authority as the forty-six of us foreigners walked in. Their efforts were somewhat undermined by an inability not to break into friendly grins whenever they were addressed. The dining area was a bombed-out ground-floor hall, open to the elements save for uneven sheets of corrugated iron over trestle tables covered in plastic cloths.

Haniyeh entered without pomp, but in a frenzy of media flashbulbs. I had cleverly made sure I was at the back, well away from the cameras. The last thing I wanted was to be photographed with a figure so feared back in the UK. Times were changing and Britain was not the home of 'free speech' it had been when I was younger. A photo with the wrong person in the wrong place could trigger security issues. Even for a white journalist like myself. There was a scuffle of people around where I sat and I looked up to find myself surrounded by a group of Palestinian men in suits: 'Dear Miss Booth, Mr Haniyeh requests you please be his honoured guest at the top table'.

Inside, I put my head in my hands and swore a dozen times. On the outside I held onto a veneer of politeness for my hosts. This was my chance to secure an interview with the Prime Minister, though the cost would be film crews and media outlets filming and photographing me with Ismail Haniyeh, which would be broadcast around the world in moments. I stood up smiling and followed the men to the front of the hall. My fellow travellers raised their eyebrows as I was ushered past. I sat to the left of Haniyeh, a giant of a man with an easy going political style, not dissimilar to the 'hey guys, I'm just one of you' attitude Tony had made his own when PM.

Though the translator sitting just behind us, Ahmed, Haniyeh asked how the journey went and we made polite chitchat. Then he asked: 'What do you know about Muslims or Islam, Miss Laureen?'

When I'm nervous I make jokes, and I was very nervous by the situation I was in, although the atmosphere was one of a delightful picnic with old friends. A vast tray of lamb and meat was laid before us, which I shared with the PM using our hands. Then the words tumbled out before I could stop them: 'Well I know a little about Muslim clerics,' I said. Haniyeh stopped eating and turned his body to face me, giving me his full attention. 'I know that Muslim clerics love two things above all else in the world.'

'And what is that?' He asked politely.

'Lamb and women, but not necessarily in that order!'

There was a pause as the translation was whispered in this ear. Long enough for me to think to myself, 'bloody hell, Sarah, are you actually crazy?'

As I cursed my idiot tongue yet again, Haniyeh began to laugh, hard. Then he coughed and laughed some more. Two hundred people looked at us, wondering what the joke was. 'Then you know plenty enough about us already, Miss Lauren,' he said. '*Tafaddal* (welcome) to Gaza. You will be looked after here. This is your home.'

Neither of us could know just how prescient those words would prove.

After the food, there was a ceremony for the Free Gaza crew and passengers. We were lined up to receive gold-coloured medals bearing the legend 'Free Gaza', which were hung proudly around our necks The rarest thing I would ever own, one of just forty-six in the world. There was a great deal of laughter and we could tell that the gratitude for the risks we had taken was genuine, it poured from every person we met. The initially scary-looking security men slapped the backs of the male sailors and nodded shyly at the women.

After we had eaten, Haniyeh, myself and a doctor toured the tight, rubbish-strewn alleyways of his home, Beach Refugee Camp. Skinny children were everywhere and I paused to marvel at how they made games out of the rubbish around them. Five stick-thin, mucky boys under ten crouched in the dirt and donkey dung in the alleyway. They were flicking stones at tin cans. Dr Khamis was a rehabilitation specialist and as we entered the shockingly rundown slums around us, he paused to inspect the skin and teeth of the barefoot children. Their eyes, I noticed, were dull and filmy. Why? 'Due to a lack of minerals,' he said. He pointed to a little boy who looked around the same size as my seven-year-old daughter, Alex. The boy smiled up at us and I could see his only teeth were five partially formed stumps. He wasn't seven either, he was twelve years old. The lack of vitamin and poor diet had ruined his teeth and was damaging his long-term health. Dr Khamis pointed out the same signs visible in varying degrees in all the children around us. Anaemia, stunting, and in many cases, malnutrition, made the innocent scene of children playing suddenly dark and foreboding.

On the tour I was given of impoverished families and the slums, photos were taken of me sitting drinking tea with the Prime Minister. The same photos would appear on Egyptian blog sites some time later, alleging they were 'proof' Haniyeh was 'drinking whisky' and 'secretly married'. The blogs aimed to defame him, not me. In fact, I met the PM's wife in their humble home the same day. As I chatted on their sofa, without a scarf and not really modestly dressed for a place routinely called a 'terror enclave', I found them both to be kind, calm people, religious yet non-judgemental.

Too soon, the morning came when it was time for the re-fuelled boats to head back to Cyprus and the activists headed dockside, dragging their luggage behind them. The original plan outlined to me by Osama had been that the mission would be quick and I would be home in a week. I had already been away from my families for a month but the Free Gaza Movement had succeeded incredibly and against all the odds. They had sailed to Gaza, the first international boat to reach its 25-mile coastline for forty-one years. After a few days witnessing the effects of the siege on the people, my copy was ready to file. The symbolic amount of food and medical aid we had brought with us had been delivered and documentary footage was in the can. Articles and news items had made international headlines. Mission accomplished. It was time to head home. And yet.

I stood on the dock unable to move as Greta grabbed my hands and pulled me to her: 'Honey, forget work, the interviews, whatever, just come home. It's over. You may not be able to get out after this.'

My legs wouldn't move. It was as if a force was gluing me to the planks where I stood looking out at the sea, towards home: 'I can't Greta. I don't know why, I just can't. Allah bless you. I love you.'

There were calls of 'hurry up' from those waving to us already on deck. We hugged one last time as she rushed aboard the *Free Gaza*. Then, with nine others who had chosen to stay in Gaza, I waved the ships off as they sailed away on the afternoon tide. Standing next to me was a person who would remain in Gaza forever, only we didn't know it then: Vik.

Seventy-two hours after the boats left I had the interview with Haniyeh for the Islam Channel. The excuse that I needed to stay and complete my work was no longer valid. My new friend, a sweet-natured and pious man called Yasser who had watched over us in his role at the Popular Committee Against the Siege, accompanied three of us to the Rafah border. Although usually sealed, journalists and aid workers with international passports were being allowed to exit into Egypt that weekend. There would no trouble leaving, I was told. But there was trouble, and a major twist that I could not have planned for.

The Rafah checkpoint and terminal is the only viable connection to the outside world for ordinary Palestinians. Israel was allowing only (some) medical emergencies and those with international credentials to exit via the Erez Crossing, which leads to the West Bank. Even that would change. The essential gateway to the world for people and goods to get in and out remains the Rafah border crossing into Egypt. At that point in 2008 it had been open for just eight days.

Ken Keefe, Dr Bill and I joined the crush of humanity in a bus heading across no-man's land. The vehicle, like virtually all the transport in Gaza, had no air-conditioning and it was easily 30°C inside the bus. When we finally arrived at the checkpoint the terminal was in utter chaos; like Heathrow Terminal 5 at the height of summer, during an air traffic control strike, when everyone's luggage has been sent to Sudan. Families lay sprawled and dejected on the floor, men yelled at the authorities, and snappy uniformed police with riot truncheons and guns strapped to their waist looked over the scene with barely-concealed hatred of the people trying to gain freedom from the prison that was Gaza.

My passport was taken by someone in uniform and it vanished for an hour-and-a-half. I started to feel panic and wandered outside to take my mind off the chaos in the terminal building. I handed a tennis ball to the Palestinian security guard Hamas had sent to make sure I was okay, I had brought several balls to Gaza which I had given to the bored children at checkpoints, and the officer and I took turns rolling the ball at a can. A point was awarded every time it was knocked down. The Gazan children had taught me to be creative in seeking entertainment under siege. We began to enjoy the game, shouting and cheering at every loss and gain, and attracted the attention of a middle-aged man in a t-shirt and black trousers with a gun strapped to his belt. His full beard denoted authority, in Gaza your beard length was clearly a status symbol. The man began to shout furiously at my companions, then strode angrily away.

I picked up the ball, assuming our game was over, but instead Ken O'Keefe and I were led by two young Hamas policemen to a secluded patch around the back of the terminal. There were stables for police horses and a serious young policeman and his fellow officer marked a line in the dirt track, nodding towards my hand holding the ball. In one of the most bizarre experiences of my life, Ken and I began to play handball with Hamas. An hour later, we were back amongst the human misery inside the terminal.

'Read my passport,' I said a little preposterously to the Bond-villain like officer sneering over it in a side office off the main hall.

'It says the Queen of England demands that ...'

I never thought I'd ever name drop Lizzie Windsor to get out of a situation. As a republican it was a sure sign of my increasing desperation. At his desk, the scoffing security jobsworth told me that unless I left the terminal at once they would close the entire checkpoint and no one would cross that day. Complaining about mistreatment at checkpoints and 'borders' only leads to further collective punishment of Palestinian civilians. It was an uncanny duplicate of the threat which would be made to me when I tried to exit via Israel, days later. I was trapped. The government would (quite rightly) no longer support my stay at Al-Deira Hotel now the Free Gaza mission was over. Thankfully, Dr Eyad Saraj, the pioneering Palestinian psychiatrist and founder of the 'Gaza Community Mental Health Programme' (GCMHP) invited myself and fellow shipmate Ken O'Keefe, also stranded, to stay with him as long as was needed.

I spoke to my husband and children every night using Skype. The children were missing me and money was tight as I was not in London or at home to write the usual columns which would pay the bills. Writing about Gaza would always be for love, since no mainstream media wanted any more of my news from there. I looked for a job in Gaza and a local journalist, Yousef Al Helou, connected me with Press TV and I began reporting for them straight away. I looked around at everyone struggling to survive and realized my homesickness was not something deserving of self-pity. When I had appeared as a guest before on Press TV there had been no expectation that I would wear an Islamic scarf. However, as a representative of the channel on screen, I would be expected to adhere to a dress code which included the hijab. This time around the choice I made was different. If getting out stories about the appalling oppression of the people around me meant wearing a scarf it was a no-brainer, I put it on when the cameras rolled and took it off straight after. It had stopped bothering me and I no longer saw it as a symbol of oppression. I interviewed female ministers of the Hamas government who were covered, I met academics doing incredible work at the astounding al-Aqsa University in Khan Yunis. Their faith appeared to empower them rather than weaken them and the people amazed me every day.

Despite Gaza being the most conservative part of Palestine, run by a government roundly condemned as extremists by US and Israeli spokespeople, strolling down the main streets in the city centre and through the winding paths of the refugee camps, I never once heard the word 'haram' (banned/sinful) as I walked around. My blonde hair and back tattoo were clearly on display, not that I wanted to show my shoulders to religious people. I had developed more respect than in my early Islam Channel days, but my clothing had been chosen for a boat voyage and for Cyprus. I had never expected to be making a life, of sorts, in Gaza and it scared me to think of it. The greeting I received everywhere I went was the same word: '*Salam, salam*' (peace to you).

One morning, dawn was shattered by the thud of naval artillery against small fishing boats. This was normal, but the length of the attack drew me towards the dock to see what was happening. It was still before 8 am, but already the sun was blazing. Car horns screamed along broken streets lined by the art installations of rusting cars and piles of rubble. I walked thoughtfully on my own past breeze-block apartments peppered with shell holes. No cement was allowed to enter Gaza as it was considered at risk of 'dual purpose', meaning Israel deemed it could be used to build homes – or tunnels, so after Israeli shelling homes went unrepaired. I passed a group of primary school aged girls in dark green uniforms with jeans beneath for modesty. They skipped through the chaos, chatting happily, and I remembered cycling my own children to school. Would I enjoy that simple privilege again? At the port, a large crowd of men were shouting and gesturing amongst the decrepit vessels. Towering in the midst lurched a boat whose front had been ripped apart. Dejected young men sat beneath the wreckage, threading worry beads in and out of work-hardened fingers. An elderly man in a traditional white Arabic shirt shouted for anybody to take in: 'This is what Israel has done to me. It has destroyed me.' The Israeli navy had imposed a 'no-go' zone six miles from Gaza's coast. During the night, patrol vessels had attacked the small Gazan fishing fleet, which was not really a fleet more a Dunkirk-style array of battered little tugs doing their best to contribute to feeding hungry people in a conflict zone. A gunboat had smashed across and right through the upper hull of the vessel, leaving it wrecked. It was the third boat to be destroyed in that way in as many weeks. The Israeli military aboard the gunboat had shouted at the fishermen through a megaphone: 'When the foreigners leave Gaza, you will all be made to pay.' Maybe our mission had caused more pain than good? The people around the boat shrugged. As they say in the Gaza Strip: '*Hayk al- dunya,*' that's life. I shielded my eyes from the sun as the old man repeated over and over the words, 'fifty thousand dollars'. No one had that kind of money here.

Their life for the time being was my life, I thought, as I headed back to the home of Dr Eyad, his wife, Nirmeen, and son, Ali. Mocking pieces had been appearing in the British press about my situation, including on the pages of the very paper I regularly wrote for, the *Daily Mail.* I had been accused of naivety and stupidity by a veteran columnist for taking a boat to Gaza and then expecting everything to be okay. Photos taken of me smiling (I always smiled) on the streets and refugee camps had inspired her to write: 'Still, no matter how much Booth bleats behind the barbed wire, she is still managing to look quite pleased with herself.' It was partly true. Hadn't I been naive to believe that I could come to Gaza, a land where human rights were routinely ignored and abused, and expect my own to somehow be respected? Even my passport, with the Queen's precious signature on it, meant nothing anymore. I was getting a real lesson in solidarity. It means standing shoulder to shoulder with people, rather than patronising them from outside and returning to normal, to forgetfulness.

As always, I couldn't help looking for the plus points in my situation. I at least felt safe. I had been assigned two (frankly useless) but friendly bodyguards. Ali was a newly married 24- year-old and Mohamed at the same age already had three children. They both carried hand guns but all we did was joke about all the time and drive between meetings faster than everyone else because of their special government licence. Their protection seemed pretty pointless until three weeks into my stay. I awoke at 4 am to the sound of machine-gun fire. Heading bleary-eyed into the kitchen, I found Dr Saraj and Nirmeen already there making coffee. They tried to assure me that the gunfire was nothing more than Hamas police carrying out training sessions on the beach. Yet as we sipped from our mugs, the booms got louder and closer. Then the sirens began. Dr Eyad received text messages telling him of a violent clash between the police and the heavily- armed militia group, the Army of Islam, the family gang responsible for the kidnapping of BBC journalist Alan Johnston. The shooting went on and on but the periods of silence were worse – a form of water torture. We were tense in the silence, waiting for the ratta-tat-tat of the machine- gun fire to break out again.

It was an eleven-hour battle, and the British consul in Gaza called me: 'Limit your movements today, do not go to the South at all, which is not to say the North is safe. In fact, stay inside if you can.' A young attaché there had been kind enough to smuggle me in a bottle of wine and some whisky. He had felt 'bad' about my situation, he said, and I suspected more than a little embarrassed that the British consul could (or would) do nothing to help me get home. It was a decisive battle and eleven militiamen and two policemen were shot. Other members of the radical faction were rounded up, part of Hamas' pledge to clean up the streets and give some semblance of security to the people. Nothing could be done about the Israeli drones overhead, or the army border snipers, or the navy, though. For me the battle was a brutal reminder that I had to get home. Things went wrong, badly wrong, in Gaza all the time and my children needed me to stay alive.

Every day in between my filming schedule there were rounds of phone calls and emails to a growing circle of officials about my situation. I was urged not to be too proud to ask for help, and after much coaxing from local officials I unwillingly contacted (Tony's) Middle East Envoy office in Jerusalem. I knew it was a mistake and it was a chance for some petty vengeance by officials I had always been openly critical about. The envoy's office response was a round telling off: 'Why didn't you leave when you had the chance?' This was followed by the parroting of the official line: 'Israel says you can leave, so why haven't you left though Israel?' I called the number given me to 'coordinate' with Israeli officials. They were even more delighted at my call. Leaving via Erez, I was told, would be out of the question as I was 'illegal' in Gaza in the first place having sailed in without a border stamp in my passport. And so it went on.

Everything happens for a reason. Nothing is an accident and there is no such thing as coincidence. I was meant to sail to Gaza and I was meant to stay at that precise time. On 1 September, the holy month of Ramadan began. It's an integral part of the thirty days to increase in good deeds. One way to do this is to provide food to the fasting. My cameraman, Abid, told me doing such things carries great blessing. One night, in mid-September, I carried bags of still- warm shop-bought kebab meat to a desperate family in Rafah refugee camp. It was incredible to me that I should be walking the same rickety back lanes which Faris Odeh had tried to defend with his stones. I was in the same part of the world in which the boy had lived and died. I wandered the unlit darkness of another power cut, marvelling at the miracle which had brought me to the precise place that had affected me so much on the news, almost eight years before. I was meant to be there.

As I approached the broken wooden door of the family's crumbling cement dwelling, Abid whispered: 'Lauren. Whatever food they try to give you, don't eat it, okay? You can eat at my home later. Anything you eat will come out of the mouths of children. Sorry for that.' I knocked at the door. Um Mohamed (meaning: Mother of the eldest child, Mohamed) greeted me. Parents took the labels 'Um' and 'Abu' (father of) for a dual purpose; to keep their own names private as a part of modesty in public and, as with so many cultural practises in the Muslim world, to preserve the sense of closeness between generations.

Um Mohamed beamed at us, her face shone in the moonlight and her glowing eyes seemed to suggest she didn't have a care in the world. Perhaps she wasn't as poor as her doorway or the slum's exterior suggested. Maybe her family had some hidden wealth that allowed her to smile despite her clean, yet frayed abaya. There had to be a secret I couldn't see, for in this ragged slum street there was no visible reason to be happy. '*tafaddal*,' she said, moving slightly and inviting us inside. I hovered just inside the doorway, my stomach suddenly in my shoes at the full horror of the room. I stood in the middle of a cement cell which was entirely empty; no furniture, no TV, no decoration to brighten it at all. Not even a picture on the wall or a dash of paint anywhere, apart from a small rug surrounded by some cushions on the bare stone floor. On the rug were three plastic plates, the family's *iftar*, the meal they took after the day's 12-hour fast.

Abid chatted to Um Mohamed. '*Masha'Allah*,' he said on discovering she and her husband had eight children. I looked at the small plate of hummus, salad and pitta bread. There was hardly enough to fill me and my daughters for a snack, and for ten people after fasting it was nowhere near enough. I was pleased we had brought the bags of lamb, the children would sleep on a full stomach for once. I was shown to a cushion and poured a Coca Cola, cheaper than bottled water in Gaza. As Abid had feared, Um Mohamed immediately began piling a plate with food until it was full. Little to nothing remained for the parents or children.

'No really,' I said when the plate was offered, 'We've come to bring you food not to eat it! Anyway we really have to go, sorry!' Um Mohamed put her hands firmly on my shoulders and I could feel the weight of her determination stopping me from standing up.

'Eat!' she said in Arabic and again urged the plate towards me. I didn't take it, so she lifted my right hand and placed the plate into it, curling my fingers one by one around the rim until I was holding it. I felt foolish for refusing her kind hospitality, but I knew I must. 'Eat and welcome!'

She was smiling, but at what I wondered? At the empty, awful space? At the dreadful, seemingly-hopeless existence that was her life? I felt anger rising in me at the stupidity of it all.

'Stop, please!' I stood up and handed back the plate. I'd had enough. I was tired of the shattered fishing boats, sick of seeing children playing with dirt. I was nauseated by the generosity, the patience and the goodness of the people. I was disgusted at the idiotic starvation and the thirst inflicted upon the poor and called 'fasting'. None of it made any sense to me. I was out of my depth and I just wanted to be home in Britain, where things made sense. Where you turned on the tap and clean water came out. Where people minded their own business and weren't so concerned for ... me.

Um Mohamed was confused at her guest for refusing to eat the food she had offered. She expected me to play the whole grateful game that these people constructed inside themselves in order to survive from day to day. Weeks of withholding anger and with nowhere to set it free came brimming to the surface. I was convinced the Gazan people were suffering a combination of Stockholm syndrome and cultural low self-esteem.

The dam broke and my thoughts poured out all at once: 'Tell me please, what is the point of your Allah making you hungry for four weeks and then in week five you will still be hungry? Tell me why your Allah makes you go thirsty for four weeks then in week five you still won't have enough water anyway? Tell me what adding hunger and thirst to hunger and misery adds to life, because I just don't get it. Just tell me why are you going hungry right now? What is the point in Ramadan? What is it all for?'

Abid, disturbed at my outburst, gave me a concerned look then quickly translated for the confused mother. As I stood there, I spotted children's faces peering curiously, hungrily, through the only other door of the cement hut. I knew the type of room they were in, I had seen it a hundred times already. There would be one, if they were lucky two, filthy mattresses on a bare stone floor where all eight slept. In one corner there would be piles upon piles of clothes on the floor because there would be nothing as luxurious as a wardrobe. Their little faces were hoping some food would be left by this noisy guest.

The translation was repeated, just to be clear. Um Mohamed walked to me and took my hands lightly in her own, which were soft and warm. She looked me in the eyes: 'My Allah tells me to remember others who have less than we do. That is why we *enjoy* not eating or drinking for so many hours at this time. We fast to remember the poor.'

Time stopped and the sounds of life were suspended as my mind rested on the meaning of what had just been said. I was being told that only the present mattered and the good that could be gained in it. Everything else: wars, poverty, hopes, and doubts were outside our immediate control. In Ramadan, Muslims were refocused on the one thing, perhaps the only thing that mattered: the atom at the heart of all deeds. The understanding that made every other pain easy to bear: You can please God by pleasing the people. By being grateful to God your heart would know ease.

A door in my heart felt like it had been opened by these magic words: 'I fast in Ramadan to remember the poor.' Yet Um Mohamed was poor herself, catastrophically, appallingly, permanently, desperately poor.

'I fast in Ramadan to remember the poor.'

Of course, now it all made sense. If you recognised there were always those worse off than you, how could you sink into self-pity and endless speculation about work, money, the future? How could you envy when you were blessed? If you cared about your neighbour like yourself, if you were busy with their concerns, it took the edge off your own. What a remarkable system! A welfare state of human empathy, flowing from household to household and all with one purpose: To love and to please God.

Perhaps they saw something on my face of the internal dialogue, as no one said anything else. When Um Mohamed guided me back to the rug, I sat down quietly on the cushion and we ate enough of the food for her to feel satisfied that she had fed the strangers; the special visitors on the blessed night in Ramadan. I left enough to know the children would have enough as well. At least for that meal. I was in a beautiful daze and then the thought came to me clear as day: 'If this is Islam, I want to be Muslim.'

***

Unsurprisingly there wasn't much fun stuff to do in Gaza. The beach was the main place families went to enjoy themselves and I was keen to swim, but I was told that as a woman the only time I could go was at dawn, when I wouldn't be seen by the general public. I was taken out to sea by a fisherman on a rowing boat with a small engine. Dr Mona El-Farra, the dynamic physician and author of the acclaimed book, *From Gaza, with Love*, came with us. We chugged out to about half a mile from the shore, where it was deemed modest enough for me to splash about. I was wearing black jogging bottoms and a long baggy t-shirt, and aside from the school swimming exam in year five, I'd never swam in my clothes before. I was expected to climb into the boat after a few minutes, but seeing the shoreline I couldn't resist the idea of breaking the siege of Gaza by sailing *and* swimming. It was a twenty-minute freestyle swim to the shore in the beautiful morning sunshine and the sea was as blue as any other part of the Mediterranean. I could hear the boat driver shouting in panic behind me, I'd probably get him into trouble with the authorities, poor man. I emerged onto the beach, my salty clothes clinging to my body. It was 7 am and a group of fishermen watched as I walked ashore, from where they couldn't imagine. I traipsed down the beach, squishing in my wet clothes with my blonde hair drawing even more attention than my sudden appearance. As I passed the stunned fishermen, a toothless elder offered me a bit of whatever seafood speciality they were frying. I thought it best for them not to be seen with a blonde in clingy clothing and politely declined.

It was my day off, so I dried and changed back at Dr Eyed's then went for a wander around the city. The intense feeling of the night before had vanished, leaving only the memory of Um Mohamed's generosity and piety but not my own longing for the same. I carried on with life and God was yet again a forgotten dream. On my route, I stopped at the PLO flag shop. Like all the non-essential stores in Gaza, there was never anyone inside when I turned up except the dejected store owner. The white haired 'uncle' leapt to his feet and handed me box after box of incredible trinkets. Some like the Yasser Arafat keyrings, I'd seen in Jerusalem, others like Hamas bookmarks and the pins of dead martyrs could be found nowhere else. I settled on buying a t-shirt that read: 'Free Gaza' and a mug with iron bars printed over the obscurely cheerful: 'Smile – You're In Gaza, The Biggest Prison In The World.'

My phone rang, it was Ghazi Hamad, a top government official: 'Lauren,' he said, 'Get your things and go to Rafah. Now!'

My original intention on coming to Gaza by sea had been to stay just under a week and then head home to France. I hadn't bargained on the vagaries of the Egyptian border authorities. Having a passport plus an oral agreement that you can pass through the crossing had counted for nothing twice before. Now, after two months away from my children, I was utterly desperate to get across this time. It was 8:30 am and the centre of Rafah was heaving. Mohamed, my personal security guard, blasted through the traffic of donkey carts and school children. His driving was even more crazed than usual and he was almost as tense as I was. It was the third time we had driven to the Egyptian border and I was hoping this time I would be freed from this concentration camp. Previously, I had been turned back each time, my passage refused by the Egyptian authorities. The students I had been with had managed to escape from Gaza by paying the all-important *bakshish* (bribe) to someone on the Egyptian side. Today I had only three hundred dollars in various pockets, would that be enough?

It started well enough, and within half an hour of entering the airport-style terminal building on the Palestinian side I had an exit visa stamp on my passport. Next I was led by Gaza police officers to the same building I had spent thirteen hours previously: 'Not the room of doom!' I said, trying to make light of the situation even as my heart sank to my dust-covered toes. It had been seven and a half weeks since I had seen my daughters, Alexandra and Holly, or my husband. I didn't allow myself to think of them for more than a moment. I had met several women who hadn't seen their children or their homes in the West Bank for a year. One poor lady hadn't seen her parents for fifteen years. What was my suffering but discomfort when compared to theirs? In the 'room of doom' I laid out several chair cushions on the floor and forced myself to sleep. A better option than the anxiety the Egyptian authorities wanted me to experience. I lay there for nearly three hours before raised Arabic voices turned my blood to ice.

'What do you mean they must *all* go back to Gaza, NOW?!'

I looked at my fellow detainees in the laughingly-named VIP room; a highly-respected Sheikh and a young man with bullet injuries. Both Palestinian and both needing medical treatment in Cairo. Suddenly, I was surrounded by armed guards: 'You can go. Only you, Ms Booth. Leave now, now, now, now!'

I turned to my new friends: 'What? Sorry it's like this! Why me and not them as well? I can't leave them behind, they have families too!'

That is how it is at Rafah, *divide et̄ impera*, divide and conquer. There was no time for warm handshakes or kind words. When your 'co-ordination' came you couldn't miss your chance to go home and see your children, to leave this concentration camp. The atmosphere of powerlessness and despair was dizzying. Suddenly I really am a VIP, it seemed. A large man in a sweaty shirt smiled and took my passport as we headed downstairs and he asked me if I was okay. The small pleasantry in this hellish place suggested that a call had been made from somewhere high up the political food chain. I found out later that the Jimmy Carter Center in the US, who I had contacted for support, had used their channels to help get me home. So had a Labour Minister and a LibDem MP from North London.

In the final room before freedom, I faced one of the loathsome Mubarak regime representatives. Outside in the main building, names were shouted out by officials: 'Hussan ... Ahmad ... Dijani'. Husbands and fathers who had somehow pleased their jailers would be allowed to work or study or visit family in the world beyond the twenty-four by four kilometre stretch of the Gaza Strip. I asked the obese man behind the desk who was sifting through piles of green Palestinian passports if he spoke English. He didn't.

'Your system is a disgrace,' I said to him in English in a friendly tone, as if I was reading to very young child. He looked across the desk at me. 'You should be ashamed of your part in this. Are you proud to be destroying lives today?' I waved my hands randomly around and chuckled just for good measure.

The official shook his head and went back to sorting Palestinian passports into piles which decided whether the people outside would be freed or not. He handed mine back to me and I left his office and walked to a window in the midst of the noisy misery. I paid for an exit visa and stepped outside into the sunshine. It had taken seven hours to get through the border but I had made it. I was finally in Egypt.

A battered bus drove me eight hours through the Sinai desert back to Cairo. On my flight home, a single thought was going round and round my mind: Would I ever see the people of Gaza again?

CHAPTER 13
THE TEST OF LIFE

'Whatever has befallen you was not meant to escape you,
and whatever has escaped you was not meant to befall you...'

Prophet Muhammad PBUH

People collect all kinds of things: teapots, autographs, Pokémon figurines, soap bars. I am a collector of curious life experiences and I had picked up several interesting souvenirs working at the Islam Channel, then Press TV and on my travels to Palestine as a journalist. In the same way it took two years to shake off an Australian accent on returning from that continent, certain phrases appealed to my actor's tongue and my traveller's mind as I toured the Muslim world.

At an event held by the Islam Channel, singer Abdullah Rolle had given me a CD of his album, *Patience*. I played it to my daughters as we baked in the rustic stone kitchen at weekends and they loved it straight away. Cycling to school, Holly was snoring, as always, in her special seat on the back of my bike while Alexandra pedalled ahead of me. Heading towards the rustic town of Vergt, she joyfully sang the chorus to Rolle's song, 'There is None Greater'.

'There is none Greater. Than the Creator. All-a-a-ahu Akbar, All-a-aa-hu Akbar!'

I fell into the habit of greeting people locally with 'salam' (peace) instead of 'salut'. In hindsight it was bad enough they had 'les Anglaises' buying up the best properties in the region and refusing to learn French, whilst opening up shops specializing in 'le tomato sauce', but to then have an English woman greeting them in Arabic I was lucky not to have been lynched. As a writer I somehow forgot that words had power. A cruel word from a partner can feel like a heart attack in the making. When we argue needlessly and hang up on a loved one, doesn't our spite hurt us as much as those at whom we vented our spleen? Singing that song made me feel light and made me smile. Alex and I agreed that somehow it even made pedalling uphill past the chicken farm at the corner of our country road easier. Down the hill we went, month after month, winding our way towards school: 'Allahuuuuuu Akbarrr, Allahuuuu Akbarrrr!' We were unconsciously praising Him, every morning.

Yet I thought those weighty words would have no effect on me, and I never considered they might be heard. It was a time of encroaching sadness: My husband was travelling back and forth to the UK for legal advice, seeking a divorce, and the end of a special period in our lives was coming to an end, though I had no idea how suddenly and tragically that end would arrive. At 1:30 am on 24 April 2009, I was awoken from sleep by my phone buzzing endlessly. The insistence of it made me reach across my daughters, who were sleeping with me, and feel about on the floor for my mobile.

'Mrs Darby?'

'Yes?'

'It's the police. Your husband's had an accident. Can you tell us how to reach you from the village?'

The next hour passed in agonising slow motion. Eventually, two policemen appeared at the front door. I remember the pouring rain streaming off their black uniforms as they asked to come in, I somehow remembered to be polite and made coffee, then I was handed a black leather jacket. Beneath it was the t-shirt my husband had been wearing when I had left him hours earlier in the local bar. He hadn't wanted to come home with me, or to leave his beloved motorbike. The clothes were torn and ragged.

'Your husband came off his motorbike,' one of the policemen said. 'He was found in the road unconscious. He has been taken to Bordeaux hospital.' They looked at each other and came to some silent decision. 'Please prepare yourself. He is in a coma.'

The soaking wet jeans were torn from ankle to hip, the t-shirt still smelt of his aftershave. I was too shocked to cry. I called his family and then prayed from 3 am until the girls woke up, around 6:30 am: 'Don't take him, let him live, please, please, save him ... Allah!'

***

The former national cricket captain and leader of Pakistan's Tehreek-e Insaf (PTI) opposition party, Imran Khan, described in his book, *Pakistan*, finding faith through sport. On certain match days, he wrote, everything about his national team would be in free fall. There were injuries to star players and dressing room arguments, but the other team would be in perfect form. Yet despite the 'natural' odds being against him at that point, his team would enjoy a great victory, with every bounce, every catch and every wicket being gifted to them. On other days he felt the squad couldn't possibly lose. Everything had gone to plan; team health, training, reactions, yet Imran Khan would watch an inexplicable defeat unfold. In this, he felt an 'unseen hand' in charge of success and disaster. Gradually, he began to ask the One he felt had the power to effect outcomes by praying. He began to rely on God above machismo, confidence or even training.

I was about to learn the painful reality that I had no control over major events in my own life. There are things you can never mitigate for and sometimes they all come in one agonising period of time.

Between April 2009 and April 2010, all that I had built up over two decades – the stuff of life; marriage, home, love, safety, family would be stripped away. Six months after the accident, for reasons I choose not to discuss here, I knew we had no choice but to return to the UK, for all of our well-being. With my friend,

Anne, I packed up the house into cardboard boxes, though most of them would have to be left behind. My younger sister and her husband came over and doubled the amount I could afford to transport back to the UK from one car to two. One precious front seat of space was reserved for the girls' gerbils, Fluffy Mcguffey and Jessica. We tried to release them into the woods (I know it would have been murder), but wisely they refused to run away. We all said goodbye to our perfect life, our dream home. My husband returned to his family in Highgate, north London, to continue his convalescence. I rented an apartment within walking distance so he and the girls could easily see each other. I found local schools for the girls and continued hosting a series I had helped create, *Remember Palestine* for Press TV.

A few weeks after settling into a crumbling flat, carless and penniless, at 7 am one morning there was another ominous knocking. I opened the front door to find a court officer in a stab-proof vest who asked my name then demanded to be allowed inside. My husband's family were accusing me of 'removing children from the jurisdiction' where they were resident, without permission of both parents: A form of 'interstate kidnapping'. The case would be heard in the High Court in London. Before leaving, the sympathetic court officer said gently: 'You seem like a nice lady. Get yourself a good lawyer, quickly. One other thing, I'm very sorry but I need to take all your passports with me.'

Shakily buttoning up a little cardigan for school an hour later, I pushed away the whispering voice that wanted me to ask: 'Why me, why is this happening to me?' Part of me wanted to take to my bed and embrace my self-pity, but instead I forced myself to recall the horrors which had been suffered by other families, like those I had met in Gaza and the West Bank. Parents I had met there had shown patience in hardships which were far greater than my current difficulties. Their houses had been bombed or bulldozed, yet didn't my girls fall sleep in comfort and warmth every night? Gazan people had no work, I had a job I loved. Refugees in camps didn't have enough food from day to day, my children never went to bed hungry. Instead of focusing on the problems we faced, I sought out reasons to be grateful. I began to say 'Alhamdulillah' (thanks be to God), forcing myself from the bottom of the emotional pit I woke up in every morning to recognize blessings in everyday things. Stuff like health and love that for too long I had simply taken for granted.

A few months earlier I had considered duck breast and a £10 bottle of Château Margaux were the essential basics of life. That was when the joy of a swim in our beautiful pool overlooking the green of the Dordogne valley had become a part of my daily routine. Now, I needed a positive thinking strategy to get through our reduced circumstances. The car had been taken back by the person who owned it, so I turned that situation into a bonus. When the girls were upset, realising it was gone, we went for a walk. In Highgate Woods it was spring and the trees and bushes were in full bloom, abundantly green. They ran and played amongst the oaks and chestnut trees. We wandered into the children's playground and were delighted to find a mini zip wire amongst the climbing frames. On our way home I held their hands and remembered how my own father had, in his blunt way, made me recognize that being financially 'broke' was nothing like being broken by real poverty. 'Girls, we have another wood to walk through, just like in France and this one goes all the way to your new school!' They were thrilled by our twice-daily walks – extra time with Mum watching the glories of the seasonal changes. We splashed through puddles, kicked up leaves and slowly walked in the magnificence of London rain.

I was forced to face this life head on. For weeks during the trial I wanted to stay in bed and ask over and over, 'why me?' Instead I forced myself to work, as so many single mums do around the world. What kept me going was a thought that at first seems negative, but proved very powerful: 'Why *not* me?' Why shouldn't calamities hit my family when they afflicted others? Life wasn't about building castles in the sky, clinging to material goods thinking that wealth would keep disasters at bay. A positive outlook, kindness, the giving of love even in the midst of a personal drama, I found these things mattered more. Illness, financial pressures, divorce, and loss were the things of life. All I now had to ask was: how was I going to deal with them? Every spare penny of my wages, plus money I had borrowed from my sister, Cherie, to try and keep the house in France, went instead on lawyers fighting my High Court case. For months, I wrote cheque after cheque, for six, eight and ten-thousand pounds at a time.

I remembered a Qur'anic prayer of protection. It was one that I had heard so often in homes from Jenin and Jerusalem, in Ramallah and in the Rafah refugee camp: 'Hasbuna Allah wa-Ni'ma al-Wakil'. Allah (alone) is Sufficient for us, and He is the Best Disposer of affairs (for us). After six months came the final hearing in the High Court in the Strand. I entered a courtroom where the decision would be made whether the children stayed in London, or returned to France without me. Before leaving the house that morning I got down on my knees. 'Allah,' I pleaded, 'Just my children, I get it now, nothing material matters. Please, just my children, Lord.' The case was dismissed.

Due to their father's injuries I did not make an application for my right to claim the tens of thousands of pounds in legal fees I had paid. Then came another blow. Sitting at my kitchen table going over the figures yet again, I realized that with thousands of pounds still outstanding in legal fees and a huge overdraft, I had no choice but to file for bankruptcy. A month later a French bank filed repossession papers for our home. My ex-husband immediately filed for a court hearing over custody of the children. I had to find another lawyer, and the money to pay them. 'Hasbuna Allah wa-Ni'ma al-Wakil'.

The Prophet Muhammad is reported as saying: 'The situation of the Muslim is amazing. His situation is always good! When hardship befalls him, he is patient and when ease befalls him, he is thankful.'

CHAPTER 14
THE GREEN LIGHT

'Let yourself be silently drawn by the strange pull
of what you really love. It will not lead you astray.'

Jalāl ad-Dīn Mohammad Rūmī

That September I travelled to Tehran for Press TV to report
on the largest protest in the world calling for the reunifica-
tion of Jerusalem. After my reports had been filed, I travelled by
car from Tehran to Esfahan on a road trip with my new friend,
Nargess. As the sand flats rolled past, I looked out of the taxi
considering how my fledgling respect for Islam had been damaged on the trip. The suburbs on the northern side of the Iranian
capital reminded me of the northern suburbs of London. It was
a prestigious enclave of media workers, bankers and the upper
middle-classes. I was staying in a five-star hotel.

It was Ramadan, not that you'd really know it from the continued commercial atmosphere in the city. This part of Iran appeared to be a post-Islamic society. My colleagues at Press TV
embraced the month's religiosity at work and there was a calm
patience, not at all like the buzz of a western newsroom with ripe
swear words emanating from the editing suite. It was the end of
summer and the days were too long and too hot for fasting, some
days it was more than 35oC. The pre-dawn call to prayer arrived
shortly before 5 am and the call for the dusk prayer, known as
Maghrib prayer, and the breaking of the fast came after 7 pm.

The length of fasts didn't matter, I had discovered, whether you were in Nova Scotia or southern Australia, the daylight rule of no food or drink applied for an entire month. There were other rules to be abided by – spiritual ones. Muslims were expected to avoid gossip or 'vain talk', no wonder our office was so quiet. Journalists live for chitchat about politicians, yet the modern stock and trade of news media channels was perfectly summarised as 'vain talk'.

Everyone was expected to fast from the age of puberty until illness or infirmity made it physically unsafe. Until recent years, the chief of Iran's national police would warn that anyone breaking the fast in public would be arrested. But now more people were grumbling and their hearts appeared irritated rather than cleansed by the policed spiritual marathon. On my way to work, I stopped at the lobby shop to buy some toothpaste. The owner was bent double beneath his glass counter, sneaking sweets and sipping water from a bottle. Seeing that I was watching him curiously, he stood up, wiped his mouth and shrugged: 'It's not my religion to fast. It's "theirs"'. Shopping appeared to be the major (if not the only) pastime for the Tehran middle- class, who were without doubt the worst drivers I had ever had the misery to passenger with. The roads were so chaotic they beat Cairo's legendary traffic anarchy. I even saw cars reverse up a motorway if an exit was missed. Before I flew out, friends and family had asked if my life would be at risk in Iran. My answer when I got home would be, 'yes, every day', though not from kidnapping or hijack, but from dangerous driving.

I wanted to visit the city's mosques, so I asked 36-year-old single mum, Fatimah, who worked in a government department, if we could visit one on her day off. Her response was the kind of look teenagers give to parents: 'What's wrong with you?'

Unable to avoid it any longer, I shopped. I was dropped off by a friend at the Panzdah-e-Khordad St bazaar, an ancient domed marketplace. Passing through the throng, I experienced a pang of homesickness for Palestine. A wall of coldness existed between me and the Iranian public which I couldn't seem to melt. Where Ramallah was a summer's day, Tehran was an ice sheet of aloof shoving. With little of beauty to look at in the main city centre, I sought out my usual pastime – human tourism. I had to succeed, I decided. If I didn't connect with the people I met I felt I had never visited their country at all. The next time, I carried the Islamic greeting, 'salam', on my tongue. An old lady was my first effort. She tottered along in a black scarf, laden down with plastic bags of fruit. 'Salaam,' I said. The change was instantaneous. A road full of suspicion was transformed into an esplanade of charming smiles. Success! Everywhere I visited, from museums to ornamental gardens, I was suddenly wished well by the passers-by.

More than half of the young women (and nearly as many guys) had neat, skin-coloured, almost invisible plasters across the bridge of their nose. In Tehran, my colleagues laughed when I asked about them: it was the 'nose-job capital of the world'. Alongside the operation to remove the hated Persian 'hump' nose shape, the ladies headscarves rose up to half a foot above their foreheads, something I had never seen anywhere else. More and more women were buying large pieces of foam, which they put on top of their heads then clipped hair over them at the front. Then a scarf was put over the odd combo when they left the house. The effect had me almost falling over giggling. One woman I passed appeared to have the entire star ship *Enterprise* under her scarf. What stopped me from collapsing in fits of laughter at the foam/hair mutation was that it was clearly a desperate attempt at freedom of dress. Those women were seeking an individuality that challenged society's demands and expectations, whilst not crossing the 'line' expected of women in public or contravening the modesty laws.

I had the growing urge to seek out calm spaces when I travelled to Muslim lands for my work and I asked yet again to go to a mosque, but with no luck. Even when Muslim kids used the long carpets for their athletics, sitting down quietly speaking to God my heart still found a new kind of equilibrium. Now Tehran was pushing me away from Islam. In the small rich suburb surrounding Press TV's main centre, I was meeting women who wished nothing more than to escape the confines of their society. They had been repelled by enforced prayer times, they loathed the dress codes. The women I spoke to used the same phrase: 'we are made into religious hypocrites.' I felt sad for them. I felt angry at the men who thought religion, like taxes, could be enforced and policed in the same way.

In the taxi en route to Esfahan, I was pleased to leave the conflicted social atmosphere of Tehran behind us. My colleague, Nargess, and her mother chatted on the back seat. Nargess had grown up in Britain and the combination of (quietly) devout Muslim in her mingled (at times hilariously) with the loud Londoner she liked to show to the outside world. The spiked landscape of 'Planet Persia' whisked past and soon we would stop in Qom, one of the most religious cities in Iran. We arrived exactly at *iftar* (dusk), the same time of night in the same holy month that I had been moved by the words of the Um Mohamed in Rafah, two years earlier. There was no such thing as coincidence.

On a sandstone paving outside the Mosque, Nargess handed me a plastic bag hanging from a hook in the middle of the entrance: 'For your shoes.' She could see I was nervous of the sheer number of Iranian pilgrims around me. 'Just enjoy this experience, Lauren. These nights are special here, lots of people come from all over Iran to pray.'

I was concerned about being arrested.

'You'll be fine, don't look so worried. We'll stay an hour then head to Esfahan okay?' The side door of the Mosque opened straight into a large room with glass pieces on every inch of the ceiling and part way down the walls. The light was almost blinding. There were thick red rugs on the floors and without noticing we had separated from the men. Women and children read together or ate and chatted. I risked losing sight of Nargess in the crowd, where she became yet another black-draped head amongst thousands. Reunited, we sat down. I muttered 'Allahu Akbar' several times, closing my eyes for a short prayer: 'Thank you, Allah, for all my blessings for this amazing life that brings me here to you, please bless my children. Thank you Allah. Please bless Palestine.'

Opening my eyes, the room seemed sharper, yet heavier than I remembered. I swayed, feeling I was about to faint sideways onto the carpet. Nargess was at my side. 'Are you okay Lauren,' she asked.

I honestly didn't know.

When I was nineteen, I had an emergency appendectomy. I was petrified, on my own in a hospital bed. Everything had happened so suddenly. That morning I had gone to the doctors after a few days vomiting. Hours later I was being prepared for an operation. The surgeon came to see me. I was hyperactive, fidgeting and wringing my hands anxiously. He called the nurse and said he would not operate without 'this young lady having a pre-med before you send her to theatre.' Ten minutes later I was given an injection of morphine. The moment the needle left my arm I was embraced by a feeling of sublime joy. I got out of bed and wandered up the hospital corridor as an orderly tried to get me to lie on the trolley. I was singing a made up song: 'I hope I die that would be great, see what happens at the Gate.' At that moment I felt no fear of death at all. I was utterly certain Heaven existed. Redemption would be so beautiful that nothing in this life, this realm would matter once it was tasted. Of course that was just the effect of the drugs.

On the floor of the Qom Mosque, the feeling came back again. I was heavy, like a stone at the bottom of warm, clear river. Everything around me was in perfect focus, yet blurred as if taken by a camera far away. I was able to recognise the 'pre-med' rush – I was experiencing a general anaesthetic but my eyes wouldn't close. I felt the stress that had lived in my chest for two years, since the accident, suddenly, gently, leave all at once. I was in the deepest meditation of my life, yet all I'd done was sit down. My breath came and went and I felt a smile on my lips. Was I laughing? Sighing? Nargess was close by my left side and I was aware of her. But my body had no substance. I sat on the floor, legs crossed, covered in layers and layers of clothes, no longer irritated by the chador on my head. I didn't want to move and break the enchantment. Everything was very, very lovely. Ah, to live with no pain. Isn't this what every human craves?

I found myself repeating quietly, 'This is lovely, this is lovely, this is lovely. Thank you Allah, thank you Allah, thank you Allah, Allah, thank you Allah, Allah akbhar ...'

A young woman's face came close to mine. The girl was bending down staring at me. She spoke in Farsi. Nargess said, 'this lady wants to know if you are at peace, Lauren.'

What a silly question, I thought! What else was there but peace? Could I even imagine what not-peace felt like anymore? From within me came the words, 'Yes, I am at peace,' pushed through floppy lips. Would you understand if I said that I was no longer Lauren at that point? That my sense of self had melted away and been replaced by a feeling of just being a part of a universal energy too great to countenance? All those years of trying to be 'someone'. I understood that being a part of everything was better.

A word was passing between the girl and Nargess: 'meditation'. How clever, I thought, that they knew how I was feeling. The girls sat with me for a while until Nargess spoke again: 'Lauren, can she take your photo to show her husband the lovely thing that has happened here?'

'Yes' I said from my distance. I saw the girl's dark, black eyes as she sat close to me on her knees.

'I love you,' she said. Such love!

'I love you too,' I slurred. At that moment I did, utterly and inexplicably love her. With all my heart as if ... as if we were the same family. As if she were my child, sister, mother rolled into one. As if we are the same being made entirely out of love's energy. The young women backed away, bumping people as they left so we could look at each other for as long as possible. Sometime later Nargess' voice woke me.

I was surprised to find myself sitting on the floor of the main room. My head felt full of cotton wool. It was almost 10 pm, two hours had passed. As we headed out so she and Mamma could eat a proper meal, a wave of panic came over me. I took a sharp breath as we weaved through glass hall after epic glass hall.

'Lauren, are you okay? Do you need to sit down?' I sat down. Mamma was reading the Qur'an in a nearby corner. It took us a while to weave the short distance to her, so intense were the crowds of black-draped women.

'What do you want to do now? We will be really late getting to Esfahan,' she said, 'which is fine. It's your choice, this is your visit. We are with you.'

I was amazed to hear myself say, 'I want to stay here, in the mosque, tonight. Is that possible?' Nargess' face showed no hint of surprise, as if a western journalist having an out-of-body experience and wanting to sleep in her home town mosque happened every other day.

'We'll find a place to lie down later. Lots of people stay here all night, don't they Mamma? But for now let's eat!'

The air in the splendid courtyard revived us all. A melody of doves fluttered from minaret to minaret. Qom's high street was old style stalls along a bustling highway, and thronged with locals and pilgrims browsing mobile phone stores and clothes racks. A man was selling underpants outside the main mosque, which made us giggle without reason. Even back on the street I felt as if I were cocooned in a bubble of happiness. It was as if I had the best lover of all time and he was about to ring. I was expecting his call and that was why my heart was so full. Men rode motorbikes with young women on the back. The wives (surely not anything else!) held one hand on their chador, the other around their husband's waist. 'Salam,' I said to everyone we passed. These women smiled easily, they were happier than anyone in Iran I had so far met during Ramadan. But then the streets of most towns are more relaxed and friendly than capital cities. Only in Qom were the ancient culture and customs of Persia and Islam more keenly celebrated. Besides, it was too conservative for nose plasters and space ship hijabs.

After eating our burgers we walked back into the mosque, passing once more beneath reflected light from glass shards on the high domed ceilings. At last we found a space by a wall outside the main prayer areas, the stone floor covered only by a thin rug. It didn't matter and I felt rather than heard myself snoring. After midnight I awoke again, stretching in the new quiet, and Nargess took me on a series of walks. We wove out into the splendid courtyard and a little girl tugged at my sleeve and took my hand in hers. She was cute, a dark haired version of my eldest daughter, Alex, all bright-eyed sweetness. She asked Nargess where I came from. Without waiting for an answer she looked me in the eyes: 'I love you,' she said. Bemused, her mother apologized and told her to leave me alone, but she wouldn't let go easily. Finally pulled away, she watched me with solemn eyes. Like the women earlier backing away into another room never taking her eyes from my face.

Turning to Nargess I said that I shouldn't think about converting until I could observe Muslim lads chanting Islamic prayers without seeing potential jihadists. I was only partly joking, though the word 'converting' silenced us both. It fell onto the marble of the courtyard like a rock. I rolled the pebble-word 'conversion' around my mind. A universal narrative was happening all around me and I was feeling the pull towards its unifying centrality: The oneness of God. This Muslim unitarianism was rolling round in my mind and I thought of Prophets with dark skin and long beards. The men in scriptural stories were brave. What about the women, though? I now met so many ground-breaking, brilliant women who were also able to submit to family and to religion in a way that expounded joy. I had seen them commit to their marriages in a way that proved love, they accepted hardships in a way that showed faith. I was not, could not be like them. How could I ever be like them?

My inner voice offered a quiet series of counter thoughts: 'Are you happy in this moment?' Yes.

'Do you like this feeling and have you felt love in this mosque?' Yes. Then you have nothing to fear.

'Nargess,' I said, 'I'm now in my forties and I'm beginning to realise how little I know about existence beyond getting through every day'. A large elderly lady was swaying to and fro next to us on the stone fountain ledge in the cooling pre-dawn courtyard. The old lady's cheeks were tear stained. She caught my eye and I smiled back, 'salam'.

'What's this lady's name,' she asked Nargess in Farsi.

'Sarah,' I said. Sarah was my birth name, Lauren the work name I'd selected aged twenty just to join the actor's union, Equity. Sarah seemed right again, authentically me.

'This lady knows less now than when she was younger. But tell her it's okay, she is doing fine'. Nargess translated for me, her eyes wide.

'She has just said what you said, except in Farsi.' The lady was rapidly repeating other things I had been saying all evening to Nargess.

'Are you getting this, Lauren?'

Another thought panicked me: Am I getting the 'call' to faith? My inner voice was swearing like crazy. My mind was telling me I did *not* want to convert to this faith. 'You have gotta be kidding, no please, this is crazy, stop this,' I thought. Followed by: 'Don't ever let this stop, it's lovely!' My thoughts tumbled over each other in a rhythm of hope and terror. Sat on a soft red carpet with my back to a vast white wall 'something' had taken root inside me. Something big – vast – which wouldn't go away. I was no longer a tourist–reporter seeking an exclusive scoop on what happened inside an Iranian mosque in Ramadan. I was someone else, something else. The peace in my heart told me I was invited into the global family of Muslims, that I was now a part of the *ummah*. I fell deeply asleep. There were no dreams, just a deep silence.

At dawn I was woken by the *adhan*, the call to prayer. Inside the mosque it was much louder than I had ever heard it before. 'Time to pray,' I said aloud, then I jumped. I wanted to pray like it was the most natural thing in the world. Nargess was nowhere to be seen, so rubbing my eyes and pulling my robe straight, I wandered outside to a sink. Cold water ran off my hands, then my face, my hair, my forearms and finally my bare feet. I went back inside to the thousands of women pilgrims lined neatly row behind row. I stood between them, relishing the body's warmth after the water's chill. The recitation started, it was relayed from the men's prayer area by speakers. After a while everyone bent at the waist and I did the same. I stood up again, repeating 'Allah is Greatest' before falling to my knees and putting my forehead against the soft, musk-smelling, carpet.

In the car on our drive to Esfahan, Nargess and Mamma left me to my thoughts. Every so often the long dusty route was broken up by a petite dome above a neat roadside mosque, there for the travellers' convenience. I remembered that in France they had drive-through bread shops, and in Australia they had used to have drive-through 'grog' (alcohol) shops. In the Muslim world they had emergency roadside places of prayer.

'Do you want to stop and pray here?' I asked Nargess after yet another passed by.

'No, Lauren. We are combining prayers as we are travelle s. Do *you* want to pray?' She didn't quite smirk. But almost.

'No thanks,' I said laughing, a little nervously. 'I'm *not* Muslim.'

***

Forty hours later I was back in the midst of the morning school run. Never had the stressful normality of a Monday morning been so welcome. I was back to being just a working mum, struggling to make sure my children had everything for the complex needs of a London school day. On the plane from Tehran to Heathrow I had reviewed my time in Iran though the calm lens of distance. It was clear to me that I had been on the verge of a nervous breakdown. Odd to consider that a mental collapse seemed preferable to converting to Islam, but that was how I felt. I had, I told myself, been through a pretty tough couple of years. In a mosque, some kind words from strangers had tipped me over an emotional precipice: A nice precipice, but clearly what I needed was some 'me time'. Not a new faith!

'Alexandra sports shoes!' Alex pounded up the stairs bringing our poor, elderly and understandably grumpy neighbour to his door.

'Would you mind ...'

'... telling the girls to walk up the stairs quietly?' I finished the sentence for him, as he pulled a face. 'I'm really sorry, I'm late which ...'

'... you always are in the mornings?' Harry helpfully concluded for me.

Holly came downstairs, pulling on her duffle coat. 'Holly violin!' She pounded up the stairs before I could stop her. Harry wordlessly slammed his front door.

Finally both girls ran outside. I put my keys in the lock then froze. I didn't have a headscarf on. The weird thought shocked me. I tried to dash after the girls, who were already sprinting towards the woods. I couldn't do it. There was as much chance of me leaving the house 'undressed' without a scarf as there was of my doing the school run in a onesie. I didn't have time to debate the peculiar thought with myself. I ran upstairs, tutting on Harry's behalf with my noisy clumping, dashed into my bedroom and rooted through the unpacked case for a scarf to wear. Belting downstairs I looped the scarf, which had been a gift from Iran, awkwardly around my hair and neck. At the entrance to Highgate Woods the girls did a double take when they saw me.

'Mamma why are you wearing a scarf?' Asked Holly.

'I don't know,' I said.

'Oh,' she replied, skipping away.

At the school gates my cheeks turned red with embarrassment. The usually chatty, coffee- morning parents didn't say a word when they saw me, which was a mercy. The political editor of the *Jewish Chronicle*, Martin Bright, raised an eyebrow silently as we passed each other. His paper would soon be the one of the first to take aim at my newly-found faith. I could no longer deny what was happening, I was being drawn towards Islam. No one needed to coerce me, I was not being 'groomed' online by fundamentalists, nor was I being tempted to join the latest trend, because Islam was seriously uncool and not in the least chic. Plus, it would pretty much be a disaster if I came out as 'one of them' and tried to continue working in the mainstream. Who would take seriously a white woman dressed as an Arab?

All day I simply couldn't push away the feeling that like Jim Carrey in *The Truman Show* I had lived my whole life on the set of a reality show, until then. Only I hadn't realized how much of the script or the scenery was fake. I had a feeling that I wanted to see things as they really were, to see the real world and experience a deeper life and a different level of liberty. The conflicting thoughts rolled around in my head, making writing impossible. That evening I made the girls pancakes for tea, then I sat the two bathed pyjama-bundles on the living room carpet where our best chats took place: 'Mummy's thinking of becoming Muslim and this will affect you as well. So I want to ask you what you think about it.'

Ever since my first trip to Palestine, and throughout my work at the Islam Channel, they had become used to hearing one sentence said over and over: 'Nice people Muslims, seriously lovely people.' They had their own experiences of Muslims. Osama from the Free Gaza movement had kept in touch and become 'Crazy Uncle Osama' to the girls. They weren't afraid of the word Islam and knew Muslim people as individuals rather than an amorphous group to be suspected – or feared. I explained my feelings to the girls as best I could, considering I didn't really understand them myself. The girls listened carefully and when I'd finished I said: 'So what do you think, kids?'

They asked for a few moments to talk it over and went into a private huddle that I was excluded from. At last Holly, with a seriousness only an 8-year-old could manage, said: 'We'll be back in a bit. We are going to our bedroom to write down questions for you.'

A while later as I cooked dinner, Holly tugged on my apron: 'Mamma, we have three questions to ask you before you can become Muslim.'

I wiped wet hands on a tea towel with a solemn manner, it wouldn't do to giggle when the children were being so grown up and serious. I sat back on the carpet ready for my inquisition. Alexandra began: 'Mamma. Question one: when you are Muslim will you still be our Mummy?'

The depth of the words stunned me, I was touched. Their most urgent thought was whether I would be with them always or if a new faith would take me away from them. I had done my best to devote time to family life as a single parent. But until then my weekend evenings were still about getting a babysitter so I could go out to openings or alcohol-filled events. If I gave those up and devoted myself to quiet nights of cooking and prayer that would be a big change for our family life. Plus, there would be an end to grumpy hungover mornings.

'I will definitely still be your mummy,' I said. 'In fact, I think I will be a better mummy!'

They huddled and ticked their bit of paper. Alexandra continued: 'Mummy, if you are a Muslim will you still drink alcohol?'

How did they come up with this stuff in only ten minutes? I had been interviewed dozens of times by press and TV journalists and I had never been asked anything so deep. I had tried to go 'cold turkey' in recent years and had managed to reduce my drinking to just one night a week. But to go teetotal in British society? Was it even possible? Right up until that very moment the idea had been as laughable as it was improbable. Had there been such a thing as a high school 'Yearbook' when I was a teenager, the title under my photo would have read: 'Least Likely Ever to Embrace a Religion Prohibiting Anything She Enjoys.' A feeling of tranquillity was still inside me after my last mosque visit. Would it be enough though to control the lusts of my lower self? Cravings and desires which had, for decades, held me in their grip. I could hardly believe it when I pledged: 'If I become Muslim I will never drink again.'

The girls looked at each other. They told me later they had longed for the toxic effects of alcohol on the mind, body and soul to be gone from their parents' lives. I remembered feeling the same hatred of booze when I had been a child. Society has trained me to accept it. Now I would reject it.

Stepping forward, Holly showed her usual potential for the drama in a situation (inherited from her grandfather, no doubt). In her crisp, clear voice she read out the final question: 'Mamma, when you become Muslim will you still show your chest to men in public?'

'What?' And. 'Still!?'

Since my mid-twenties, I had used my looks as a kind of unwritten bonus at job interviews, although I would never have admitted that to myself. I had coaxed famous male interviewees to speak in a less guarded fashion using a flirtatious manner. Like many female professionals, modern sexism dictated that whilst I could choose what to wear, when I was around men in power the more my clothes clung attractively to my shape (in the days when I was skinny), the more success would come easily with those same decision-makers. It was like training a monkey, getting young women to dress in a way that aroused men whilst also making it invisibly 'worth our while.' My 8-year-old daughter was still lecturing me for all the times I had worn low cut tops to parent's evening. They were both saying they didn't like it. Holly emphasised the point: 'And last week when you came to school you bent down to pick up my bag and I saw the Maths teacher looking and he could see ...'

'Okay Holly, thank you. I hear what you are saying.' Blimey, this was hard! I ran a hand through my hair trying not to snip the first response that came to me. I knew what the expectations of Muslim women's public dress code was. It was similar to the way I had seen the Jewish girls dressed in Golders Green when I was a child: Ankle-length skirts, loose blouses. Muslims replaced the wigs of Orthodox Jewish women with a scarf, like the Catholics used to wear.

'If I become Muslim I will dress modestly whenever I leave the house,' I told the girls. There was a pause. They looked at each other. Then they jumped up, clapping their hands: 'We love Islam!' They announced.

Now my children were accepting of Islam, would I actually go through with it? A few days after my interrogation, I decided it was time to formalise my decision. That Friday, my friend Anne and I stood nervously outside the Islamic Centre of England in Maida Vale. Anne has the sweetest nature of anyone that I know. She is all about 'energy', 'nature' and 'spirituality', tenets that make up her personal path to understanding human existence. Entering the large double doors, I had no idea what to expect of the conversion ritual. But I knew that Anne would treat whatever that might be with the utmost respect. If only she and I could stop giggling like schoolgirls every time we looked at each other.

I was blissfully unaware of the schisms and sectarianism which was rife in the Muslim world. The term 'Sunni' or 'Shia' did not hold any relevance for me, whatsoever. Why should they? I was focused on the fact that by the end of the afternoon I would no longer be a Christian, but a Muslim. That was at the forefront of my mind. Behind that realization, which was nerve- racking enough, another was hitting home. Once (if) I took the testimony of faith, God could genuinely expect me to do the stuff that Muslims did. Islam was not the passive 'anything-goes' faith which modern Christianity had morphed into. It had boundaries that I would need to navigate and adhere to, if I cared about God being happy with me ...

I held Anne's hand as we walked up the large stairs towards the offices. I was not in a spiritual frame of mind. I was focused on what I was about to lose. Would I really be able to quit bacon sandwiches, red wine

CHAPTER 15
WHICH ROAD TO TAKE

Which Islam is best? 'To feed the hungry and to greet
with peace those you know and those you do not know.'

Prophet Muhammad PBUH

I had no thought as to what 'kind' of Islam I would be following. I didn't have any idea of what options were available. My
faith was simple and based on basic articles of faith: God was
One and was not a part of a trinity; He hadn't had a child; He
wasn't born and would never die. All of the prophets, starting
from Adam and ending with Muhammed, peace be upon him,
had brought mankind the same message, which was: there is
only One true God and He alone is worthy of being supplicated
to and worshipped.

There was a book to believe in too. Muslims believe that God
revealed His wisdom and instructions through one main book,
but also through the many connected scriptures which came before it as well, like the Psalms, Torah, and the Gospel, although
the original teachings of those books had been distorted or lost.
The Qur'an is God's final revelation to mankind, given to Prophet Muhammad, peace be upon him. It was easy to accept and it
had remained unchanged in 1,400 years. In my visits to mosques
in many different countries, I had noted Muslim women in the
lines chanting sometimes vast-seeming sections in unison. Once

or twice, when I had visited in Ramadan, the imam had stumbled in a recitation. Dozens of voices knew precisely where he had been and were able to shout out the precise cue to restart or correct the verse.

As for belief in angels, it was interesting to find research from America that showed the majority of people believed in the unseen beings. At the same time, people had stopped asking a basic question: If angels existed, who were they working for and to what purpose. Islam, like Christianity, named angels as God's obedient beings who worked to administer His kingdom. Similarly, I had never stopped believing in Judgment Day. To me it was the only way that human existence made sense. The life of this world and all that is in it will come to an end on an appointed Day. At that time, every person will be raised from the dead and God will judge each person individually, according to his faith and his good and bad actions. The pain, the apparent unfairness so many go through because of abuse, war, or famine, would all be justly dealt with at one time. And the bliss of eternity when compared to the pain of months or even decades mean that the pain never existed, because eighty into eternity is a non-existent, meaningless amount of time. As for belief in Destiny and Divine Decree, since God is the Sustainer of all life, nothing can happen except by His will and with His full knowledge.

Anne and I were shown into the cleric's office. The sheikh who greeted us turned out to be a Canadian. He was over six-feet tall and wore a white shirt and trousers covered beneath a brown cloak. He bore a striking resemblance to the US actor, Samuel L. Jackson. Out of the corner of my eye I saw Anne's shoulders begin to shake at the surprise presence of a Hollywood icon in a white turban and brown cape. Sheikh Ahmed Haneef tried to put me at ease. He made small talk about family and the weather, then he posed soft questions about the background to my decision. He drew out whether I understood the basic tenets of the faith. I did.

'You're ready, sister,' he said.

He guided me to say two phrases, first in English, then in Arabic: 'I testify that there is no Allah except Allah alone without Partners. And I testify that the Prophet Muhammad is the final Prophet and Messenger of Allah.'

The words were transparent and clear. I was not being called to follow a half-man, half- God, a concept I had never grasped. I was vowing to be obedient to the sole God of all existence. The room had the heavy, woollen quality I remembered from the night in the *masjid*.

'Are you feeling this?' Anne asked, sensitive to the atmosphere.

I had just taken the greatest oath of my life, to submit myself to the God of all creation. I acknowledged the Might and Majesty of the single force behind life and death and rebirth. I was taught to recite the first section of the Qur'an, *al-Fatihah*, and Anne joined in supportively, repeating line after line of the strange Arabic words.

'*Bismi-Llah al-Rahman al-Rahim*', in the name of Allah the Most Merciful, the Most Compassionate.

From time to time the sheikh interrupted us saying: 'Roll your 'r's' more, ladies, like this: Bismillahirrrrr Rahmanirrrr ...'

Feeling like an illiterate child, the words began to work their beauty upon us. I tasted each syllable, thirsted for the meanings, savouring sounds eternal and deep in flavour.

'*Subhanaka Allahumma wa-bi-hamdika*', O Allah, how perfect You are and praise be to You.

We had done our ablutions, *wudu*, earlier. It was already one of my favourite things to do. There was a real excitement as I ran water over my hands and face with the intention of purification. By the time I ran my fingers from the back of my head to the front, I was covered by a tingling sensation.

Muhammad, the Messenger of Allah, said: 'When a Muslim, or a believer, washes his face (in the course of *wudu*), every sin which he committed with his eyes will be washed away from his face with water, or with the last drop of water; when he washes his hands, every sin which he committed by his hands will be effaced from his hands with the water, or with the last drop of water; and when he washes his feet, every sin his feet committed will be washed away with the water, or with the last drop of water; until he finally emerges cleansed of all his sins.' (Narrated by Muslim)

Now that I was Muslim, my duties began right away. We were taken downstairs to the vast prayer hall where a short partition wall allowed men and women to pray separately. As an outsider this 'segregation' had always seemed outrageous. Now, preparing to pray it made sense. I didn't want to be watched by men as I crouched down. A younger girl would have been shy, bending over before hundreds of men and going into prostration. I was glad of the single gender privacy. People cried too when they made *salah*, I'd seen that happen. Would I want a stranger of the opposite sex seeing me so openly emotional? At the same time, a man trying to pray could have his thoughts wander far from the divine realm if a young woman were in his eye line. I preferred gender separate privacy in my moments of deep reflection and emotional vulnerability. I had been subliminally led by press headlines and a constant stream of negative attitudes towards preconceptions and prejudices about Islam and what little I had known of its practices. The religious observances of Muslims were not explained in rushed news bulletins about 'extremists' or 'fundamentalism' to offer the 'why' of the faith. I was finding out to my surprise and relief that each step, every recommendation made to the believers came from both common sense, and beneath that a 'wow' factor of spirituality.

Salah is poorly but usually translated into English as 'prayer.' My prayer as a Christian had become the equivalent of asking a bank manager (who didn't trust my collateral) for a loan: it was a half-expectant whine for things I wasn't in desperate need of in the first place. *Salah*, on the other hand, recognized God's Mastery of everything in existence, for all that was and all that is to come in the future until and beyond the 'Day of Judgement'. It is a vast acknowledgement that no one and nothing else is worth asking for help except for The One. Anne and I both prayed in the near empty hall at Maghrib time.

When I got home, it was 10 pm on a Friday night and my first weekend as a Muslim stretched ahead of me. The girls were visiting relatives so I was alone. What did I do with my time now that drinking and meeting friends (for drinking) was not an option? On my bedside table was the copy of the Qur'an in English I'd taken from France. Despite it being there since my return from Iran, I hadn't opened it. I opened it now to chapter two, Surat *al-Baqarah*. I was face-to-face with the same verses which had judged me so harshly five years earlier. There in Arabic, and besides that in English, were the words which once upon a time had made me want the book to be as far out of sight as possible. I read out loud:

This is the Book, wherein there is no doubt; a guidance to those who are al-Muttaqun (the pious and righteous persons who fear and love Allah). Who believe in the unseen and perform al-salah (worshipful prayer), and spend from what We have provided for them [including caring for their parents, their children, and charity to the poor]. And who believe in that which has been sent down to you (Muhammad) and in that which was sent before you and they believe with certainty in the Hereafter. They are on (true) guidance from their Lord, and they are the successful. (Qur'an 2: 2–5)

I was reading the book as one seeking guidance rather than seeking fault within it. My new faith didn't mean passive muttering of some lines on a page before closing my eyes. Like every believer I was now called upon to change my life, to positively affect the lives of those around me. Words without action were a redundant litany. I read again: '*Who believe in the unseen and perform* al-salah *(worshipful prayer), and spend from what We have provided for them.*' After accepting Islam with my heart and with the words of testimony that afternoon, the Qur'an had turned from being a book only of warning and Divine wrath into an astounding tribute to the Creator who wanted to give me care and guidance.

I was astounded.

I was *very* relieved. I was in love.

I believed.

Lying in bed, I thought back to the first winter my family spent in the French farmhouse. Despite having travelled around the world, I was basically a suburban kid who had never grown a flower, much less a vegetable. We had arrived in the south-west corner of France at the tail end of summer. The garden had been bursting with colours and late fruits such as figs and grapes. But within weeks I watched in confusion as the jasmine vines which wrapped around the gables of the front door began to lose leaf after leaf. The peach tree went from an abundance of fruit to a measly stick. The flower beds looked like graveyards for dead foliage. By January, I was convinced that my poor gardening skills had killed every growing thing on the three-sided garden around our home. One icy day, Roget, the elderly farmer who had made us instantly welcome (despite our Englishness), stopped his battered car outside our house and knocked on the door holding a bag of dead pigeons he had just shot. They were still warm. He gave them as a gift, telling me gruffly in French: 'pluck next to a burning fire and throw the feathers into it.'

I took the chance to ask him a question that was bothering me: 'What happened to our jasmine vine and our peach tree? Why have they died?'

He had looked at me, nonplussed. So I said it again, trying every French phrase I could think of to describe our entire garden's demise. Each time I finished my question he would just say: 'Quoi? (What?)' Finally Roget looked at me like I was crazy and said: 'It's winter.'

Never, until taking my *shahadah*, had I fully grasped the profundity of the dying of vegetation that comes about consistently to most plants, flowers and vegetables. I had walked to our fig tree, staring, then to the walnut trees, past the destitute strawberry patch and at the back door stopped by the brown sticks which weeks earlier had yielded vast (but sour) grapes. This was all going to come back? Impossible!

He sends down water from the sky from which We bring forth growth of every kind, and from that We bring forth the green shoots. (Qur'an 6: 99)

In mid-February, after a dozen brutal frosts and a foot of snow, the first peeping shoots of recovery began to appear. I walked with the children around the garden, examining the miracle of rebirth first-hand. They cried in excitement: 'Look Mamma over here, even this one is alive!'

***

I decided to 'come out' to my fellow Muslims. The opportunity came via the Islam Channel and Mohamed Ali, who had invited me to their annual boat party for VIP guests attending the weekend's Global Peace and Unity conference at the ExCeL Exhibition Centre in the Royal Victoria Dock. I remembered sneaking alcohol into Muslim events, of meeting Sheikh Raed Salah with a low neckline. Now my stomach churned with embarrassment.

Getting ready, I dreaded the idea of Muslims who had known me for years as 'about-town' Lauren seeing me as 'one of them'. My ego hated the idea that somehow they had 'won' and I had 'lost' in the battle for the best way of life. I forced myself to an extra prayer, asking God to take the petty thought away. That morning I had begun the process of removing plunging necklines and clinging clothes from my wardrobe. I had dragged two bin liners of newly inappropriate tops all the way to the local Cancer Research shop. Had I done my clear-out with Nargess she would have told me to keep them all, I only had to add a long sleeved t-shirt underneath or a jacket over them to 'halalify' them. For the event I chose a long black skirt, red shirt and black suit jacket, nipped at the waist, topped by a loose red hijab that let my fringe show. I had absolutely no idea how to dress or what my 'style' could be as a Muslim. It would take almost a decade to find out.

Why had nobody told me sooner about how much nicer life would be for me as a Muslim? Okay, I had warned colleagues not to try and convert me, but still. They had left me to wander amongst them for years in the spiritual darkness. Was that friendship? All those Muslims I had met in the UK had been silent, out of respect for my English culture, and now I wished they had spoken to me earlier about the faith and its clean and simple moral guidance and way of living. Despite having worked for half a decade at Muslim-led TV channels, I had few close Muslim friends. They kept to themselves and I hadn't been invited into a single home by colleagues or to any gathering outside work. Had I been so awful an example that their children had needed to be 'protected' from my entering their home? I began to wonder if that's what some people had thought.

It was an icy October evening when I boarded the Thames boat moored on the Embankment. The first person who saw me was Yusuf Chambers, co-host of the Iraqi families fundraising event, who looked aghast at my hijab. There was no cool pretence, my change was not going to be greeted quietly. Weaving through the throng, Yusuf came over grinning from ear to ear.

'Blimey, Lauren, you did it then? I knew you would, *masha'Allah*! Congratulations on the best decision you will ever make! What a bargain you have just made! Have you any idea? The fakery of this life for eternal bliss, what a win!'

He seemed so pleased for me that I forgot my earlier trepidation at coming along. It had been four weeks since my *shahadah* and I wore hijab every day. Often I felt anxious about appearing in public in the scarf, I had been waiting for the wrong person to see me and report it to the newspapers and for the floodgates of opprobrium to be opened. Here it felt different, I could relax for a couple of hours with members of my extended Muslim family. Everywhere I walked people were shaking their heads in amazement and congratulating me as if I had won a Nobel Prize.

Carl Arindell spotted me as we both towered head and shoulders above everyone else. I joined him in the buffet queue and with typical dry humour he said: 'Well, well, well. Sheikha Lauren. You know you won't be able to drink wine any more right?'

Mohamed Ali of the Islam Channel was next: 'Lauren, you must come to the Global Peace and Unity conference tomorrow. We will give you ten minutes on stage, fifteen! Make your *shahadah* public!'

A clear head, free from alcohol, was giving me the space to examine my life, my choices, my interactions with others, and above all the intentions that were behind my actions. Intentions are the 'why' of what we do. They are an important element in Islamic understanding where the 'ends' do not justify a series of corrupt 'means'. The intention is the reason we embark on any new course of action. It must be made at the start of things, and then carried through at the heart of the process. That's why you will hear a Muslim about to eat or drink murmur, 'Bismillah.' It means 'in the name of Allah' and is both a reminder and a pledge to eat with the purpose of staying strong in order to be a better mother, father, colleague, or community member. Worshipper. The Prophet Muhammed (peace be upon him) said: 'Any important work that does not begin with *Bismillah* is devoid of blessing.' The best way to achieve blessing in our deeds is to remove the ego from the process, making the action for the purest and recommended reasons – solely for the sake of Allah.

I told Mohamed Ali that I wouldn't go on stage the next day, I wasn't ready. After only a partial reading of the Qur'an, and still learning the basics of *salah*, I felt to go fully public with my conversion now would be too soon. Also, the media blowback could be painful not only for myself but my children. If the press were interested in you in any way, better by far to announce being a member of Alcoholics Anonymous, or to admit having a gambling addiction or to having an affair than to admit belief in Allah. The other admissions could be dealt with in a double-page spread seeping with sympathy and understanding. Announcing I had converted to Islam would mean a barrage of aggressive questions on matters I had not even begun to look at in detail. I just wanted to privately tread along the road to learning the ways and manners of my new faith.

***

And (the unbelievers) plotted and planned, and Allah too planned, and Allah is the best of planners. (Qur'an 3: 54)

The next day Alexandra went with me to the Global Peace and Unity (GPU) conference, the largest Muslim and multicultural event of its kind in Europe. Over the weekend it is said that up to 100,000 people pass through the shopping souk and the vast performance arena which seats 4,000 people. We went to the backstage guest area at the GPU for her to meet Mohamed Ali and the other guests. There had already been controversy as Baroness Warsi, the most senior Muslim in government and the keynote speaker, had according to reports been 'forbidden' by Prime Minister David Cameron from attending.

Backstage we were introduced to Jermaine Jackson, brother of Michael and part of the Jackson 5, who to my surprise was wearing a red keffiyeh and I was amazed to learn that he was a convert to Islam as well. His journey began in 1989, he said, whilst on a visit to Bahrain. He had asked a group of children what faith they were and the way they spoke so joyfully and enthusiastically about their love for Islam led to him to seek his own answers from scholars. Reading books about Islam dispelled his previous, media-inspired misconceptions.

As Alex and I were leaving the backstage area, Mohamed Ali caught up with us: 'Lauren, what are you doing? You are on next.' He knew very well I had said no, I had tried to argue for privacy, for time to learn, for protection.

He countered this would be an opportunity to connect with the global *ummah*, that support may come from many unknown quarters as a result to guide me to greater knowledge. After all, wasn't this the 'peace and unity' event and weren't those elements the basis of all my activism?

I squatted next to Alex, who even aged ten was proving a great source of wisdom and could sniff out a fake intention a mile away. I wanted to escape the vain lures of celebrity attention-craving, Islam was private, a subtle inner tonality.

'Alexandra,' I said, 'I don't want to do this.' She squeezed my fingers.

'It feels really right, Mamma. Allah is with you. And I'll be next to you.'

I prayed inwardly, asking for Allah's guidance and protection. My heart felt perfectly at ease and I trusted this would be the right moment. Holding Alex's hand we strode onto the podium before thousands of people. I had no speech, no notes, and I spoke with the intention to only, as the famous Christian theologian, St Francis, put it so beautifully, be a 'channel for peace.' I wanted to express love for people struggling for their rights in Palestine. To express love for the Muslims who had been kind enough to accept me into their homes when I travelled. I wanted to share a flavour of the immense love I had found for Allah and His Prophet Muhammed, peace upon him. I spoke for three minutes, which felt like hours.

I stood on stage before an audience of more than a thousand in the hall, and unknown to me, millions globally.

'My name is Lauren, and I am a Muslim.' I announced.

CHAPTER 16
TOWARD THE STRAIGHT PATH

'Those who look for seashells will find seashells;
those who open them will find pearls.'

Imam Al-Ghazali

About a year before the GPU event, when I stood onstage and made the first public declaration of my new Muslim identity, I met Farukh and Raz – two Muslims from the north of England – on Viva Palestina, the organization founded by George Galloway to break the siege of Gaza by land. Almost £1 million worth of humanitarian aid was raised in just four weeks and in February 2009 a convoy of 110 trucks left the UK, driven down through Europe and entered North Africa on the 5,000-mile route passing through Belgium, France, Spain, Morocco, Algeria, Tunisia, Libya and Egypt. In Libya, the Gaddafi Foundation donated seventy more trucks of aid. I had joined the convoy at the port town of El Arish, just as negotiations with Egyptian authorities to complete the delivery to Gaza broke down. It was dusk and I was in the dusty, run-down town centre surrounded by men with chest-length beards and George Formby accents. We sat together outside the Egyptian tea shop on garden chairs next to the cracked, uneven road.

'Ee, I could murder a good cuppa tea tha' knows,' said Hassan, from Blackburn. 'These Arabs 'ave nay idea how ta make a decent cuppa'. To disappointing groans, the tea shop owner brought another tray of orange liquid in miniature glass cups.

Shouts reached us from the car park where the authorities had allowed the convoy to park a second night. The atmosphere was tense and the secret police had been sending agents to harass convoy members. Sectarian graffiti, pro-Fatah and anti-Hamas, had been daubed on the sides of some trucks as the drivers slept. At the far side of the car park, George Galloway was puffing on a cigar in a better quality local cafe where he was having stand-off negotiations with regional politicians. Officials were threatening to stop the entire convoy from entering Gaza. The terms they set out were simple: they would keep half the trucks, the donated ship and a large chunk of the aid 'for security reasons.' 'For a bribe' muttered the Brits, who had been on the road for a month to bring aid this far. It felt like a state-sponsored mugging.

A sudden scream of pain ripped through the night to shouts of 'Allahu Akbar! Allah Akbar!' The Blackburn lads and I leapt to our feet, sprinting the 200 metres to the car park. A huge crowd of Muslim men from northern cities of the UK were shouting insults in English (and Urdu) at a mob of Egyptian men in leather jackets, some with bandanas covering their faces; secret police. Two of the convoy members were injured, lying in the dust with blood pouring from head wounds. British medics who had come on the convoy were giving on-site treatment, applying bandages and cleaning wounds. Rocks were still being hurled at us from different directions.

From nearby streets, hundreds of riot police emerged armed with weapons and shields. Their colleagues drove vehicles to blockade the convoy in the car park so no one could leave. A scuffle broke out behind me and like arrows from a battle scene in *Gladiator*, rocks began raining down on us. Convoy members were now in full fight, not flight, mode and instantly picked them up as they landed and hurled them back. I saw water cannons being rolled out and just metres away the police were putting on masks, preparing to deploy tear gas. Dozens of Viva Palestina volunteers were lying injured around us on the ground. Like the men around me, I was undeterred. Our mission to bring aid to the people of Gaza was paramount. What was personal safety when compared to the human suffering being endured just 53 kilometres away? 'Sister Lauren ...' I was being gently pushed back through the angry convoy members towards a London fire engine whose lights were illuminating the bloody scene. 'This is not women's work. It's dangerous. Let the brothers handle things.' Hassan walked me over to where George Galloway was having a coffee break from the fun and games he was going through with men from the North Sinai council.

'George, Lauren wants to be in the middle of that lot. I said she ...'

'I'm not a little girl I can take ...'

George put a hand up and patted the bench with red cushions next to where he stood surveying the anarchy. Puffing away on his cigar, he said: 'Lauren will make notes about what is going on so she can report on the Mubarak debacle. Won't you, Lauren?'

I was being reprimanded by a powerful uncle who everyone wanted to impress. Muttering under my breath, I pulled the notepad from my backpack and sat down to watch and make notes. It took all the tactics George had in his political toolbox, but thirty-six hours later all vehicles made it across the Rafah border. With the exception of the fire engine donated by the Fire Brigades Union (FBU) and the boat. Both of which were blocked by the Egyptian government.

At Rafah, the passports of all the drivers and fellow volunteers were returned but I was still waiting to receive mine. I bitterly recalled the fun and games when I had tried to return home just seven months earlier. The trucks started up and the convoy began to move on its way into Gaza, leaving me standing in the one place I hated more than anywhere else, Rafah checkpoint. My initial unease was turning into panic, and one lorry remained when my passport was grudgingly returned to me by the Golem official. I knew he recognized me from the previous September but it would be eight years later, in 2017, that the head of a major UK charity explained how close I

had been that night to not entering Gaza at all. He had spoken with Egyptian officials, who were adamant I was banned from the region, and it had cost him more than £1,000 of his own money in bribes to allow my entry into Gaza. 'We wouldn't leave you behind, sister,' he told me.

It was a hellish period for the people of Gaza. On 27 December 2008, Israel launched a major military offensive called Operation Cast Lead. According to the UN's Goldstone Report, during the twenty-two day offensive the Israeli military killed more than 1,400 Palestinians, 82 per cent of them innocent civilians, including 333 children. Thousands more were left with life- changing injuries, orphaned or homeless.

The day after our arrival, we were treated to a night of celebrations as thanks for the convoy's success in bringing much-needed humanitarian aid so many thousands of miles. Raz and Farukh were social care workers from Birmingham, and outside the conference centre in the warm March air, Farukh opened a backpack for me to look inside. It was packed with cash.

'We promised donors it would *only* go to people in need, hand to hand. We don't know who to trust here! Can you help us distribute it?'

It wouldn't be easy. Like the Free Gaza crew before our convoy was under the close observation of Hamas government security in order to monitor the actions of the visitors, probably amongst us some infiltrators out to cause trouble. I knew what to do. I called a friend with a car and in the melee after the event, as hundreds of people and cars poured onto the main street all at once, the three of us snuck away. Sometimes we felt were followed but we managed to dodge security for three hours and complete our entirely charitable activities. We drove to Jabaliya camp, which was without power so it was pitch black. My Palestinian friend, who was driving, called ahead and then took us to a household of six blind children, whose mother was also blind. In the flickering candlelight of her bare room, she sang a song she had learnt on the internet and adored. It was the Christian hymn, 'Amazing Grace'.

Just before dawn, as we were searching for a family who we had been told were in urgent need of finance for medical aid, we walked single-file down the tight back lane of a refugee camp. The only light was from a mobile phone and my eyes were on my feet as I tried not to break an ankle on the uneven, stony ground. A sound made me look up and I caught my breath. I was faced by six men in army fatigues and balaclavas with large guns slung across their shoulders. The man in front ignored me and led his troop forward in silent formation. As they marched past I noticed they were shorter than me. I glimpsed one of the hands holding a gun strap, a teenager's hand. Children like Faris Odeh, trying to protect their refugee camp when they should have been asleep. The next day I left Gaza with the convoy members, wondering how long those boys I had seen in the back street would survive.

Soon after the GPU event I received a surprise call from Farukh and Raz, who wanted to drop by my flat to say hello. They were on a working visit to London and were driving down from their native Birmingham. It was good timing as I needed the company. The reality of becoming a Muslim in London on my own had started to hit me quite hard and I had a growing feeling I'd made a mistake. Had I really glimpsed through the curtain of reality in the Iranian mosque? With the perspective of time that now seemed unlikely. Praying five times a day seemed too much as well; I was struggling to manage three times a day. I was in the most challenging period of being a new Muslim, my heart longed to immerse itself deeper in faith, but my mind was filled with conflict and doubt. The temptation to return to my old ways was immense. I had no male company; how did you even find a husband when you couldn't speak to men on their own? So far, I had stayed on the straight path. Just. How much longer I could last, only Allah knew.

I loosely pulled a scarf over my hair as the Birmingham lads rang the bell. When I answered the door they exchanged a look, but made no comment about the hijab as we chatted on our way to the kitchen. Making them coffee, I looked in the fridge and saw the unopened bottle of wine, there since before I said my *shahadah*. Defiantly I opened it and poured myself a glass. I wanted to challenge the men at my table to judge me; I wanted to challenge Islam to control my lusts; I wanted to know and to make it clear that I could still do what I wanted, when I wanted. No one and nothing controlled me. I had had enough! My friends watched in an uncomfortable silence as I sat down with the glass in hand. They laughingly recalled our night in Gaza spent handing out charity and hiding from Hamas. As they filled me in on all their news, I finally raised the glass to my lips. The crisp white wine met my tongue, rolled across my taste buds like a visit from a long-lost friend. It touched my throat and I gagged. I ran to the sink and spat it out, close to vomiting.

'Oh my God,' I gasped, 'How did I ever drink that stuff it's vinegar, disgusting!' I sat back down wiping my lips with a napkin.

Raz couldn't hold his silence any longer. In a thick Brummie accent he asked: 'Wharrar yow playin' at, Lauren? What's going on! You're in a hijab and trying to drink alcohol, are you feeling okay?' His tone was one of concern rather than judgement so I began to laugh, embarrassed at my confusing behaviour.

'I've accepted Islam, brother. I'm Muslim' I said.

Their faces lit up instantly. Even as the wine question lingered between us, Raz still had tears in his eyes. They shouted a chorus of 'Allahu Akbar, Allahu Akbar!' Which can only have terrified and further annoyed poor Harry in the flat below.

'Why does it make you so happy I'm Muslim?' I asked over yet more strong coffee at the pine table.

'Because after years of helping others, you've finally done something for you,' Raz said.

My work was going well. I was researching, interviewing, scripting and doing the voiceover for a series called *Diaspora* on Press TV. It documented the forced expulsion of 750,000 Palestinians from their homes and lands by Jewish terror groups in 1948, led by the first leaders of Israel. I had searched for survivors of the catastrophe known as 'al-Nakba' who were now based in the United Kingdom. In Bristol I met with an eyewitness, Mr Hammuda, originally from Lydda. It was a painful and moving interview. Mr Hammuda recounted how 19,000 townspeople, plus civilians fleeing from other areas which had already been invaded, were forced onto what became known as the Lydda Death March. On 11 July 1948, Jewish soldiers moved into Lydda and the men of the town gathered in a mosque and surrendered. Later 176 bodies were found, they had been massacred. Mr Hammuda told a horrendous account of the looting of family goods and jewellery by the invaders, of the shooting of his father and the loss of his homeland.

Towards the end of the interview in the Hammuda family's living room, I felt rather than heard somebody enter out of my eye line. Whoever it was brought with them a presence that made it feel as if all the energy in the room had been pulled towards them. My neck yearned to bend and see who was there, until it became almost painful not to turn and look. As I wrapped the interview, I thanked the elders, both Mr Hammuda and his wife, and finally turned around to see who had been behind me. It was a young man of just over twenty years old, kneeling silently. He was in a white thobe (robe) and skull cap. His beard was neatly trimmed but long for someone so young. His name was Ali, and in our brief introduction and during some outdoor shots with his grandfather, Ali told me he was a student of knowledge, an ustadh. I knew from our meeting that whatever he was studying gave him an air of profound peace that reached out to those lucky enough to be in his presence.

I was looking beyond the Shia community for knowledge about the Prophet Muhammad and the Qur'an. I felt too shy to go to a mosque and ask for assistance and I had no idea what help was valid or available to converts online. Eventually, through a Facebook post I asked Muslim sisters who I was in contact with if they could recommend someone to take my children and I forward on 'the straight path'. I quickly received a response from a young sister called Abrar. She said her cousin, although in high demand for his teaching skills, had said he would be honoured to visit our home once a week and help. I made lots of *du'as*, prayers, asking for Allah's support in sending someone to enlighten our household.

It was a Tuesday evening in February 2011, after school, when the doorbell rang to our flat in Muswell Hill. Standing before me was the young man, Ali Hammuda, from the Bristol interview. He was Abrar's cousin and I felt that Allah in His Mercy had chosen this gentle person to be our first Islamic teacher. Weekly, for some months, Ustadh Ali sat with my daughters on the living room floor as I prepared dinner. All I could hear over the rattling of my pans was the Ustadh's voice, which was always followed by my girls' joyful laughter. Were they learning anything useful and deep, I wondered. Wasn't Islam supposed to be learnt in the serious, rather sour way I had seen on TV? YouTube clips and documentaries on TV showed children rocking back and forth as they recited the Qur'an, I had never seen a clip which showed an Islamic lesson where there was laughing. My daughters, though, couldn't wait for their weekly lesson.

One evening, after Ustadh Ali had gone home, I asked Holly what she had been learning. Incredibly, she began to rattle off stories from the Qur'an about Moses. She gave me a touching description of the Prophet Muhammad's kindness to children and there was much, much, more she knew as well. I felt embarrassed. The children now knew more than I did. After that, the Ustadh kindly agreed to teach me the basics of Islam as well. For months we stayed on only two subjects, *al-Fatihah*, the opening surah (chapter) of the Qur'an, and its deeper meanings. Classes were combined with a report of an incident which happened to the Prophet in front of a gathering of many of his friends and companions, known as Hadith Gabriel (Jibreel). In the hadith (report), the angel Gabriel visited the Prophet Muhammad in public to go over the inner and outer aspects of true faith. In a to-and-fro exchange, the basics of belief were deeply yet succinctly described.

In Islam, what we learnt from the encounter meant:

Testifying that there is none worthy of worship except Allah and that Muhammad is the Messenger of Allah.

To establish the prayers.

To pay the zakat (charity from your wealth). To fast (the month of) Ramadan.

To make the Pilgrimage to the Kaaba in Makkah (if one has the financial means and health to do so).

The Angel Gabriel also asked, what is belief? The Prophet Muhammad, peace be upon him, confirmed it means to believe in Allah, His Books, His messengers, His angels, the Last Day, and Divine Decree.

Never had I experienced such deeply spiritual lessons. I was being taken on a journey that encompassed all of the knowledge given to mankind about the reason why we exist and how to navigate all our vital relationships. This included the way in which Muslims are expected to relate beautifully with people of other faiths, to our children and even to the natural world. At the same time this understanding meant diving deep inside myself to begin chiselling away at the usual character flaws, like backbiting, ingratitude and bad temper.

During a break in one class, I noticed the Ustadh glance at my bookshelf. When you have a teacher whose knowledge you greatly admire, you automatically wish to show them the highest respect. It was therefore inconceivable for me to want to own *anything* regarding Islam of which my teacher would disapprove. The very idea of disappointing such a teacher becomes hideous.

I watched, stomach lilting, as Ustadh Ali tilted his head slightly. He never frowned nor showed disapproval in all the time I had known him, but that head tilt was enough to trigger in me the unholy suspicion that I had books of which he disapproved. Most of my new books had been donated by Shia imams and they focused on the life and times of Ali, the highly esteemed young cousin of the Prophet Mohammed. Ali was the first young person to accept Islam, he was a brave warrior who was so loved by the Prophet that he was married to his daughter, Fatima, herself a brave figure of devotion and courage. I knew Ustadh Ali was from the majority *Ahl al-Sunnah*, or Sunni school of Islam, and I was becoming more aware of the sectarian struggles between the Sunnis and the Shias. It was a painful realization that men and women, all of whom believed in Allah, could be full of fear and hatred for one another. After a while, Ustadh returned to our lesson at the kitchen table with the children.

Nervous questions poured from my lips: 'Are the books wrong to own, shouldn't I read them? Will they confuse me? What should I do?'

Before he spoke on important matters, or rose to leave, eat, or open a book, Ustadh began with: '*Bismillahir rahmanir Raheem*'. In the name of Allah the Most Merciful the Most Compassionate.' He began the same way now: 'Ukhti (sister),' he said, 'I am not going to tell you what to read or what not to read. All *hidaya* (guidance) is with Allah. But if you don't mind I would like your permission to ask some questions of you and then perhaps to follow your answers with a small piece of advice.' His politeness and tone were immaculate, as always. The questions he asked me were simple:

'Have you read the Qur'an completely in your own language?'

'Almost,' I replied. That was a good start, he said.

'Can you read, speak and understand classical Arabic yet?' It was a rhetorical question as he knew I could not. 'Then this is my advice for your consideration. Once you have read the Qur'an in its own language of Arabic many times. Once you have taken on board and learnt to live the meanings and lessons it holds. After that you should move on to study the life of the Prophet Muhammad, peace be upon him. You should seek to know as much as possible about him. Once you have done that, do your best to implement his daily practises as your own, in manners, behaviour, relationships, in all things'. He paused and sipped the water I had poured for him, thoughtfully. He was so measured it was hard to believe he was just twenty-three. '

Once you have done these things to the most excellent standard which Allah allows, then you may be ready to explore, with understanding, the sad events which took place after the Prophet's mission in this *dunya* (world) was complete.'

It was remarkable advice. For the greatest scholars and imams of Islam throughout history would never have had the arrogance to say such a thing as: Qur'an – done! Hadith – done! Okay, I have mastered the divine text and lessons from the *Sirah* – what next? The knowledge was so deep it was never ending, and I had not even – in terms of textual understanding (or any other basis) – taken my first sip to quench the soul's thirst. The Holy Qur'an summarizes how infinite is the divine knowledge of the Creator and how paltry our own efforts at understanding the multiple realms of existence, by comparison:

And if all the trees in the earth were pens, and the sea, with seven more seas to help it, (were ink), the words of God could not be exhausted. Indeed, God is Mighty, Wise. (Qur'an 31: 27)

My teacher's simple message was clear. I would make the intention to begin my journey (and stay) on the straight path of Qur'anic knowledge and Prophetic example. Nothing could be more beautiful or beneficial to my understanding or my inner growth. He also advised me to pray 'istikhara' in all things. This is the particular prayer that asks God to guide us to decisions which will benefit in this life and the next.

From that day onwards I felt guided to follow the Ahl al-Sunnah school of belief, the Islamic tradition of more than 90 per cent of the world's Muslim population. Sadly, however, my appearances at Shia events would be used by some as 'evidence' that I followed their school of thought. Although how I prayed and what I believed was really no one's business but my own. Later, other social media trolls began using talks where I mentioned the Prophet's Companions to somehow justify their own vile verbal attacks on the Shia community. I strongly believe that believers are united by *shahadah*, the belief in One Allah and in Muhammad as the final Prophet and Messenger. That is greater than what is being used to divide our communities and to set us at war with one another.

CHAPTER 17
STAYING HUMAN

'Often love between two people intensifies
not because of beauty or some advantage but
because of sheer spiritual affinity.'

Imam Al-Ghazali

My short announcement at the Global Peace and Unity event went viral and the media interest and predictable mocking began the next day. I quickly wrote two pieces outlining my feelings about my new faith and a little about the journey which led to my decision to convert. In the current climate, the response to them was on a spectrum which varied only between outright mocking and hate-filled prejudice. After my first appearance in hijab, the producer on Sky News rang about my regular (ten year) slot as a monthly newspaper reviewer: 'You won't be needed,' he said, 'due to unforeseen changes to the way we want to go forward. Thanks for everything, Lauren.'

I was about to sample the reality of life as a Muslim woman seeking work in Europe whilst wearing hijab. Like millions of others, I would see the impact on my own family of the fact that Muslim women are three times more likely than other women to be unemployed or looking for work. We are 71 per cent more likely to be jobless than those who have the same educational qualifications and skills, but who happen to be white and Christian. However, I was still a great deal luckier than many sisters suffering what was finally being recognized as an economic 'triple bind', where race, gender and faith goes against them at interviews for employment.

I was expressing exactly the same political views on Iraq, Palestine and on Islamophobia as other colleagues and a growing number of academics. They were views I had held before my conversion, yet now they were painted as 'extreme' when covered by the press. It took me a while to realize what was going on. I had just lost something I had barely recognized when I had it: white privilege. As a journalist I understood I would certainly now face being discredited and denounced in public by my former friends and employers. Since 9/11 it was career suicide to attempt to publish an article showing Muslims or Islam in a truly positive light. 'Balance', I had been told when writing about Palestine, was what readers expected. It was the integrity upon which all news output relied. Yes, ideally that would be the case. Only the reality of 'balance' was increasingly redundant in modern journalism. Mainstream news channels and newspaper publishers such as Associated Newspapers, Fox News and Rupert Murdoch's stable of TV channels and publications, had an editorial 'line' to be followed on political, social and religious stories. Where was the idea of 'balance' in that mode of output? Everything fits in with editorial policy reflecting the publisher's point of view. There is no such thing as objective 'balance'.

Take that first article I had written from the West Bank. True, it had been published as contracted by the *Mail on Sunday* magazine. My editor kept his word regarding the content of my copy remaining unchanged. In fact I was so convinced that I had beaten the system by this point that on the day of publication I called Afif Safieh, telling him to buy the paper. I just might have subverted the entire media system of inherent bias relating to Palestine and Israeli Apartheid! Then, I rushed to the newsagents to buy a copy. On the front cover of the magazine was the photo of myself with the shoeless kids I'd interviewed in the rubble of their homes. And right across their innocent faces, the headline read: 'Which of these children will be a doctor, which a terrorist?'

Yet, the children in the photo had told me they wanted to be doctors, teachers and psychotherapists. They wanted to help their people but not to harm others. Despite living in tents after Israeli forces had bulldozed their homes in Jenin, not one of them had said they wanted any part in future violence. It was one of the things that had so moved me about meeting them. I felt anger at what had happened to them and to their families. It was their faith and kindness which had calmed me down. Faith helped them to cope using patience and rejecting hatred or revenge.

Was that heading unbiased or prejudicial? It was certainly not borne out by a single interview with a single child I had met and was not related to the article's findings in any way. But there it was, just the same; a clear reminder for the paper's readers that Palestinian children were as likely to blow themselves up on jihad as to want a decent life. After seeing the headline, I went home and curled up into a ball on my bed. The editorial machine had used my experience to reinforce the stereotype that Muslim Arab kids want to kill. I felt sick. So I had no illusions that my spiritual journey would be treated with any less brutality. I never expected it to be examined in a fair or balanced way which would invite genuine consideration and discussion, nor did that fact make me angry in the least. I understood the situation of former colleagues and friends: If you have invested years of commercial resources into asserting to your consumer base that Islam makes people crazy, violent and extreme, you cannot possibly give serious credence to one of your own journalists accepting that same religion. The narrative about-turn that would entail would be like reading the entire *Harry Potter* series only to find out on the last page that Voldemort was a great bloke who had just been misunderstood. News consumers would feel rightly cheated and the public would lose faith with the editors. As I saw it, the media had only two choices where the story of my conversion was concerned, either to paint me as emotionally unstable, thus letting them off the hook for having published so many of my articles for so many years, or destroy my credibility, so that when I challenged their agenda it would not matter to the general public anyway (see above).

I would get emails asking if I had read the latest attack piece and the appalling comments beneath. I read none of it, I had found my truth and it was beautiful. Nothing could interfere with the clarity and peace I was enjoying. Or so I thought.

***

On 16 April 2011, the body of Vittorio Arrigoni, was found murdered in Gaza City. One of the brightest lights in human rights activism of our time, for most of the three years since we had sailed to Gaza, Vik had remained behind to help the people. He was part of the International Solidarity Movement (ISM) and his special area was standing side by side with the farmers and fishermen whose livelihoods were blighted by the blockade. Seeing his blindfolded and beaten face on news bulletins was agony. I remembered how we had gone to the Erez crossing together in solidarity with an injured grandmother in a wheelchair. Despite having guns pointed at us from the Israeli turrets, everyone taking part felt safer around Vik's cheerfulness, not to mention his powerful shoulders. His presence at protests and demonstrations allowed him to document the impact of the blockade. It also made him a target for arrest and brutalization by the Israeli military. During my month in Gaza, he twice had bullets miss him by mere millimetres as he was working alongside Palestinians trying to fish or farm their land and sea. He left behind a deeply moving eyewitness account of the appalling massacre carried out by Israeli forces against the people of Gaza from December 2008 to January 2009. Vik served as a human shield whilst working with the Palestinian Red Crescent ambulances. Israel, he wrote: 'Turned the hospitals into morgues.' He reported hundreds of civilian casualties pouring into Al Shifa hospital against only a handful of actual fighters injured in the deluge of bombs pounding homes, camps and schools from the land, sea and air for twenty-two days and nights. Vittorio's memory would be honoured in Gaza by a street and a school carrying his name.

It was the first great test of my faith. I felt sick at the news he had been killed and I cried until I had to stop out of sheer thirst. Feeling devoid of the emotional energy required to fall on my face in thanks or praise, I stopped praying. As the days wore on, it felt as if a curtain had been drawn between myself and the opening I had experienced in spirituality and belief. I was not only grieving for Vik, I was grieving for my soul as well. On the third day not praying, I took the London Underground to Press TV where my show, *Remember Palestine*, would be dedicated to his memory. Sitting miserably on the train, I was internally begging Allah over and again to forgive me for my heedlessness in abandoning *salah* at my very first challenge. Utterly defeated, I was begging Him under my breath to bring me back to His closeness. Tears welled in my eyes and my throat was burning with the desire to break into sobs there and then. I carried on praying silently, through the entire forty-minute journey towards Hangar Lane.

Three stops before my destination, a young man in his twenties who looked Pakistani, stood up to disembark. He stopped directly in front of me, looked me right in the eyes and asked my name: 'Are you Lauren Booth?' He asked. I nodded. 'Then this is meant for you.' He put something into my hands and I watched stunned as he left the carriage and headed for the station exit. Looking down, I saw on my lap a red hardback book. The title on the front cover almost stopped my heart from beating. *The Disciplines of Prayer*, by Imam Khomeini. It was open to chapter four and my eyes fell upon the guidance I needed at that very moment: 'One of the significances of the repetition of worships and the increase of supplications and invocations is that the heart is affected by them ...'

I walked quickly to the studios, arriving out of breath, shut the door of the dressing room behind me and began to make up for the prayers I had missed the previous days. The message I had been given by the surprise presentation of a book on a train seemed clear to me: A terrible thing had happened and other disasters would also happen. '*Hayk al-dunya*' as they said in Gaza, that's life. But instead of stopping prayer, moments of pain had to be the catalyst to increase my worship, not to decrease it.

CHAPTER 18
HUNGRY FOR TRUTH

'If a person does not avoid false talk and
false conduct during fasting, then God does not
care if he abstains from food and drink.'

Prophet Muhammad PBUH

A year after becoming Muslim, the girls and I entered our first Ramadan. They were far too young to be required to fast, which begins at puberty, but they were excited at the idea of joining me for *suhur*, the pre-dawn meal, at weekends throughout the Holy month. During the first week they tried to fast, half a day here and there (in reality missing breakfast), with the spiritual benefit of doing so to please Allah. Their efforts were adorable and my heart swelled with gratitude to Allah every time we prayed together, hearing their high little voices lifted in praise. They had mastered Arabic far faster than I had managed and quickly began to help me with my memorization and pronunciation.

I had not done any research into the deeper meanings of Ramadan. Having seen fasting in Palestine I knew how my day should look and what I should do but I had no idea of the 'why' element in the ritual. As a result, I had no clue about the inner dimensions of fasting. Instead, in the lonely night hours eating alone during the week I was reminded that I had been *very* single for eighteen months. I stewed over my own day-to-day issues and missed the precious moments of wakefulness to make extra prayer and read the Qur'an. As with all elements of Islamic teaching, there is an inner and an outer dimension to the pillar of fasting. Not eating or drinking from dawn until dusk controls the body's desires. That is the starting point towards the end goal which is *taqwa* – increased closeness to and reverence of God. Major religious traditions, including Buddhism, Christianity and Judaism, all contain a recommendation to fast in order to reach a higher level of understanding and to control the lower self, known by Muslims as *al-nafs*.

As a result, I went to work at Press TV, did my shows then came home and did my household chores before eating in a completely exhausted state. After several long days like this, I could feel myself falling into a lower, not a higher state of *iman*. I was missing out on the greatest blessings of the month, including things I had no idea I should be profiting from and sharing: communal prayer, known as *tarawih*, was one recommended element. Above all, the month was a time of exerting time and effort to do extra charitable deeds, such as visiting the sick or joining programmes to feed the homeless and the needy. But I did nothing of that kind, no one called us and no one was there to advise us. It was horribly lonely and confusing.

If our first Ramadan was testing, then the first Eid for my daughters was nothing short of a disaster. The two festivals of Eid are times for Muslims to relax together and enjoy themselves. I was unsure how to have 'fun' anymore. I made up parameters that removed singing and music, going to the cinema, dressing up, just about anything girls and women like to do. No one had told me I could do this. I was creating a life which 'looked' religious but was a mutation. Meanwhile the two Eids, Eid al-Adha and Eid al-Fitr, are periods which every Muslim is guided to enjoy. They are times which come after arduous spiritual labouring, the month of Ramadan and the first ten days of the month of Hajj. Allah knows mankind has a need to laugh, to enjoy different foods, to make jokes and smile. Didn't he create those things for us too? I didn't ask for advice when I should have. It was a cursory lesson in how it is possible through human error to make something joyful into something miserable.

Some things I had less control over; we had no family who were Muslim to visit and the wonderful Muslims who welcomed us with open arms and such sweetness the rest of the year were now too busy with their own families to remember to invite converts who were on their own. However, I thanked Allah for letting me experience that isolation for in the coming years it would allow me to connect with many new sisters and families with a better understanding of what they were facing as new Muslims in western communities. As a result of that experience I now attend and hold gatherings, including Eid, for new sisters and their children.

After the confusion of my first Ramadan and the loneliness of my family's first Eid, a great gift was already on its way of which I knew nothing and had no part in planning.

CHAPTER 19
CALLED TO PRAYER

'Never have I witnessed such sincere hospitality and
overwhelming spirit of true brotherhood as is practised by
people of all colours and races here in this ancient Holy Land.'

Malik El-Shabazz (Malcolm X)

Days before the final flights were to leave from all around the world for Hajj 2011 CE, I received an email from a brother I didn't know. Shazaad Mohammed, president of the Canadian Dawah Association (CDA), wrote to say they had a last-minute fully paid place with his group for Hajj. This would include a follow-on visit to Madinah, where the Prophet Muhammad, peace be upon him, spent much of his later life and is now buried. My heart began beating with hope as I read the lines of the email over and over again. I wrote back, thanking brother Shazaad for the invitation but saying that I was unfortunately, unmarried. A woman making Hajj needs a *mahram*, a male relative with whom marriage is forbidden, to accompany them. He wrote back saying that as with other certain groups, CDA guests were covered by a fatwa (ruling) allowing single or divorced women to make Hajj as part of the specially-permitted group.

My mind was running overtime. My daughters could be cared for by family, but even then there were two things which seemed impossible: With less than ten days before Hajj I needed to obtain a special pilgrim's visa from the Saudi Embassy and to find and pay for a return flight to Jeddah. Every flight to and from Hajj terminals in Saudi Arabia had long since been booked by the more than two million pilgrims en route there from every corner of the globe. I found one ticket available online; first class and at a price that was way beyond my capacity. One of the many beauties of Islam is the allowances made so that religious duties are not a burden on people in their varied circumstances but a bonus to your life. If you are sick, or pregnant, or a traveller, you are either pardoned from fasting (e.g. if you are suffering from diabetes) or you can 'make up' (complete) the missed fasts when you return home from your travels. New mothers do not have to fast at all, or make up any they miss due to pregnancy and motherhood, until their baby has been weaned after up to two years of breastfeeding. Hajj is no exception in this, it is a pillar, a cornerstone and an expectation only on those who can afford it, are free from debt (or have agreements for debts to be paid) and who are healthy enough for what is an arduous physical and emotional task.

I settled my heart to accept I was unable to go due to financial responsibilities. The next day, Saturday, I made a simple post on Facebook, thanking Allah for the invitation and making the intention to save and go as soon as He next permitted. Many kind people going on Hajj said they would remember me and my children in their prayers. Then a sister I didn't know based in Birmingham, called Hind, asked me to direct message her. We made our introductions and then she asked to call me as she wanted to speak to me directly. Hind was a single mother who had just gone through a painful divorce. She had a young son and a little money saved. In fact it was the precise amount for the first class flights and she wanted to pay for them. I absolutely refused: 'These are your savings for you and your son, sister. It is not allowed to get into debt to make Hajj so I couldn't take your money as a loan either at this time.'

She was insistent. Allah, she reminded me, made things happen for His will and to His perfect plan. If it was His will for me to attend Hajj that year, then it would happen. 'I don't even have a visa!' I reminded her. I should not resist, she said, Allah was in control of all things. She wanted to pay, to have me pray for her and her son at the Kaaba, the square building draped in gold embroidered black cloth which millions of Muslims walk around as part of this important ritual. I refused to accept the money but she continued to insist. After much urging, I finally agreed to send her the flight details with a scan of my passport. 'If Allah wills,' we agreed.

On Monday morning, just five days before final flights to Jeddah for Hajjis (pilgrims), I received my plane ticket. The sister had paid for my flight and her only thanks, she said, must be my prayers to Allah, during Hajj, for her and her son. I prayed two *rak'ats* in thanks, then I rang the Saudi Embassy in London. Before my call was answered I made another prayer: 'Oh Allah, all life is in Your hands. You alone do I worship and You alone do I ask for support.' The Hajj official all but laughed aloud at my request for a last-minute visa. As the phone call went downhill rapidly, I bit my lip from trying my old persuasions. I did not say my name was 'Lauren', in the arrogant hope to cheat the system with bogus celebrity. I stuck to the name on my passport, 'Sarah Booth'. On Hajj, our social status is deliberately stripped away: men dress in identical white towels, women without make up in plain long abayas (robes). Be it low or high status, in business or the community, we were all the same before Allah, except in levels of dedication, and my 'celebrity' name was meaningless before His greatness. Once upon a time I had used 'Lauren' to get into nightclubs, for free passes to Glastonbury Festival, for free designer clothes and more. I would not degrade this beautiful Islamic rite with the same pride. I remembered reading the Prophet warned his friends that the person who has a particle of arrogance in them won't even smell the fragrance of Jannah (Paradise).

'There are no visas, madame. The lists were finished last week. You are too late.' 'If Allah wills,' I repeated again.

There was a long pause. 'We have one appointment with the person responsible, Jummah (Friday) at 9 am. We close at 10 am. It won't happen, I assure you, but you can come in for an appointment if you feel compelled.' The flight to Jeddah was Friday evening, the day Hajj would begin. I would need to do my show at Press TV then go straight to Heathrow.

'If Allah wills,' I repeated.

On Friday morning, the Saudi visa office at the Embassy appeared empty. Wheeling my case behind me and clutching my passport I went through the scanner at the front door. The man at the desk looked at me: 'Name?'

'Sarah Booth, slave of Allah'. He raised an eyebrow, picked up the phone and spoke in Arabic to an official in the offices above us. After handing over my passport, I was told to take a seat in the hall. By 10:30 am I knew two things would have to happen: I would have to leave in order to rush to work and record my show. And the visa office would close for the last time before Hajj.

As 10 am came and went, I made *dhikr* under my breath: '*SubhanAllah, Alhamdulillah, La ilaha illAllah* (Glory be to Allah, Praise be to Allah, There is no God but Allah).' I had seen my passport taken upstairs from the security desk thirty minutes earlier. A young lady in a business suit and hijab called my name and motioned for me to follow her. In a pleasant, bright office a high-ranking Saudi official (judging by the fine cut of his suit) showed me to a seat before his desk. He asked my name and I told him: 'Sarah Booth'.

'You are too late for Hajj, Miss Sarah.'

'Allah can do all things,' I said.

'Are you Lauren Booth?' He asked. What should I do now? Was this a test of my humility by Allah who was the All Knowing? What should I say? I stuck with my intention to be honest and trust God.

'My birth name is Sarah Booth, all praise to Allah.' The official looked at me thoughtfully then picked up the phone. He spoke in Arabic to someone else. We made small talk for a few minutes without Hajj or visas being mentioned again. When the clock on the wall said 10:27 am, the young lady in the suit who had brought me upstairs came in and handed back my passport.

'Remember us in your *du'as*. Congratulations, you are going on Hajj,' I stared blankly for a moment looking from one to the other.

'*Subhan'Allah.*'

I thanked them profusely over and over then ran to Kensington High Street Underground station dragging my suitcase behind me with tears of gratitude running down my face, soaking my scarf. Fourteen hours later, at 2 am in the morning, I would land in Jeddah.

In 2005, I had entered the Holy Land of Palestine as a Christian, full of excitement at visiting places talked of in the Bible as the birthplace, areas of preaching and learning of Jesus, peace be upon him. Six years on, I was walking in the footsteps of the Prophet Muhammad, foretold by Jesus as following him to deliver mankind's final revelation from Allah. I was nervous about my appointment with the black-shrouded mystery known as the Kaaba. A monolith thousands of miles of away in the centre of a harsh desert land, whose stone had been placed in position as a place of worship by the father of faith, Ibrahim (Abraham) alongside his son, Ismail.

After landing in Jeddah late at night, it took me two days to find my group after a not- unusual debacle at the Hajj terminal. No one there spoke English and the phone numbers I had been given for my Hajj tour leader appeared to be out of service. After three hours of uncertainty, I was ushered onto a waiting coach by a security official with the words 'English okay – go!' Thinking my tour had been found, I left the terminal on the coach only to arrive at a rustic set of apartments almost an hour from

Makkah with a group of international Hajjis who had no idea who I was. I was humbled to be invited to stay in one of their rooms overnight whilst they sought my actual group. On the second evening, as I tried to exercise *sabr* (patience) in light of the mix up, my phone finally connected with the CDA group. The other Hajjis I had stayed with were so sweet to me it brought tears to my eyes. They all kept saying in different European languages: 'stay, stay, you are most welcome with us.'

The van arrived and after a tearful goodbye and much waving I set off to meet my group with the CDA. Who knew what the coming days would bring? We were all emotional about the chance to make *du'as* – to ask Allah – for blessings for those we cared about. I had a list of special prayers to make, which included my parents to accept Islam, my children to flourish in every way, for the sick sisters and brothers who had contacted me for prayers to be given health, for success in this life and the next, for a good husband who loved Islam and always, always, peace and justice for the people of Palestine. I arrived at the comfortable hotel where my group was staying, and it cheered me to see it was within walking distance of the Kaaba.

I was sharing a room with three other convert sisters, as excited and nervous as I was at the undertaking of Hajj. One by one we showered with the plain soap someone had thought to bring with them. It was important that perfume and make up were not used, pilgrims need to be in a state of plainness and simplicity for the rites to come. Imams participating and guiding our group explained the rituals. They would teach us the history of why they took place and protect us from a very real risk of harm; in recent years stampedes and fires had injured hundreds. I had taken off all of my makeup and redressed in a state of *ihram*. Suddenly there was an urgent pounding on the door:

'Please sisters, open the door, it is an emergency I need to see my wife!' I opened the door to a large, very tall Arab man standing distraught in the hotel corridor, blushing bright red and hopping from foot to foot. Looking down I was shocked to see large amounts of chest and legs on display as he clasped onto what appeared to be dishtowels where his clothing should be.

'Sorry, what?!' I was too stunned to speak.

'My wife is in there, she has my *ihram*, she gave me our son's instead!' His European wife ran to the door and hurled two large white towels, still in their plastic covers, at her husband and slammed the door. There was a moment of stunned silence. My knees buckled, as they do when something slapstick happens around me (which is a lot), and I collapsed to the floor unable to stop myself howling with laughter. We were about to begin the greatest spiritual ritual of our lives but we were only human, after all. The others sisters joined in, with the man's wife repeating over and over: 'But why did he leave his room like that?' Which kept setting us off again. Eventually we wiped our eyes and calmed down and I apologized sincerely to the man's wife and asked her forgiveness.

'I forgive *you*,' she said, 'but only Allah can forgive my husband that display!'

Later in the hotel lobby I found her husband and sincerely apologized to him as well, which he accepted graciously. Our group headed out into the night.

It was 2:30 am and 75 degrees, I was shivering with anticipation as we wove our way towards the Kaaba, amongst people of all nations and cultures, on a run-down main street of hooting cars and unfinished high-rise developments. The whole area, for at least a kilometre in every direction, was heaving with Muslims who had heeded the call from their Divine Master. We were chanting in a thronging unison: '*Labbaik Allah huma labbaik* (Here I am at Thy service O Lord, here I am),' accepting the most important invitation of our lives. Islam is for all people of all times. Allah made it clear there is no racism in His favour to mankind. He has no preference for either gender, for the rich over the poor or vice versa. The way the believer behaves, and displaying good manners at all times towards the Creator and towards one another, are the factors which divide us into levels before Him. And He can do whatever He wills.

It was incredible to me as I walked, face scrubbed and plain, to think about how my life had changed in just twelve months. A year earlier I would have viewed this march of Muslims from the mind-set of journalistic anthropology. I would have thought, 'how interesting', or 'how amazing and odd is this dedication to ancient rituals'. I would have been interested, removed, detached and bemused. I would also have been horrified at my appearance, muttering, 'what did they do to you?' Anyone who had known me before would have agreed that I was not one to give up habits I enjoyed, no matter how bad they were for me. I had failed on a million diets down the years and battled to contain a liking (possibly an addiction) for alcohol. Yet now I found thirty-day fasts exciting. I'd even (virtually) stopped swearing, which having grown up with a father from Liverpool is pretty much a miracle in itself. I was walking alongside strangers and people who knew me from TV and newspaper articles with my true facial age on display. The cracks and lines of truth were on show. Once someone knows you from your professional sphere, TV folk have a 'currency' that needs to be protected. Your personal weaknesses are challenged one by one on Hajj: vanity swapped for humility, comfort for physical hardship, arrogance for patience, and all in the face of huge challenges in a crush of sleep-deprived humanity.

I trod as gently as possible over pilgrims sleeping on the dusty streets between acts of worship. What sacrifices had they made to reach the Kaaba? It's not unusual for an entire village to save for decades so one amongst them can make the blessed pilgrimage to Allah's House, where they pray for those left behind. There were men from villages across Africa and Asia on the pavements. They used backpacks as pillows, their loose clothing as bedding. Their food, boxes of snacks handed out by state-sponsored teams from the Hajj department of the Saudi government, was provided free, three times a day. Though I wished they didn't include yogurt in the meal containers, I thought, as we gently jostled through the vibrancy of the *ummah*. Our eyes feasted on the colourful vista, noses soured by curdled lactose.

The vast white marbled courtyard suddenly blazed around us. My eyes winced at the stadium-sized floodlights making day of the night. The sisters and I were barely keeping each other in our sights, plunged as we were into the ocean of humanity flowing in one direction. At last I reached the vast arched doorways of stone and grey. Removing my sandals was an epic struggle, as other Hajjis attempted to do the same with no room to bend in the crowds. I managed to wrangle my sandals into my backpack alongside bottles of water without being knocked over. The water was essential as the lesser pilgrimage of 'umrah still took many hours. Inside the vast prayer compound I heard my ragged expectant breath as my feet accepted the cool of the marble beneath the white hall of pillars. My eyes darted here and there, wanting to take it all in. As we got closer to our object of desire, my eyes prickled with tears. I saw the backs of heads, and brown male shoulders against the whiteness of the *ihram* robes, all shuffling forwards like one body, step by step. Litanies in Arabic were flying upwards all around me: A million appeals for cures to all mankind's ills heaved in sobs of repentance. Where was it, where was it?

The sound changed and a light breeze brushed my overheated cheeks, crushed in the human flow. Above my head the orange-black sky fought with blazing neon lights for dominance. Ahead I glimpsed cranes, and above them the giant clock tower. I was not interested in such paltry displays of human arrogance or fleeting riches. I lowered my head and focused on the space between the shoulders ahead of me. Then, right in front of me rising out of a chaos of humanity, as silent as it was solid, was the Kaaba. I froze. Hajjis tutted as they manoeuvred around me, stopped as I was just outside the main throng of worshippers circulating in a never- ending flow to my right. I could not take my eyes off the square building, sixty feet in length, width and height. This was 'Baytullah', the House of Allah, its sanctity older than history. Muslim tradition states the first stone building of praise was ordained by God to be built in the same proportions as the House in Heaven, al-Bayt al-Ma'mur. Prophet Adam, peace be upon him, was the first to build it. Later Prophet Abraham re-made the holy shrine in Makkah, helped by his son Ismail.

The first house (of worship) appointed for people was that at Bakka; full of blessing and of guidance for all kinds of beings. (Qur'an 3: 96)

All I could do was stare at the layers of ink-black stone hewn from the hills surrounding Makkah then intricately smoothed by skilled craftsmen. The four corners were roughly the four points of the compass. I stumbled, allowing myself at last to be taken around the heart of the Muslim pilgrimage. I grappled with the guide book hanging on a string around my neck, which told me to say different litanies whilst on my *tawaf*, circumambulation of the Kaaba done in sets of seven. I couldn't take my eyes off the four walls, thirty-foot of crushed humanity from my arm's reach. How I wished to caress and kiss those walls, to press my face against its coolness and sob my heart out with a thousand, a million, appeals. I walked in that stunned state, round and round seven times, anti-clockwise.

I saw other pilgrims place their hands on the Yemeni Corner of the Kaaba. There was no way I could make it through the crush, so I joined the Malaysian sisters in their pristine white floor-length capes and raised my right hand towards it instead. The curtain of black brocade (*kiswa*) covering the actual stone of the Kaaba bares the testimony of faith: 'There is no God but Allah and the Prophet Muhammad is His final Messenger' in the weave. Near to the top, I could see the vast gold embroidery covered with Qur'anic text. Beautiful does not begin to describe the sight nor the feeling the believers' heart receives to be near the transmitter of Divinity at the centre of the world's landscape.

The grand marbled floor beneath my feet was dirt 1,400 years ago. In the time of Prophet Muhammed, peace be upon him, there was no great complex, just the black stone building surrounded by 360 and more icons. Pilgrims from across the desert would deliver gifts to their gods, yet at the same time pray to Allah, who they remembered from tradition but had forgotten His Oneness. Small huts or stone homes were dotted here and there overlooked by hills. I stumbled, my legs suddenly weak. Prophet Muhammad himself had trodden this same path. Him! That beautiful man of mercy. The man who not wanting to disturb his cat as it lay on his cloak, cut his clothing to save waking it. That blessed man who when the very person who had thrown rubbish and abuse at him every day fell ill, he went to visit to see if they needed help. I started to cry, unable to stop the sobs wrenched from deep within. He had been here and I had missed him. How I missed him! I want to see you oh Muhammed, Mustafa, guide, beloved.

We reached our beds at dawn, had four hours sleep and rushed back to the Kaaba. Every breath away from it wasted existence.

***

The next day our Hajj rites began in earnest with another 'umrah, a repeat of the night before.

We completed the seven circuits of the Kaaba then moved to an area alongside where millennia before there were two small mountains called Safa and Marwa. Today, only the very top stones of the peaks are visible, immersed within the vast complex for ease of passage by the many millions making the rites each year. The purpose behind these rites is to remember the story of the mother of Ismail, Hajar. Prophet Ibrahim brought his second wife, Hajar, and their infant son to the midst of a lonely desert. There he left them with dates and a leather bag filled with water. When Hajar noticed that Prophet Ibrahim was about to make his way back to Palestine alone, she followed him saying:

'O Ibrahim, are we to be left alone in this valley with no water, or food or companions?' The Prophet Ibrahim did not respond. Hajar kept posing the question without getting an answer from him. Finally she said, 'Did Allah order you to do this?' He replied, 'Yes.' Upon hearing this, with utter faith and complete reliance on Allah, she said: 'Then we will not be lost.' Hajar, knowing her husband to be a Prophet and being a pious woman herself, didn't complain. Instead she began to eat the dates and drink the water, and breastfed her son.

When Prophet Ibrahim was a distance away from Hajar and their son, he looked back and he made the following supplication: 'O Lord! I have settled some of my offspring in a barren valley by Your Sacred House so that they would perform the Prayer. O Lord, make the hearts of some people yearn towards them and provide them with fruits for which they would give thanks'. It astounded me to be standing in what was now one of the richest places on earth, because of the oil beneath the feet of the Arabs. It felt as if I were seeing the prayer of the great Prophet Ibrahim answered.

I was at the end of my third lap between the mounds. A young man was handing out cups of Zamzam water to thirsty Hajjis. I sipped the incredible liquid, which has bubbled up from deep in the earth for thousands of years in the midst of the desert. It was the lightest water my mouth had ever tasted and seemed to evaporate on contact with the tongue. I felt immediately invigorated, despite the fact it was now almost Maghrib, the dusk prayer, and we had been praying, moving, walking for hours. I felt like running! The American brother accompanying our group told me to slow down as I was almost (almost) sprinting, as light as a feather. As if years of aches and pains, of worries and fears had been removed. I felt my spiritual load lightened on that first day of Hajj.

Later, I took a break to eat fried chicken on the floor of a nearby shopping mall. Beneath the giant escalators I watched an incredibly elderly man in the white towels of a pilgrim bend towards a plug socket in a pillar next to his prayer rug and plug in a Nokia mobile phone almost as old as himself. He sighed deeply then placed gnarled brown toes onto his green prayer mat. I stopped eating, entranced. The ancient monotheistic rite was taking place at a shrine to the modern worship of materialism. It struck me that some would spend more time in the malls of Makkah during Hajj than they would in the Haramayn.

By his simplicity and wiry physique, I supposed him to be a villager from the Asian subcontinent. Slowly, he raised his hands to ear level, dismissing the noise and bustle, the bright lights and family chatter around him. His shoulders relaxed as he said under his breath, 'Allahu Akbar (Allah is greater than all this)'. Across the atrium shopping mall life went on, oblivious to the profound act of humility quietly taking place. Twice he repeated the prayer circuit. He painfully rose to his feet and started again. At that moment, a uniformed security guard walked over to the pillar, yanked the phone charger from the wall and threw it and the phone noisily into a bucket. The elderly man's neck twitched slightly to the side, knowing his precious phone and charger were taken. He did not break his prayer. He carried on. The security guard yelled in Arabic in his direction, words which clearly meant: 'No charging phones here!'

My heart broke at the breach of etiquette towards a vulnerable, elderly worshipper. I rushed over to the security guard. Without thinking, I plunged my hand into the bucket, pulling out the man's phone and charger. 'How dare you! *Astaghfirullah!* What's wrong with you, can't you see this uncle is praying? Hajji Hajji! (he's a pilgrim!)' People were watching now.

The guard pointed to the plug socket in the wall: 'Him NO! You – ok!' He gave me the thumbs up. I felt sick at the racism that made my pale skin greater in significance to this racist than a beautiful act of worship.

I plugged the phone back into the pillar. 'Why are you like this? Shame on you!' The security guard pointed again at the

Asian man and then at me. 'You, yes. Him, no.' I sat down, keeping my eyes on the phone. All the time the elderly man was silent, sitting on his knees, hands raised to Allah, pleading. He had not budged. I watched his partially bare, undernourished back. Then I closed my eyes and also began to pray. I begged for forgiveness for myself with all my faults, for my family, for the sick, the elderly and for Allah to forgive the terrible selfishness entering the hearts of Muslims and replace it with love for Him and kindness to others. I became oblivious to the surroundings. The world is a prayer space to the believer. After a while, I opened my eyes. At the pillar the old man was unplugging his phone. Shyly he turned his head towards me, placed one hand on his chest and lowered his head slightly. I did the same, saying under my breath, 'I hope to meet you in Jannah, uncle. May Allah accept all your prayers and mine.'

A person's prayers are accepted not on the basis of the comfort of where we rest our head at night, nor the quality of the materials we wear. None of that matters in the space where the prayers flow towards. It is sincerity that separates us into levels. The old man had shown trust in Allah at a moment of vulnerability. I often think of him and wonder, would I have done the same? I made my way back to the hotel, troubled by the prejudice I was beginning to notice from our Arab hosts towards the Asian and African pilgrims.

At 9:30 am the following morning, we headed by bus to our next stop on the Hajj journey. Our group was bonding, getting to know one another better. The Muslim converts came from Denmark, Japan, America, the Philippines and Canada. The women were all in abayas for comfort and whatever we did for a living, whatever airs and graces we may have held in our daily lives, all were put aside for these acts of worship. Mina, seven kilometres east of the Masjid al-Haram, is the place where all pilgrims must sleep overnight. It contains the Jamarat, the three stone pillars that are pelted with stones in a symbolic rejection of Satan and his attempts to encourage human beings towards every kind of evil deed, large and small. I heard it was not unusual for some passionate believers to take the attack on wickedness literally and to throw chairs and huge rocks at the pillars. Injuries were not uncommon.

The sign 'Mina starts here' appeared on the highway, I felt like weeping – at a signpost! I was thinking of the early Muslims, just a few hundred faithful, who first went there 1,434 years ago at a time when they were physically tortured and rejected by their own families and the wider community. The white tents I saw covered miles and miles – a canvas city – another testimony to the success of Prophet Muhammad's mission. I found it overwhelming to watch tens of thousands of men, ancient-seeming in their white garb, flocking on foot towards the stones as our bus passed by. Many would sleep for days beneath motorway underpasses to and from the points of ritual. Conditions for us were easy, the tents provided even had air conditioning units and there were rugs and fold out cushion-beds to sleep on. Each section of the specially-built tent city had shower units, toilets and water taps for ablutions. Our group even had one tent dedicated to snacks and tea and coffee, which were available day and night.

After a short rest, we were woken for the dawn prayer. Then we hurriedly packed our belongings for another 20-minute coach ride, this time to the campsite at the base of Mount Arafat. There the niceties really vanished. We had arrived at the Day of Atonement, when our sole focus was asking Allah's forgiveness. Not just for ourselves but for an expanding circuit of needy souls; our loved ones, our communities, our neighbours, our country folk, all believers, and all of humanity. I sat on a hill under a makeshift awning amongst a sea of similar structures at an event which dwarfed anything I had ever attended. A poster of prayers in Arabic hung from the rafters beneath the canvas, which was all that stood between us and the glaring sun. At some point around midday, I took a break from my own prayers to walk outside. I witnessed the most incredible pilgrimage in existence. A rugged mountain of vast stones, smashed into being millennia before, stood before me, Mount Arafat, the Mountain of Mercy. It was on this site that having completed the structure he had been commanded to erect, God commanded Abraham to call the people to make pilgrimage to that spot.

'O Allah! How shall my voice reach all of those people?' Abraham was in the middle of this same vast desert. How could his own small voice reach anyone hundreds of kilometres from where he stood? He didn't doubt Allah, but he doubted his own ability to complete what he had been commanded. Abraham then climbed Mount Arafat and called out in his loudest voice: 'O People! Verily Allah has prescribed upon you Hajj, so perform Hajj.'

Thousands of years later, there I was, standing in stunned silence, watching 2 million pilgrims answering Allah's call to do exactly that.

And proclaim the Hajj to all mankind. They will come to you on foot and (mounted) on camels, lean on account of journeys through deep and distant mountain paths. (Qur'an 22: 27)

It was from here that Prophet Muhammad, peace be upon him, gave his Farewell Sermon in his final year of life. Before accepting Islam, I had always taken two great orations to heart as a call to goodness and fairness. The first had come from the New Testament: Jesus' famous 'Sermon On the Mount.' I will never stop being moved by its verses. It begins in such a clear and beautiful way:

'Blessed are the poor in spirit, for theirs is the kingdom of Heaven. Blessed are those who mourn, for they shall be comforted.

Blessed are the meek, for they shall inherit the earth. Blessed are those who hunger and thirst for righteousness, for they shall be satisfied. Blessed are the merciful, for they shall receive mercy.

Blessed are the pure in heart, for they shall see God. Blessed are the peacemakers, for they shall be called sons of God. Blessed are those who are persecuted for righteousness' sake, for theirs is the kingdom of Heaven...'

The other speech which has moved me since childhood was the Reverend Martin Luther King Jr's famous cry: 'I have a dream'. The simple endorsement for us to understand that God has created all humans equal. The bravery of a soul who didn't fear dying for the best cause: human dignity, justice and freedom.

Now I learnt of Prophet Muhammad's Final Sermon. When he seemed to know he was in his final year of this realm, he sought to summarize clearly and unequivocally the main message of Islam to humanity. A sister recited it to me under the bright sun as we watched the weeping crowds climbing Mount Arafat:

'O People, lend me an attentive ear, for I know not whether after this year, I shall ever be amongst you again.

Therefore, listen to what I am saying to you very carefully and take these words to those who could not be present here today'.

It continues:

Remember, one day you will appear before Allah and answer your deeds. So beware, do not stray from the path of righteousness after I am gone. All mankind is from Adam and Eve, an Arab has no superiority over a non-Arab nor a non-Arab has any superiority over an Arab; also a white has no superiority over black nor a black any superiority over a white except by piety (taqwa) and good action.'

It was the first call to equality and the first global rejection of tribalism over justice. I thought of the elderly man's experience and the return of 'Jahil' racism to the *ummah* who had been blessed with the message and wept. From dawn until sunset Muslim pilgrims, myself a mere dot amongst them, stood, kneeled or made prostrations in earnest supplication and devotion, praying for Allah's abundant forgiveness. Tears shed like waterfalls by those begging to be pardoned. We committed ourselves not to repeat them again.

After a too-brief visit to the Prophet's city of Madinah I returned home, physically aching like an old man with eight types of arthritis but spiritually as pure as a new-born baby.

As he was called to become a full-time teacher in Wales, Ustadh Ali had ended our classes. But our new way of life was becoming second nature. I had not connected the TV to the antenna for months, which helped, and the children and I enjoyed weekend treats of Laurel and Hardy movies or Little House on the Prairie box sets. It was an idyllic time and a quaint sweetness entered our household. I sometimes felt like an Amish woman with modern appliances.

These were regularly broken up by Abba-nights and kitchen dancing, which Holly and I called our 'mad half hour.' Everything was just more balanced, and music was a joy once more, rather than an obsession. Dancing was hilarious, for fun, and was no longer linked to lewdness or needing alcohol to be experienced and enjoyed.

CHAPTER 20
BACK HOME IN GAZA

No soundbite, no soundbite, no soundbite,
no soundbite will bring them back to life.'

Rafeef Ziadeh

The April after Hajj, when the girls were with family, I was invited to a conference in Gaza on the issue of prisoners. I hadn't been back for three years, since the Viva Palestina land convoy and the night delivering cash to needy families with the brothers from Birmingham. It was also to be my first visit to a Muslim land as a Muslim woman. Previously, I had been given a special status locally as a 'foreign journalist', and as such I could speak and act in a way that was void of Islamic and cultural expectations. As videos of my talks about my journey to Islam continued to circulate around the world on social media, trolls accused me of living 'an orientalist, untrue version of Islam'. Would my visit to Gaza be the time I came face to face with rules and strictures I could in reality never live with?

The delegation on our bus to Rafah were from Bradford in the north east of England and Derry in the north of Ireland. There were many cheers from everyone the coach from Cairo as our passports were stamped at Rafah and we passed the legendary sign: 'Welcome to Palestine'. For me it was a homecoming, and in the coming days I would make documentaries on the experiences of al-Nakba survivors who had fled to Gaza from Palestinian villages invaded by Israeli troops in 1948 for my series *Diaspora*. In Gaza our delegation of twenty students and politicians were welcomed into the home of Walid H. We gathered in the large main living room for coffee so strong it would normally have kept me awake all week and we devoured luscious home-grown dates and chicken shawarma – a feast! But I was itching to get out onto the streets for a walk in the Gazan evening air. I asked around and eventually I was accompanied by Maphaz, a 20-year-old student.

The drone of generators, the only source of electricity in the area, assaulted my ears, a dour throbbing which drowned out the birds' bedtime chorus. The streets were dusty, just as I remembered, and boys surrounded us – pushing each other or kicking around stones instead of footballs – were as cheeky as always. Yet something was amiss. I sniffed the air for the warm, sweet smell I remembered, but instead my nostrils were assaulted by a faecal stench. Without constant electricity there could be no sewage management. The main road was as dark as it was deserted and I began to realize what was missing from my memory of this place; evening laughter, shouts of enthusiasm and greetings to strangers as we passed by. Now, at barely 7 pm, Rafah was shut, silent and preparing to sleep. What had I expected in a semi-perpetual blackout? I supposed I had imagined families would stock up on candles and sit around them, bravely carrying on with the traditional outdoor life Arabs had always relished. But how could it be the same now? Without a hot evening meal to prepare or to collect from takeaway stands, without greeting relatives and other guests, the noisy washing up of the women and the chatter of extended family life, the evening was silenced. A few young men, cold and sullen, their hands shoved deep in their pockets, walked past without a cheery 'marhaba!' as they headed back to cold, damp rooms for a night of quiet gloom.

Da-da-da-dadadaaada! I looked at Maphaz: 'What was that?' 'Israeli gunfire,' she smiled. 'They are telling us what they want to do to us tomorrow at the Land Day March.' She shrugged and we walked on, her straight back showing her defiance. Later our coach drove us through Khan Yunis en route to the hostel where I would stay. On previous visits the evening had been abuzz, but now everywhere was virtually empty. Our route was a long silent caravan of despair, as area after area passed us by, invisible in the darkness. At Khan Yunis there was noise: car horns and the shouts of frustrated drivers. We drove past a petrol station where hundreds of cars were queuing at the only place that still had fuel. Fathers, taxi drivers and workers, all desperate for petrol so they could get to work on Monday morning, would sleep in their vehicles that night. The men at the end of the queue would still be there at Fajr, then go straight about their daily business.

My best friends in Gaza, Yassir and his wife, had waited three long years, as I had, for us to meet again. Hamas security, ever conscious of infiltrators' threats to the well-being of visitors, especially after the murder of Vik, did not let me leave the hostel to stay with my friends. They stationed men outside with guns, knowing I was likely to bolt. Yassir came to the hostel to meet me and we tried again to negotiate permission for me to leave. We failed, and eventually with acceptance, 'Allah wills it so,' I headed to my room. It was time for the night time prayer, Isha', so I made my ablutions, cleaning my mouth, face, forearms, head, ears and feet. As the tap water hit my tongue I spat it out, immediately disgusted: 'Ugghhhhh!' The salty taste was a shock.

The hostel had light when we arrived, but as I put the prayer mat (a bath towel) away on a shelf having completed my *salah*, the area entered another blackout period, plunging us into profound darkness. I only had a vague idea where the bed was and I felt about in the dark. The lights blinked on again, then off, then on again, three more times. Then whatever power source they were using gave up the ghost and darkness reigned. Good night Gaza, it was still great to be home. After the twelve hour blackout there was no hot water to shower the next morning and no internet to find out what was going on. As the days passed I felt dirty, tired and emotionally wrung out. Gaza was so different from even the short time before, the silence morbid and desperate. Alongside the near empty roads more shops were boarded up, and the pavements which were once jammed with people were also empty. There was simply no way to get to work for those who had found anywhere near paying wages.

The camera team from Press TV were well used to the power cuts, but I found the working environment impossible. I recorded an important interview with an elderly member of the Dawan Council in Jabaliya Camp. His time was precious, as he sat daily to give advice on family, relationship and monetary disputes requested by neighbours, friends and locals. Half way through our interview, the power died. 'Seriously?' I said, unable to contain my frustration. I was offered tea, to 'calm my nerves', and I could only wonder what I would do if I had to make a living there with time-related deadlines.

It was dusk, Maghrib prayer time, as Yasser drove us to Beit Hanoun on the border. Not long ago, Beit Hanoun had been a flourishing agricultural area and historically it had vast orchards stretching as far as the eye could see, where adults worked and children sheltered from the heat of the sun, playing games only children understood. This evening, the sun set over what remained: a tank- and shell-decimated scrubland of weeds and thorns. Occupation bulldozers had deliberately destroyed old trees and old orchards. To my left, across the potholed 'road', was Gaza's front line with Israel: the enemy it professed to fear so much were families living in the roughshod apartment blocks facing the border. There were so many children in the area it was hard to fathom for the first time visitor. Large families are the norm in Palestine, and in Gaza they remain a symbol of tribal success and a source of pride. Beside each and every window of the family apartments was evidence of strafing by automatic gunfire, intersected by or with larger impact damage from shelling. On my previous visit I'd asked a poor mother in Gaza why she had so many children:

'We need at least seven to each family here,' she had said. 'At least two will be killed by Israel, two more will be kidnapped and put into prison for a long time or will be disabled by rockets. Two may (may) have a chance to get educated and will leave Palestine and never return. Which leaves just one child to look after us in our old age ...'

Turning a corner on foot, two young guys came over and greeted me as if I were a long lost cousin. Their welcome was so warm I wondered for a moment if we had met on a previous visit to Gaza: 'Okay?' Said the tallest brother, after introducing himself. 'Nice to meet you. Now you come to our home to spend the evening. First tea, then you stay with us. Yalla come!'

I laughed.

'Why you laugh?' Asked the younger brother in his late teens. 'We don't joking, you come for tea now, really, *tafaddal!*'

It was funny to think how scared my friends were of the risk of 'kidnap' when I mentioned my trips to Gaza. Kidnapping was a risk – to be force-fed only tea and treats. The young men were brimming with a vibrant generosity which was undiminished by their circumstances.

I had just finished a wonderful book about the 1920s conversion to Islam of Leopold Weiss, a Jewish journalist from Austria who became Muhammad Asad. He described in his memoir, *The Road to Mecca*, the ennui, the spiritual malaise, he had experienced and encountered, which in his age had gripped European society. Ethical values, he wrote, had become confused under the terrible impact of what had happened during the First World War; there was no new set of values in sight to replace the old. In his early twenties he had travelled to Palestine where he landed a job with the news agency United Telegraph. He set off as a reporter across the region, exploring and meeting the Arabs and the Bedouin on the border-free route between Jerusalem and Makkah. He spoke with touching potency about the beauty of the friendships made in the lush green of Palestine and the dusty desert which he navigated on camel back. Here I met eyes that had something of that same energy and light of welcome in them that Muhammad Asad had encountered nearly a century earlier.

Through a broken wooden gate behind a crumbling stone wall, my friend Yassir, silent, grim-faced, guided me towards a cement building which had no right to be standing. It was once a PLO prison and was now 'home' to a family of one father, his two wives and their seventeen children. Before the second Intifada the father used to work in Israel, earning enough money for his growing family. When Gazans were banned from entering for work, he became a taxi driver on an income which was just enough to get by. Then the siege came and food prices shot up to parity with those in European nations whilst incomes fell to third-world levels. In 2015, unemployment in Gaza would be the highest in the world and its economy on the 'verge of collapse', according to a World Bank report. For the family, the political situation was a personal catastrophe. The father's car began to develop small problems which he couldn't afford to repair. I passed the vehicle's rotting carcass and we entered a large unplastered room with a bare cement floor. There was no furniture, no pictures, no adornments of any kind. Besides two plastic chairs, the freezing space was utterly destitute except for a small TV on a crate in one corner. Children with hollow eyes were milling about, expressionless yet wide-eyed at the surprise entry of so many unknown faces. They looked exactly as they were; shell-shocked.

One of the wives made an attempt to smile but her lips had clearly forgotten how. The husband, in his shame at the poverty of his family, muttered 'salam' and looked at the ground. I was there to see their situation, so I put on my reporter's head and spoke professionally to the family members one by one. Their 16-year-old son had a limp and I asked what the matter was. Had he hurt himself playing football? Instantly, his mother unceremoniously pulled his trouser leg up, ripping down a large plaster to reveal a freshly-stitched, ten-inch wound. Two years earlier the boy (then 14) had been collecting rubble in the wasteland where orchards once grew and now called a 'buffer zone'. His job was to sell the rocks for whatever he could, to salvage them in the hope of making some money for his hungry family. An IDF sniper shot him in the leg at long range, shattering the bone. After twenty-four months he finally had pins put into the shin, but he would limp for the rest of his life. A smaller boy of around ten was brought over. His mother pulled his filthy tracksuit bottoms above the knee to reveal strange light patches of skin. They were white phosphorous burns, the napalm of the twenty-first century, which had rained down on this densely populated area by the tonne. Another son, of around seven, shoeless and silent, clung to his father's legs.

'This boy,' he told me, 'Had developed mental problems since the attack in 2009. Now he doesn't talk and doesn't act normally. Doctors can't help him.'

Food was cooked at the farthest end of the garage-like space. It was a kitchen area only by dint of having a fridge, but it was turned off and was no more than an empty cabinet. Inside were four cauliflowers of questionable age. On the dirty floor was an ancient electric camping ring on which a pan of chips bubbled, enough for three children in the UK. Tonight it would have to feed a family of twenty.

It was *salah* (prayer) time and the younger of the wives, Iman, took me to yet another bare room. This one a bedroom because there were blankets on the floor. She carefully laid out a prayer mat for me and as I prayed images of my home and my educated, thriving, safe, daughters interrupted my train of thought. All the luxuries of London flooded my mind. In *sujud* (prostration), head on the floor I angrily sobbed. Besides me the mother was also making her prayer and behind her a daughter held a mobile phone over us, the bleak light breaking the unending darkness.

'*Habibti* (my dearest),' said the mother when she finished her prayer. 'Please don't cry.'

I couldn't speak with the weight of my grief. Oh Allah, I thought to myself, don't let her be kind to me, please, I can't take it. But she was kind, of course she was.

'My dear, why do you cry? Are you alright?'

'I ... I hate this for you ...' is all I managed.

She looked into my eyes. Mother to mother: 'What? Don't cry for us, it's okay, you can stop now, shhh.'

Then she said words that threatened to break me, right there on the cement floor.

'Don't cry for us. We are so happy. We are Muslim. We know this is our test and we must be patient. We are happy, really sister we are. Allah will reward us if we can just be patient.'

Those words, I have heard repeated in so many besieged homes in Gaza.

Those words that led me to beware of ingratitude in my own, pampered, ease-filled, life.

Thanks to a *masjid* congregation in Manchester, I had brought a donation with me provide for homes in need. That evening, the Beit Hanoun children had new shoes, footballs, table-tennis kits. Plus tracksuits for the boys and the father. The older girls each received a new abaya to wear to university. The mothers were given tapestry and sewing materials to teach the girls the Palestinian art of sewing. Everyone had a hot meal during our visit and wood was provided for cooking in the coming weeks. Before leaving, I asked the youngest boy, aged four, what his dream was, what he wanted to be when he was older. All around the world, children have creative, hope-filled dreams to be doctors, teachers, astronauts, you name it.

'I want to eat,' he said finally. As we sat down to enjoy a feast of chips and kebabs, somehow his natural honesty made us all laugh.

Two days later, the accompanying soundtrack to the coach drive back to the Rafah Crossing was fighter jets and drones buzzing overhead.

CHAPTER 21
IMRAN AND WAZIRISTAN

'Service to others is the rent you pay
for your room here on earth.'

Mohammad Ali

China cups clinked amongst pots of Earl Grey tea and silver bowls of cubed sugar. Across tables of white linen, the scent of freshly-brewed coffee and newly-baked croissants made my stomach rumble as I crossed the breakfast room of the Mayfair Hotel. The first glimpse of Imran Khan was enough to take my breath away. He sat straight-backed before a plate of porridge, talking animatedly to three other men whose faces couldn't help but blur into insignificance besides such charisma. My inner voice gave me the urgent reminder: 'You're Muslim!' and I politely averted my eyes from the handsome weathered face once described by fashion model Marie Helvin as 'devastating'. I walked towards the cricketing legend turned heroic anti-corruption politician with one thought on my mind: I hope he doesn't recognize me.

We had met once before, in 2008 at the Global Peace and Unity event. I had been browsing the stalls as a guest with my daughters when Mohamed Ali from the Islam Channel had spotted me, tall and white in the sea of scarfs and shiny black hair. He led me along a side corridor in a hurry without explanation, demanding 'follow me, it's important'. We went through a door in an ugly industrial corridor behind the scenes and straight onto a makeshift TV set. 'What is going on? You haven't asked me to give an interview to anyone, you can't just expect me to ...' Ali put his hands up.

'We are in a situation. You have to interview Imran Khan because the presenter hasn't shown up. Just do it, please.' I had little make up on, I was in my mum-on-duty outfit and had no idea what to talk about. On the notepad shoved into my hands I scribbled the key words I had heard most frequently by the UK media regarding news stories from Pakistan. They would be the basis of my hour long interview because I myself knew absolutely nothing else about the place: 'Failed State', 'Floods', 'Drone Attacks', 'Taliban'.

Imran Khan strode in, throwing himself impatiently onto the chair opposite me on the makeshift TV set. In a grey City suit with well shone shoes, he was every inch the political player. He wriggled irritably as the crew miked him up, he had been kept waiting an hour already, and he didn't smile when I introduced myself. Pulling on my years of experience, I began as if I knew everything there were to know about Pakistan and his ambition to lead: 'So the news reports that US drones have ...' I managed to make it through the interview but only because Imran Khan spoke non-stop about his beloved country. Answering questions I had made deliberately vague in the hope that he would do exactly that.

Now he had invited me to breakfast, Introductions were made and coffee poured. Eggs Florentine was ordered for me and Imran smiled over his sportsman's breakfast of porridge and fruit. This was the first time I had seen him smile, considering the tension of our first meeting. Imran's life as a Pakistani politician was constantly under threat, yet I was shocked to see he had no visible security with him. He told me he was ready for whatever 'destiny' had in store. Decades of facing fast bowlers clearly made him an unflinching political opponent.

The meeting's focus was on the continued displacement of people in Waziristan due to the US-led drone campaign on the tribal lands. Far from destroying radical elements, Imran Khan was convinced the attacks were fuelling extremism. He put forward that if a far-off enemy you had barely heard of destroyed your village from the air for reasons you could not fathom, murdering your entire clan, you would hate them, wouldn't you? 'It's inconceivable,' said Khan, 'that Obama does not realize the effect of this policy. Therefore, the only sane conclusion is that this must be what America wants: Islamic extremism.'

Imran invited me to Waziristan a month later to take part in a road convoy protest against the drone attacks where we would meet the families of the dead and injured. I raged to Imran and his colleagues against US policies which continued to write-off great swathes of humanity as 'collateral damage'. Lives less important than white, Western ones.

Yet.

Inside I hesitated from immediately accepting the invitation. Being in Palestine had never scared me, but Pakistan was a different thing altogether. I mean, they seemed a bit extreme that lot - the head bangers of the Muslim world, right?

Imran changed the subject. He asked about how I had come to accept Islam. I told him about Palestine, the land of *baraka* (blessing) and of the *sabr* (patience) of the people I met. He listened intently, and at some points I noticed tears in his eyes. His passionate defence of his people removed my initial doubts about going on the convoy.

The convoy's mission was to drive thirteen hours so as to hold a protest against the CIA drone programme amongst the very people who had suffered as a result. It was joined by important names from the world of human rights activism: Clive Stafford Smith of Reprieve, Medea Benjamin of the US women's group, Code Pink, and retired US colonel, Ann Wright, would be there in solidarity. We spent several days hyping up media interest via various Islamabad TV studios. One of the interviews was with the national news channel, Geo News, hosted by the legendary presenter, Hamid Mir. My husband and I sat in the green room, with Imran sprawling on a sofa nearby. Hamid Mir briefed us on the kinds of questions to expect and told me he had interviewed both Tony Blair and Osama Bin Laden. As usual, my cheek got the better of me and I couldn't help asking: 'Who did you like more, Blair or Bin Laden?'

Mir was clearly flustered. He ummed, he ahhed, his hands twisting on his lap: 'I only met Blair once and Bin Laden several times, so it wouldn't be fair to, er ... compare the experiences.'

I turned to Imran. 'What is that answer in cricketing terms, Imran.'

'Well left,' he said smoothly. 'You don't have to play every ball.' The room exploded in laughter.

Finally, the day arrived for the convoy to head off. We were collected from the home of Fawzia, one of the PTI senior members and our most charming host. Our 4x4 transport was driven by a dapper man with a curled moustache who was under strict orders to keep his car close to Imran's at all times for security reasons. There had been threats against the action from across the political spectrum, and a confusion of stories had hit the local media with the aim of persuading us internationals not to leave Islamabad. The government was angry because it made them look like sell-outs for supporting the US military campaign on its soil at a massive cost to the people. The Taliban had also reportedly made threats because they didn't want foreigners on their home soil, whilst another section of the Taliban had offered Imran Khan its protection in what the media called 'militant infected tribal areas'. South Waziristan is a stronghold of Hakimullah Mehsud, head of the Pakistan Taliban. None of the internationals withdrew, our cause was to highlight the suffering of innocent civilians who lived not only with threats but suffered real harm from the internal security actions and the drone programme. The Bureau of Investigative Journalism had recorded at least 2,570 deaths since 2004 in 346 drone strikes.

We set off at a crawl in our car, and the task ahead became clearer. It would take a full day to travel even part of the 300 miles to the border. The convoy of hundreds of cars and trucks wound its painful way through the Mianwali region. Mountains jutted out of the lush greenery like sharp teeth, interspersed with dusty plains. After eight hours, night had fallen and the cars and trucks we had been amongst had dispersed en route. We had become separated from the main convoy in a 'red zone' – Taliban territory. It was pitch black and our driver lost his debonair edge as he cursed into the phone trying desperately to reach member after member of the PTI to find out where we were supposed to be sleeping. The phones were either blocked or out of range in the remote region in which we were now stranded. The darkness outside the car was intense, and the only sound we could hear were the crickets in the shrubs along the barren route. We held our breath each time a set of car headlights came towards us, half expecting men with guns to pull us from our seats.

Zaheer, our driver, decided that moving around looked less suspicious than sitting still, however that risked him running out of petrol. After several hours of feeling like sitting ducks interspersed with aimless driving, Zaheer finally received emergency directions to the home of a local PTI member who lived inside a military compound. As armed soldiers closed the compound gates behind us, we laughed with relief.

The next morning at 8 am, we set off on the bizarre hunt for the rest of the convoy. As the sun rose over another day of never-ending road, we finally regrouped outside a local town and the atmosphere was incredible. More than 500 vehicles made up the mile-long train of peace activism, surprising local people as we passed through rustic villages and farmlands. Buses beeped and men shouted greetings in Urdu, crammed inside vehicles like sardines or on the roofs of the cars, singing and waving red and green flags. Scooters bumped alongside on the uneven roads with entire families somehow packed onto the seats and handlebars. I was stunned at the reception which greeted my waving and smiling. Once again, I now realized how the media had given me a none-dimensional view of a complex people. Weather-beaten men wore robes which brushed their shins. Turbans were on almost every male head and long beards touched the chests of the shalwar kameez, the local dress of baggy trousers and long shirt. None of us could keep from grinning at the amazing reception.

'Look there ... up there, over there!' The army that we had been told to fear were waving and cheering at us from every rooftop.

Shouts came in Urdu: 'We are with you all! Allahu Akbar!'

Mid-afternoon we came to a complete standstill, for reasons we would understand later. Ignoring Imran's express instruction not to, I climbed out of the car. To me solidarity work is not to drive through an area waving like royalty. It means meeting the people, hearing their experiences first-hand, getting a sense of their community and struggles in order to stand shoulder to shoulder with them. I began to walk up the middle of the dusty route lined with roadside shacks of corrugated iron or wood. The dusty children looked like they should be featured on magazine covers. Adorable toddlers of three and four went about their business, surprised yet pleased to see the tall *gura* (white) woman. They were wearing kohl eyeliner, in all shades of light brown to bright blue, making their eyes sparkle intensely with the luminous quality of the truly alive. Two smiling soldiers approached me, walking either side and offering protection should I need it. The friendly attitude from the men was completely unexpected as again a remote Muslim region confounded my expectations as a western woman. I walked amongst men in turbans, old and young, and was greeted with 'salam, salam,' peace to you.

The plan was to assemble for a rally at Kotkai, but under orders the army had blocked our way. Giant cement obstacles and abandoned vehicles blocked the route between the town of Tank and the border. Despite attempts at negotiation by Imran Khan, the army's Frontier Corps said it could not ensure the security of the several thousand rally-goers as the convoy had arrived too late in the afternoon to risk allowing people to gather after sunset. Earlier, the Taliban had distributed leaflets in the nearby town of Dera saying they would 'welcome' the motorcade with bombs. Undeterred, Imran and his team led the convoy into a nearby field. He quickly climbed onto a bus, preparing to give the speech and rally we had travelled thousands of miles to support.

I was told to 'run' through the crowd which stood between us and Imran. This seemed impossible, some 20,000 Muslim villagers and thousands of convoy drivers blocked our way. Zaheer, our driver, pushed through the throng ahead of us and an avenue just seemed to open. At one point a hand grabbed me from behind and I stopped, instantly ready to whack the furtive abuser, but I was met with a dozen blank male stares. Finally, we reached the bus and I looked up at the eight foot climb over the coach's bumper and up the side without much hope. I got about half way up with a variety of unknown hands 'helping' me. I was about to give up when Imran spotted me, reached down and pulled me up with the strength of ten men, as if I were as light as a feather. Teetering on the edge of the bus roof, I clung to his shirt momentarily.

'Are you okay, Lauren?' he asked. 'Glad you could make it. Welcome to the real Pakistan.'

I hung on to whatever we could find (mostly Clive Stafford Smith) to stop from tumbling into the crowd below. As Imran began to speak, thousands of tribesmen and convoy drivers went silent: 'The whole world has heard your voice,' he said through a megaphone. 'The message that our government and our rulers could not get to the world, has now been spread worldwide. If the USA bombs Pakistan and I am leader they will be shot down.'

The crowd erupted with a tremendous roar of *takbir*, praising Allah over and over and sending a unanimous message to the unseen drones buzzing ominously far above their heads. Shots were fired into the air from one of the many guns.

Before the epic 300 mile journey back to Islamabad, our vehicle and two others were guided onto private farming land where armed men closed gates on the dusty road behind us. Bumping along an earth track, we were greeted at a rustic, barely-roofed farmhouse by more armed men wearing the large yellow and white turbans of the regional dress. A giant of a man came over and looked us up and down, taking in our unlikely height difference and alien appearance. He welcomed me with 'As-salamu 'alaykum (peace be upon you).'

Young men with bright smiles led me towards a gate in the far wall of the farming compound. There was barbed wire everywhere and the wall was half tumbled down as I stepped gingerly through the gate with no idea what to expect the other side.

As soon as I was through the gate, I surveyed the scene. There were cows in the distance, and herbs and vegetables planted in uneven rows nearby. As cats rushed over asking to be fed, a feeling struck deep to my core which I had only ever felt before in Palestine: home.

Women swathed in black shawls, holding them together with their teeth, ran over and embraced me with both arms. I staggered suddenly, exhausted by the tension of the past two days, and the women half carried me into their dwelling. It was little more than a hut with a fire in another room over which food was always bubbling. The bare room was cool after the heat outside; finally a place to relax away from the men. I pulled off my hijab and the women all smiled, pointing at my blonde hair. I gestured towards the bare, ancient-looking mattress in the corner. The women laid me down on it gently, as if I were a child. A shawl was pulled over me and I fell into a blissful sleep.

A while later, I was woken by a rustling sound. One of the younger women was hunched down next to the mattress staring into my face. She held a spoon to my lips and nodded for me to sip. I sat up slowly, hungrily drinking a delicious clear lamb broth. I had just finished the last drop when there came a commotion from outside. The women quickly drew shawls around themselves and returned my hijab so I could cover myself. A group of young lads in their teens came in leading Imran Khan's highly-respected older sister. She greeted the elder mother with a kiss to the forehead, then greeted the other women with equal politeness and affection. We all sat down to take tea. I noticed boys and young men of the family would come inside briefly, be shouted at very loudly in Urdu by the women and then run off again. After watching this strange parade several times, I asked Aleema Khan what was happening.

'In tribal Pakistan, the men may be kings in the village but the women run – and I mean *run* – the home. Those lads and young men are these women's errand boys, secretaries, bag carriers, you name it,' she laughed. 'In the West it is thought we are all slaves. But look around you, Lauren. Really look at them. Do they look miserable or enslaved to you?' I took in the smiles of the women chit-chatting with each other going about their daily chores, with us guests sat in the middle of the dirt floor drinking tea. They seemed content and cared for, and they were certainly giving the young men all kinds of hell.

There was a shout from outside and the women helped us stand up. I brushed dirt from my skirt and looked towards the door, suddenly filled with a giant of a man wearing a long beige shirt, a furry armless jacket and a vast turban. In the dictionary next to the word 'Taliban' is that guy's photo. I stood more formally than before, suddenly nervous, and the women backed off in deference to his status. I had no idea if he too were a visitor or the father of the family. The man's eyes were dark brown, his skin the darkest I had seen in the region, his beard flecked with white. He stared at me in a way that I interpreted as anger. Had I breached some local etiquette? He and Imran's sister were speaking rapidly. I could tell by her voice she was respecting him with her tone, but also that he knew she wasn't a woman who would take any nonsense.

Eventually, Aleema turned to me and said quietly, 'Lauren, this man is very important, the head of a regional tribe …'. Was I going to be sold into slavery? Or was I about to be imprisoned by the Taliban and swapped for a missing US soldier? Her next words were a shock: 'He asks if you won't mind having a photo with him for his Facebook page.'

Actually, looking at the man and thinking how the security services might read such a photo, it was the last thing I wanted. However, this was not the time or place to refuse such a request and so somewhere on the internet is the strangest of many unusual photos of me; in a hut in a rural Pakistan with the head of a tribe who may – or may not – be a Taliban leader.

After many hours driving, we all made it safely back to Islamabad. The next day Imran thanked all of the international visitors for standing with the people of Pakistan, his manners impeccable as always. I would have a deep love for Pakistan from then on, understanding the manipulation that goes into painting the beautiful country and her people as a broad-brush 'threat' to our 'western way of life'. It has natural resources and a wealth of skills and talent economists in the UK can only envy. I met the warmth and underlying cohesion of families and village systems lost in time to modern culture. As soon as I returned home to Manchester, I prayed to be allowed to return one day, to drink soup from a bowl with sweet-natured women, and maybe even to implement the 'remote control' of the men into my own household too!

CHAPTER 22
FAITH OF OUR FATHERS

'Goodbyes are only for those who love with their
eyes. Because for those who love with their heart
and soul there is no such thing as separation.'

Jalāl ad-Dīn Mohammad Rūmī)

The bedroom on the middle floor of the pretty stone cottage is silent. It's the end of September 2017, three weeks before my father's eighty-sixth birthday, and I have been called to see him 'for the last time'. After a noisy welcome from the small dogs, they quickly lose interest as I climb the stairs. Outside, hovering rain clouds make the room as gloomy as the atmosphere indoors. Death hovers, an unwanted guest that refuses to leave empty handed. Dad's bedroom door is open. He is sleeping, mouth open, and so emaciated I forget about the tea sitting downstairs and head straight to his bedside.

'Can I sing to you Dad?'

I sit down beside him, repeating under my breath, 'There is no God but God'. I gently stroke snow-white hair, from wrinkled temple towards the large, rounded ears of an Irish descendant. I recite surah *al-Fatihah* from the Qur'an. After a moment, my father's eyes flicker, then slowly open. He looks deeply into mine, so deeply, I wonder if he recognizes me.

'Sarah,' he says hoarsely, 'you are full of light, so honest, so beautiful.'

My hand briefly stops the gentle stroking as I pray for sincerity, for the words to give comfort to this special man departing on his solitary journey.

'Don't stop, Sarah,' he says. So I keep stroking his hair, trying to ignore the raggedness of his breathing.

I've been called here to say goodbye. Old grudges which had kept us apart for the best part of three decades suddenly as irrelevant in death's waiting room as a celebrity magazine. I consider my duty, which as a Muslim child is serious indeed. No rift, not even rejection by the parent, should stand in the way of the connection and the repayment of the debt which the young owe to the elderly who raised them as best they could.

From the sleeves of grey pyjamas, gnarled hands swathed in mottled skin poke out on thin arms. They never lost the scarring from the night of the fire, age merely blended them into the wrinkled skin of the old man lying on the bedspread before me. The skin of the forearm nearest me was a purple signpost of imminent collapse. Despite his emaciation, after twelve days my father was still unable to eat, at that moment it was hard to imagine this colossus of a personality, a vivid example of a human being, actually losing this battle with life.

His sparkling blue eyes stare deep into mine again. I know what he's thinking, he's reading me: 'The eyes are the mirror of the soul,' he always said.

And there we meet for the last time. Brown eyes and blue, in that place where ambition for life had halted, where this background reality of acting, of storytelling, of relationships of pain and of beauty are passing by.

'Sing then ...' he says.

I recite in Arabic the opening of the Qur'an, again. Angels gather where the Qur'an is recited and there is peace in this room. How odd that I don't feel like crying. We both let the resonating words settle.

'I have come here for two reasons,' I say. 'To say goodbye to you, Dad, and to speak to you about God.'

He nods. He rasps out the words, 'okay then.' But now he's thirsty, so I find the child's beaker on the chest of drawers and lift it to his mouth. Water spills across his chest and he finds his more familiar 'stage' voice, raging: 'Bloody 'ell Sarah, have you come here to knock me off or what?' Which despite everything makes me laugh. After much mopping of his neck and some coughing, we settle again. We speak together about the next life, his onward journey. His views are as honest and as insightful as those of a man who has lived a full life, made mistakes, tried to do good, fought cowards and faced many demons. His message has little changed from what I remembered as a child.

'There is no God but God,' says my father. 'And by the way! Jesus was a prophet, not the son of God not a part of God. A prophet ...'

His wife calls me from the doorway: 'Time to go. He's tired. Needs rest.' She leaves and I move next to the bed.

'Don't go, Sarah,' he says.

I place my face against those paraffin- and flame-battered fingers, rubbing my cheek gently over them. I kiss chapped knuckles. This is it.

'I'll see you again, God willing, in a beautiful place, Dad.'

As I reach the doorway my father finds the strength, to leave me with a final message to live by.

His voice raspy, yet determined, says:

'Remember always take care of the poor.' He repeats it again. 'Remember always take care of the poor.'

These are the last words I ever hear him say.

CHAPTER 23
A NEW WAY OF LIFE

'Verily, humans were created impatient, irritable when evil touches him and ungenerous when good touches him. Except for those devoted to prayer, who remain constant in their prayers.'

Qur'an 70: 19-23

My new identity took time to be secured by regular salah (prayers) and the seeking to understand what it meant to be Muslim for real - in my daily life. Gradually, I ventured out of my early seclusion from mainstream friends and colleagues. It took time. The media, including my own friends and colleagues, had been predictably vicious about my conversion. This headline was in the Daily Mail was a personal favourite of mine and summarises the British press response succinctly.

'How Cherie's sister became a Cheerleader for ISIS'. The prejudice was so blatant it was amusing rather than hurtful.

'...what prompted a chain-smoking confessional journalist, with a colourful private life and a liking for alcohol, to become a sort of poster girl for conservative Islam?' It struck me then as it does now that the nicotine addicted, drunk, was a far preferable version of myself to the media than a teetotal, mother, who stayed home nights and fasted a month a year in order to control their lower impulses.

An early bonus of the introspection required on the Islamic spiritual path was the recalibrating of priorities - who and what matters. The headlines worried my mum of course. In her usual blunt way she would ask over and over:

'Now you have made yourself completely unemployable darling, what will you do for money?' To which my answer was always 'Allah will provide.'

Gradually, I felt confident enough to meet old friends and trusted colleagues. The unwritten rule was that coffee not alcohol was on the menu. The hugely witty writer, broadcaster and satirist Victor Lewis Smith, invited to me a meeting with him at a place he liked for lunchtime chats, in a trendy area of London. He was passionately pitching a travel series we had been honing for some time. It was getting nowhere. This would be our first meeting since I had become Muslim and I was ready for some respectful teasing. I wasn't ready for the place he had booked us to meet.

Outside the 'restaurant' doors, I checked Vic's last email on my phone and sighed. With a prayer of forgiveness on my lips 'astagfirullah' (may Allah forgive me), I entered the pub.

The smell of spilt beer hit me first. Second the smell of red wine. Then came the looks as the waiter showed me to a back table in an Edwardian style, wooden compartment. Muslims are often demanded to 'just fit in' to environments which we know clearly come with toxic risks to body and soul. What is less noted are the looks of revulsion and comments we can receive should we venture out of our environmental safe zones.

Vic's face on seeing me in hijab made the whole thing worthwhile. His usual sarcastic lope was broken by first an expression of shock 'I thought you were kidding Lauren'. Then it turned to one of horror about his lapse in judgement. He could not have been kinder or more regretful of his choice. For a decade I would unrelentingly call him to Islam in a way our banter allowed. In one email he wrote:

'In my early 20s, I used to write comedy for a Christian Theatre Company - I was its only atheist - they used to pray for me before each show (I did the sound so could hear them on their radio mics). They were as edgy as it gets .. and we won a Perrier. All the great satirists were deeply religious.'

My mum found the change the hardest. She never expected (or wanted) her Jack Daniel's drinking, low neckline wearing, football supporting eldest daughter ('of all people, darling') to embrace something as 'puritanical' (her word) as Islam, and the occasional comment still slips out. One recent night, during a regular visit to stay with her, I was heading out to chair a panel discussion taking place after the screening of a film in Soho when Mum called me to the living room: 'Sarah watch this! Somethings going on in central London!' TV news reports were saying Oxford Circus station and Bond Street were closed due to a terror alert. Shots had been reported on social media, but police had not confirmed the story.

'Mum,' I said, 'that's terrible. That's exactly where I'm headed right now.'

Without missing a beat she shot back: 'Well looks like your friends have started (the attack) without you.'

I stared at the screen for a moment silently repeating: 'sabr, sabr' (patience, patience). I turned around to face her: 'There's only one thing I can say to you right now, Mum.'

'What,' she said, suddenly uncertain of my response.

'Give me five! That was so fast!' Surprised at my response to her joke, she laughed and we smacked palms, giggling. A Muslim convert and her self-proclaimed 'Islamophobe' parent, watching in mutual relief as the alert turned out to be a false alarm. I am so grateful for her patience. What love to show a daughter and grandchildren, accepting a way of life which she has been taught to fear.

In wider society a negative change was taking place to which my children and I would not be immune: the rise of the alt right rhetoric across Europe and online.

My daughters, who in their early teens chose to wear hijab. Yes - their choice. They have been shouted at and called terrorists more than once: out walking in the Lake District; at a David Lloyd gym in north London; whilst I was driving down the M6 between Manchester and Birmingham.

The online abuse continues. Murder and rape are suggested punishments for my crime of leaving 'peaceful' Christianity. Perversely, the most violent tweets and messages come from animal lovers and those who say they are 'protecting freedom'. Being mocked means asking a new kind of question. Not: 'How will society accept me,' but 'how can I be as kind and as charitable as Prophet Muhammad when it doesn't?'

Largely, these kinds of comments have abated. They are increasingly replaced by comments to my YouTube channel asking real questions about to escape anxiety and how belief is possible in this day and age.

Good and evil are not equal. Repel evil with what is better and you will see that your enemy will become as close as an old and valued friend. But only those who are steadfast in patience, only those who are truly blessed, will attain to such a blessed attitude. (Qur'an 41: 35–36)

EPILOGUE

Istanbul, 2023

It is 4.45am. The bedroom trembles with a low thunder which stirs me awake. Gradually, my mind recognises the sounds are words immortalised by a former slave named Bilal, who lived in the seventh century CE alongside the Arabian Prophet. Yet, this is Istanbul, currently my home, 1400 years on. Where, even now, millions are awakened by the epic rumbling from Europe into Asia - many still answer the role call to submission.

It's my turn to accept or to ignore the Arabic warning that 'Prayer is better than sleep….' At the foot of our bed, light from the hall forms a halo around my toes as I raise my hands to my shoulders. My breathe eases out, I announce softly: 'Allahu Akbar …' (God is Greater). Nothing else matters but Him.

This is how each new day begins.

Islam opens the mind to a vast, extended timeline, a new universe. Practising faith is like opening a door and realising your life so far has been lived in a broom cupboard in the mansion of existence. Reality actually lies beyond and beneath the nuts and bolts, the brooms and cloths of the material world. In the twenty-first century, modern society is shivering in financial and social instability. We are richer than ever before, whilst our societies are crumbling at their core. Printing new money doesn't seem to work.

Islam, with its behavioural expectations, is made to seem rigid and foreboding. Give things up? Change our habits? Say no to the lower self? Are you kidding me? How can such a demanding religion continue to exist in this time of existential lethargy? Yet, despite the onslaught against its people and its ethics from politicians, media empires and armies, Islam remains the last stubborn religion. And it's growing. In Europe and the US, three-quarters of new converts are women. Of these women, the majority in the UK are educated to degree level or above. They have found the faith not through a lack of intellectual rigour, but because of it.

My life changed because of, not despite, the Muslims who may be your neighbours, your doctors and taxi drivers, your midwives and lawyers. I have met thought-leaders and the makers of tea. I have been star-struck by the wealth of those who give to society not just from their pockets but from their precious time. I have sat with the elders of the Muslim community with ancient fine manners and commanding rhetoric. I have been moved by the recitation of Arab children that can melt the heart. It was because of their bravery and steadfastness, the refusal to feel hopeless, the generosity when I was a stranger, that my heart learned to beat with the universal love that throbs the best of names; Allah.

So, I end my journey here, for now. Thank you for travelling with me this far. I leave you with a loving reminder, as your sister in humanity. Take some time to yourself. Sit alone quietly, or take a walk in nature. Consider the intelligence that perfectly balances every form in the universe, every single process, from the complexity of your own hormones, your body's heat sensors, to the incredible blessing of water.

This is your invitation.

Read the Qur'an asking to find the truth, just once.

Indeed, in the creation of the heavens and earth; in the alternation of night and day; in the ships that sail the seas with goods for people; in the water which God sends down from the sky to give life to the earth after it has become barren, scattering all kinds of creatures over it; in the changing of the winds and clouds that run their appointed courses between the sky and earth: there are signs in all these for people of reason.

(Qur'an 2: 164)

THE END